MW00451306

THE PAPERS OF WILLIAM F. "BUFFALO BILL" CODY

SERIES EDITORS

Jeremy M. Johnston, Frank Christianson, and Douglas Seefeldt

GEORGE W. T. BECK

Beckoning Frontiers

The Memoir of a Wyoming Entrepreneur

*Edited and with an introduction by Lynn J. Houze
and Jeremy M. Johnston*

Foreword by Alan K. Simpson and Peter K. Simpson

Afterword by Betty Jane Gerber, George Beck's granddaughter

University of Nebraska Press
Lincoln

© 2020 by the Board of Regents of the University of Nebraska

All illustrations in this volume are from the McCracken Research Library Collections, Buffalo Bill Center of the West, Cody, Wyoming, and are a gift of George and B. J. Gerber.

Support for this volume was provided by the State of Wyoming.

Library of Congress Control Number: 2019053553

Set in New Baskerville ITC by Laura Buis.

CONTENTS

ILLUSTRATIONS

FOREWORD

Reflections of Two Young Lads on the Life of
George W. T. Beck, a.k.a. "the Governor"

Alan K. Simpson and Peter K. Simpson

Al Simpson

Brother Pete and I have tried to compare notes on our remembrances of "Governor Beck." They are scattered and myriad. You'll have to pump Pete further for his, but here are mine.

We well knew that "the Governor" was a dear friend of our parents, Milward and Lorna Simpson, and also my grandparents, William L. and Margaret "Nanny" Simpson. Their lives were thoroughly intertwined here in Cody, especially with William Simpson, who was one of the attorneys for Buffalo Bill and knew the Governor very well. My grandmother Nanny was a dear friend of Mrs. Beck, known as Daisy. To us she was Aunt Daisy.

They had three children—Jane, Betty, and Thornton, who was known simply as "Tee" (a nickname that came from the initial of his first name). Jane, Betty, and my father knew each other in their young lives here in Cody and also at the University of Wyoming. Betty was a real spark plug, full of energy, joy, and spirit. Jane was a bit more subdued and a little bit more studious, and she married the first ambassador to China, Nelson Trusler Johnson. From that union were two children, Nelson and Betty Jane, who became dear childhood friends of ours. You need that background to know that when Nelson and Jane, and Betty Jane and Nelson (called "Nebe," pronounced as "Nebby"), would come to the United States, they would bring one or two Chinese amahs, which would be known in these days as au pairs or even babysitters! When they came to Cody they would stay at the Beck mansion, which was located where the Mountain View Manor apartments are behind the old library today. It was a glorious old sandstone home, and we spent many joyful days in it.

Governor Beck and Daisy would often dine in our home, and he and Aunt Daisy were very gracious in including Brother Pete and I in the conversations. He would tell us of his youth. He was quite an athlete. He was a runner, and quite a physical fitness devotee. Aunt Daisy was the perfect wife because she would listen attentively and then often add her own sparkling interjections into the conversation.

The Governor was an imposing figure with a leonine head, white hair, and a white mustache, who we would see around town as young boys as we ranged through the village in those years without restraint! He was often found at the Green Front, where, when you walked by, there was a general wafting of cigar smoke and spirituous beverages of various aromas.

One would not want to draw a comic caricature of the man, but the dapper man with the top hat and the cane on the Monopoly board would come close if you felt terribly irreverent!

We would see him most often when the Johnsons would

return from their diplomatic assignments and stay at the Beck house, and he was there on the ground floor over near the fireplace in a large leather chair. When entering the house, you had to walk where he might see you, and he would see one of us boys coming and say, "Come on over here. Let's see how you're doing." He had a very bright reading light and a very comfortable, huge upholstered leather chair with an ashtray and a cigar, and in the evening a glass of fine bourbon. He seemed genuinely interested in us—but not for very long! The house of course was a mystery land to all of us. On the first landing was a complete set of full-body Samurai armor, and as kids we were a little spooked because we always wondered who was in there! Not in the house—in the armor! And of course we'd run all through the place and the amahs would try to restrain us. Various gifts would come back from China, and Pete and I would easily overturn the amahs' skills in restraining us even when they seemed to get a pretty good handle on Nebe and Betty Jane from time to time. And when they couldn't handle us they just sent us home! Or they'd call for somebody to come and get us and take us home!

The Governor seemed to me a very big man, with ever-sparkling eyes and a mustache, and a very dapper hat—not a homburg, but you see it often portrayed in pictures. He would stroll the streets of Cody, and of course he was always ready to tell stories of his friend Buffalo Bill and some of the fine men who formed and nurtured our early town, whose names today appear on the street signs—himself, Messrs. Alger, Salsbury, Rumsey, Gerrans, Bleistein—and he loved telling stories of history, of his youth, and of his business and social ventures with the pioneers of Cody.

I never saw him angered or out of sorts but understood that he could convey a most impressively demanding demeanor when the occasion necessitated it.

I distinctly remember the pall that came over this little town when everyone learned of the Governor's death. I recall that my grandmother and grandfather, and my mom and dad, were quite overcome at the news of his passing. I also remember vividly the funeral procession—and observed it from our house, proceeding on the Yellowstone Highway to Riverside Cemetery. I've seen a photo of cars wending down what was known as Sulphur Creek Hill. There was quite a gully there at that time, but of course it's now all filled to the level of the highway. Surely the longest procession of cars I'd ever seen.

He seemed a gentle giant of a man, and whether or not he really had a gruff exterior was unknown to us young boys for he always seemed to have time for us—but on his terms, and his terms were good enough for us.

One could never forget the Governor. We haven't.

Pete Simpson

Brother Al and I have compared notes on our memories of "Governor Beck." As is the way with memories, they become indistinct and lose that earlier surety as the years go by. For instance, things I have only a vague memory of, Al often recalls vividly, while some of my "technicolor" recollections are only fuzzy monochromes for Al. By exchanging what we recall between us, we have, I think, come to a better conformation of events and images that we are honored to recall in this book. As a compendium to Al's recounting, then, I'd like to offer these remembrances of our fondly regarded Governor and his family.

Though a heroic and imposing figure, the Governor for me came deliciously close to my image of Santa Claus—large, affable, mustachioed with snow-white whiskers (my imagination always added a beard), and endowed with a strong, rich baritone voice. What living person could come closer to an eight-year-old's impression of Saint Nick? No one in my memory—not before nor since.

What's more, Governor Beck's demeanor was warm and accessible. He clearly loved children. And we could feel it. Parties for striplings of our age were a wholly generous outflowing of both affection and joy. Though Aunt Daisy, the Governor's strikingly tall and distinguished wife, was hostess in her elegant and efficient ways, ably shepherding not very shepherdable youngsters, the Governor, just by being there, laughing, peering at the proceeding, and overseeing the festivities, was the iconic master of the house—the symbol of its stability and its importance in our lives.

I, too, remember that grandly ominous suit of armor at the top of the stairs, but always in association with the grandeur of the broad, expansive staircase itself. In my recollection it was as wide as a city street and retreated upward into a pair of smaller staircases to the right and left shadowed in the mystery of what lay above them farther up the stairs. I never ventured there. Al did, as I remember—all the more tantalizing, you see, having been forbidden by those ubiquitous amahs.

Winter or summer, the best parts of knowing the Beck family were the times when the family was all together at "home" in Cody. Vivacious and infinitely fun-loving Betty,

Governor Beck's younger daughter, would whisk in from somewhere else (I never knew from exactly where—she was a traveler), and her two siblings, brother Thornton "Tee" Beck who lived in Cody and sister Jane, often straight from China (an exotic thought for us grade-schoolers), together with her husband, Ambassador Nelson T. Johnson, and their two children, Nelson ("Nebe") and Betty Jane—all of their assembled families exuberant, noisy, and overflowing in that grand mansion like a scene from *Meet Me in St. Louis.*

And we would likely be in the middle of all that, along with many, many others who were always invited to participate in special events both seasonal and otherwise. Specifically I still recall Nebe asking me for horseback rides. Al and I were older and bigger, and Nebe small enough for us to give him a real mini-rodeo bucking bronco ride— both inside the house and sometimes outside where falling off was a good deal more fun for him. Nebe would shout like a veteran cowpoke on those rides and his laugh testified to his pure joy in the game.

Indeed games, as I remember, were always part of the Beck house sociable—parlor games, practical jokes, charades, and I can even remember bobbing for apples one Halloween. And these were games the adults joined in. Ambassador Johnson, Jane's husband, was not above folding paper airplanes, one of which he once threw into the midst of the ladies' tea party. Nelson himself, to my everlasting admiration, hid with me behind a closet door.

So one might imagine the heartbreaking effect of Governor Beck's passing and the later sale and dismantling of that venerable old mansion. It was Cody's western landmark, its "castle," and home to the only royalty we knew—a western, homegrown royalty of generous spirit and a real love for the community that the Governor and his family had helped to build—and had built to last. There's no forgetting the Governor. His legacy is our home, and his spirit surrounds us to this day.

The name "Buffalo Bill" conjures a variety of iconic images of people and events we identify with the Old West: cowboys vs. Indians, the attack of the Deadwood Stagecoach, Custer's Last Stand, Annie Oakley, Sitting Bull, Buck Taylor, and more. In his 1970 study of Wild West shows, Buffalo Bill biographer Don Russell identified 116 different western-themed traveling shows, yet William F. "Buffalo Bill" Cody's enterprise is the only one most people can identify. Often the celebrity status of William F. Cody masked his other contributions to the historical evolution of the American West, including his roles as irrigation developer, town founder, and promoter of tourism, activities that do not often come to mind when thinking of Buffalo Bill. George Beck's account, previously only available in fragments at various archives, offers readers a firsthand version of this often-overlooked aspect of Buffalo Bill's legacy. This work also offers readers an inside view of western economic development, one that succeeded through collaboration as opposed to individualism, where companies and agreements superseded violence and threats.

The Papers of William F. "Buffalo Bill" Cody series is the result of a partnership between the University of

Nebraska Press and The Papers of William F. Cody at the Buffalo Bill Center of the West in Cody, Wyoming. This series is dedicated to publishing scholarly editions of autobiographies, histories, and unpublished memoirs that provide more in-depth insight into this renowned, yet often misunderstood, western figure. While promoting editions of memoirs written by Buffalo Bill and his contemporaries, this series also strives to provide scholarly insight into how these historical works reflect broader themes related to the history of the American West and the global fascination with the region's landscape, history, and cultures.

One of the primary missions of The Papers of William F. "Buffalo Bill" Cody is to preserve and interpret the published and unpublished historical works of Buffalo Bill and his companions, offering readers primary resources to better understand the complex historical development of the American West and its mythic representatives. In addition to this series, readers can view historical documents on the project's digital archive: CodyArchive.org, and its digital interpretive site: CodyStudies.org. This project began with a generous appropriation from the State of Wyoming and the Geraldine W. and Robert J. Dellenback Foundation, with further funding provided by Adrienne and John Mars, Naoma Tate and the Family of Hal Tate, the National Endowment for the Humanities, the McMurry Library Endowment Fund, W. Richard and Margaret Webster Scarlett III, Deborah and Rusty Rokita, and many more private contributors. This volume and subsequent material available on CodyArchive.org resulted from a partnership with the

American Heritage Center at the University of Wyoming and was partially funded by a grant from the Wyoming Cultural Trust Fund. Our sincerest thanks to these individuals, whose contributions brought this volume, and many more, to fruition.

ACKNOWLEDGMENTS

The publication of this work has been a long, arduous journey, but one that has been greatly aided and supported by several colleagues, friends, and family, all of whom made this endeavor worthwhile, memorable, and enjoyable. We have known each other for years, as colleagues and as friends. We cannot imagine a better team for researching and editing the material found within these pages.

Through both individual and shared tenures at the Buffalo Bill Center, we've worked closely with Mary Robinson, Housel director of the McCracken Research Library, and her tremendous staff, especially Karen Preis, Karen Roles, Eric Rossborough, Karling Abernathy, Mack Frost, and Samantha Harper. These individuals located and provided many key resources in annotating this edition. Additionally we've worked alongside many trustees, advisors, curators, and staff at the Buffalo Bill Center of the West in Cody, Wyoming, who supported our work on this and many other projects. Through the Center we were extremely fortunate to discuss our work with Paul Fees, Louis Warren, Patty Limerick, Paul Hutton, Christine Bold, Bob Rydell, Bob Bonner, Beryl Churchill, and many other extraordinary historians.

The Papers of William F. "Buffalo Bill" Cody brought

together many Buffalo Bill scholars, editors, researchers, graduate students, and independent scholars, all of whom earned our respect and appreciation for their insight and advise. The staff of the Papers at the center offered tremendous support, sound advice, and emotional encouragement to ensure the publication of Beck's memoir. Linda Clark, Deb Adams, Gary Boyce, Shelly Buffalo Calf, and Sam Hanna, we could not have done this without each of you! A special thanks to our transcriptionist Kim Zierlein. Senior digital editor Doug Seefeldt from Ball State University and senior editor Frank Christianson from Brigham Young University not only reviewed and discussed this manuscript with both of us, they also offered their insights and support from beginning to end. We thank both of them for their contributions.

The Papers also collaborates with several wonderful people from a variety of academic institutions we are honored to identify as our colleagues. Kay Walter, codirector of the Center for Digital Research in the Humanities at University of Nebraska–Lincoln, and her staff, Laura Weakly and Karin Dalziel, oversee the digital archives of the Papers. This site hosts a number of digital archival resources related to this work and can be perused at CodyArchive.org. Under the supervision of Doug Seefeldt, a number of graduate students from the History Department at the University of Nebraska worked on various topics related to Buffalo Bill's life and legacy; Brian Sarnacki, Adam Hodge, and Michelle Tiedje focused on topics directly related to this work. A generous grant from the Wyoming Cultural Trust Fund supported a collaboration between the Papers and the American Heritage

Center at the University of Wyoming to scan, edit, and digitally publish George Beck's correspondence with Buffalo Bill, along with other business records. It was a pleasure working with the late Mark Greene, director of the American Heritage Center, his associate Rick Ewig, and their outstanding staff.

We are blessed so many generous donors contributed to the Papers, which allowed for the completion of this volume. A large thanks goes out to Naoma Tate and Bob and Dine Dellenback for not only the financial support they offered to the Papers but also the passionate support they demonstrated for various projects and the praise they offered for the results. Additionally we appreciate the support of all who donated toward The Papers of William F. "Buffalo Bill" Cody. Their combined contributions made this volume possible.

We appreciate the support of University of Nebraska Press in publishing this work, especially director Donna Shear, past editors-in-chief Heather Lundine and Alisa Plant, interim editor-in-chief Bridget Barry, associate acquisitions editor Heather Stauffer, and Elizabeth Zaleski and Debbie Anderson for their invaluable editorial contributions. And thanks to Roger Buchholz for his work on the cover of this volume.

We are very fortunate to be supported by residents of the Big Horn Basin, many of whom shared their stories with the authors about George and Daisy Beck. A special thanks to Brian Beauvis, Robyn Cutter, and the past staff of the Park County Historical Archives for their assistance, as well as Rowene Weems and Brandi Wright at the Homesteader Museum in Powell, Wyoming. We both feel a deep sense of gratitude to be blessed by knowing the late Ester Johansson Murray who encouraged us both throughout our early Cody history careers. We only wish she were still here to see the finished product. Pete and Al Simpson not only offered to write the foreword; they, along with their wonderful spouses Lynne and Ann, also offered their encouragement throughout the project.

We offer our deepest thanks to our respective families for their support through the years and for enduring our absences and stress in working on this project. We know they are happier than we that this work is now completed. And, last but not least, we sincerely offer our deepest gratitude to Betty Jane and George Gerber for their countless contributions to this work. The Gerbers not only provided photos, letters, articles, and other items; they also included us in many family events and were our loudest cheerleaders in successfully publishing George Beck's memoir. Their friendship is the greatest "royalty" two editors can hope to receive.

INTRODUCTION

Lynn J. Houze and Jeremy M. Johnston

The Mystery of Two Manuscripts

"My grandfather George Beck had a wonderful puckish sense of humor," Betty Jane Gerber informed us during our first meeting in Cody, Wyoming. She shared her memories of traveling through the Big Horn Basin in the backseat of Beck's car with her brother Nelson Beck (nicknamed "Nebe," which was formed by taking the first two letters of his first and last names) listening to their grandfather's stories while nibbling gingersnaps. The historical record tends to portray George Washington Thornton Beck as a serious-minded, stern businessman who lacked any sense of humor or flamboyance, strikingly in contrast to his business partner and renowned celebrity friend William F. "Buffalo Bill" Cody. Betty Jane's comment caused us both to question why this lighter side of her grandfather was missing from published histories and public memory.

Did Beck only share this puckish sense of humor privately with his family? Beck's humor comes through somewhat in the two known manuscripts of his memoir, one held by the Park County Historical Archives and the other by the American Heritage Center at the University of Wyoming, both of which were never published. The two documents contain only a few amusing anecdotes tending to make light of others, including Buffalo Bill. Another mysterious aspect was why the scope and subject matter of both documents differed considerably. The typed manuscript held by the American Heritage Center consisted of 118 pages, covering Beck's life from childhood to the founding of Cody. The document held at the Park County Archives numbered 99 typed pages, yet only covered Beck's life and business activities in the Big Horn Basin. These discrepancies raised questions regarding the source of Beck's memoir and the role Beck's immediate family may have played in editing the two versions available to the public, leading us to wonder if another, fuller typescript of Beck's autobiography existed. In response to our inquiry, the Gerbers traveled to the Buffalo Bill Center of the West in Cody, Wyoming, with four large boxes containing the Beck family archives for us to review.

The cardboard boxes were full of various archival materials, including photographs, scrapbooks, and newspapers, in addition to several more edited copies of Beck's unpublished memoir, including one version written in the form of a historical novel. Toward the bottom of the last box examined, we discovered a faded green three-ring binder containing what we believed to be the original typed manuscript. This copy covered most of Beck's life history in 279 typewritten pages, proving to be the "Rosetta Stone," clarifying the discrepancies between the two versions located in Laramie and Cody. Handwritten edits and comments peppered the pages of this document, indicating that Beck's wife Daisy and his two daughters, Jane Beck Johnson and Betty Beck Roberson, heavily edited the work. This discovery revealed the mystery of how past historians, relying on what they believed to be Beck's original manuscripts held in public repositories, missed Beck's puckish sense of humor among other aspects of his personality.

Due to concerns about their father's public image and his historical legacy, Jane and Betty intensely revised their father's original words, stripping humorous anecdotes and many playful comments. Upon reviewing the original, Betty Jane noted that she thought both her mother and aunt edited the manuscript to the point that it stripped out her grandfather's voice. This was evident on page 230 of the original text, where Beck described the courtship of his wife Daisy in self-deprecating humor: "[Daisy] was very pretty and very young and I maintain I won her with a barrel of gingersnaps. Anyway, I used to take her driving in my buckboard and she certainly ate an awful lot of gingersnaps." Handwritten edits recommended changing "buckboard" to "*buggy*" and the last line to read "she certainly enjoyed the gingersnaps." Another editor wrote "omit" and indicated all lines of text discussing gingersnaps. The edited versions available to the public formalized the courtship by changing "buckboard" to "buggy" and removed his spirited reference to the role gingersnaps played in the courtship of Daisy, obliterating from his memoir one example of Beck's puckish sense of humor that his granddaughter fondly recalled. This editorial process, along with contradictory public perceptions of entrepreneurs and town founders in the American West reflected in traditional histories and popular culture, conspired to ensure George Beck's original memoir remained unpublished until now.

George Washington Thornton Beck as Town Builder

Shifting public perceptions of entrepreneurs and town founders in the American West reflected in traditional histories and popular culture restricted the Beck family's attempt to publish George Beck's autobiography. In the first biographical study of George Beck, historian James D. McLaird noted, "In the latter part of the nineteenth-century men such as Beck developed the economy when they came west. As individuals these men were not imposing figures in the larger scene of history, thus they have been ignored. However, they assume major importance in explaining the development of the West."[1] McLaird called for more in-depth studies of western entrepreneurs such as Beck, whom he argued had been overshadowed by the more romantic tales of trappers, cowboys, and gunfighters, the primary subjects of traditional frontier narratives and popular westerns. "While the gunfighter quickly passed and left little but legend behind him, the entrepreneur bequeathed important institutions of a more permanent nature," stated McLaird.[2] McLaird also argued Beck's experiences demonstrated how entrepreneurs countered Frederick Jackson Turner's Frontier Thesis by bringing the East with them to the West while building towns, rather than creating a new, more democratic process to establish an egalitarian, frontier community. In McLaird's view, Beck stood out of the crowd. He wrote, "The usual stereotype of the man who ventured westward does not fit George T. Beck. He was neither a criminal, nor uneducated, nor a poor immigrant. Instead he was a man of education and influential connections. He could have been successful in the East. But as an economic pioneer, he used his faculties to develop and exploit the virgin land."[3]

Beck proudly touted his familial lineage to George Washington, the great-uncle of his mother, Jane Washington Augusta Thornton. Later in his life Beck showcased Washington's wax seal stamp to Cody schoolchildren on Washington's birthday, allowing them to create their own wax seals using the very tool handled by the nation's first president. His father, James Burnie Beck, was a Scot who immigrated to the United States from Dumfries, Scotland, and became a leading lawyer and political figure in Kentucky, reflecting the life of a successful immigrant who fulfilled the American dream. As a young boy, living in Kentucky and later in Washington DC placed Beck in the center of the sectional conflict brought on by westward expansion of slavery and questions of states' rights.

While in Washington DC, young Beck witnessed his father's efforts to bring about political reconciliation between the North and South. The Civil War disrupted his early years and impressed upon a young George Beck that tension and conflict within American society and politics generated the need for collaboration and compromise to avoid violence. This lesson was reinforced by his father's congressional career where he worked with political colleagues who later represented both the Union and the Confederacy. His father met with Abraham Lincoln and worked alongside many Republicans but was also friends with politicians who joined the Confederacy, including John C. Breckinridge, his former law partner and the former vice president of the United States who served as the secretary of the war for the Confederacy. Like many Americans, George Beck later viewed the economic development of the American West as an opportunity to unite a nation torn asunder by a bloody civil war.

Beck originally dreamed of a military career and sought an appointment to West Point, yet his father selected another candidate in place of his son. Instead Beck enrolled in Rensselaer Polytechnic Institute to study civil engineering but left after three years to explore the American West after inheriting some funds that originated from the sale of land once held by George Washington's estate. As an engineer Beck decided to try his luck in mining and traveled to Leadville, Colorado, hoping to strike it rich along with hordes of other miners. However, news of the Meeker Massacre and the Ute Uprising caused his fearful parents to demand his brief return to the East. After assuring his parents of his safety and a firm lecture from his father, Beck joined the work crews building the Northern Pacific Railroad across the Dakota and Montana Territories and put his engineering expertise to work.

Beck's wanderlust struck again, and he found himself leaving his railroad work and trying his luck at homesteading on the banks of Big Goose Creek that formed the headwaters of the Tongue River near the base of the Big Horn Mountains in Wyoming Territory. As did many homesteaders, Beck invested in various operations to make money, including farming, cattle and sheep ranching, a flour mill, timber claims, and mining. He also became postmaster of a small community he named after himself, Beckton, and he campaigned as a Democrat and was elected as a territorial legislator, chairing the Wyoming Territorial Council as Wyoming became the forty-fourth state of the Union. Beck later ran for the Wyoming governorship in 1903, and despite losing this election many residents addressed him as "Governor." He returned to Cheyenne as a state senator from 1913–17.

As more homesteaders moved into the Powder River region and competed for available resources, escalating the conflict over the grazing range, once again Beck found himself caught between the opposing factions in what became known as the Johnson County War. That experience may have caused Beck to look for other investment opportunities in different localities. Throughout his travels in the northern Rocky Mountains and Great Plains, Beck witnessed the many booming communities such as Leadville, Colorado; Medora, North Dakota; Miles City, Montana; and Sheridan, Wyoming. Mining, railroad, and ranching communities rapidly developed, providing investors with, at times, sound monetary returns from their various investments.

Like a giant poker game, Beck and many other western developers staked the future of their towns by drawing a winning hand of cards representing multiple economic resources, transportation links, potential settlers, and climate, as opposed to a deck of numbered suit cards, face cards, and two Joker cards. Once they selected the site of their future town, they placed their bets on what they hoped was a winning hand, hoping their settlements would boom and provide residents and themselves with a financial windfall, many times at the expense of other contenders. Playing a hand successfully somewhat depended on maintaining a keen poker face, placing forceful bets, or bluffing, to ensure they made the best of their selected town sites. The lack of only one card, be it geographical location, weather, lack of transportation routes, or limited water, often resulted in a losing hand.

Beck's future partner Buffalo Bill also played this high-stakes poker game by attempting to establish a Kansas town by the name of Rome, which quickly busted due to his refusal to work with railroad officials who then decided to bypass his enterprise. This hope and inclination to gamble on potential town sites led Beck to establish Beckton, Wyoming, only to see it surpassed by the competing Wyoming towns of Big Horn, Buffalo, and Sheridan. In 1894, on a tip from his friend Laban Hillberry, Beck investigated reclamation possibilities in the Big Horn Basin where he invested with others to develop an irrigation project under the newly passed Carey Act. Named for Wyoming senator and family friend Joseph Carey, the Carey Act partnered private enterprise with the western state governments to bring water to arid lands within the public domain. Many believed it would provide settlers with productive farmland, add funding to the states' treasuries, and provide profits to the irrigation companies—a collaboration that would entice developers like George Beck who hoped to shape new farming communities and produce a profit by selling water rights.

Even with state and federal support, Beck, along with his first partners, Sheridan banker Horace Alger and rancher Horton Boal, realized they needed a prominent spokesperson generating tremendous publicity to lure settlers to an arid region. This marketing need brought George

Beck and Buffalo Bill together as business partners. Beck's plan of using Buffalo Bill as a promoter worked exceptionally well; it placed and brought international attention to the emerging reclamation project and town. However, the decision to install Buffalo Bill at the forefront would instill in the public memory that he was the town's sole founder, eclipsing Beck's significant role in establishing both the reclamation project and the community of Cody, Wyoming.

Collaborating with Buffalo Bill to Build
the Town of Cody, Wyoming

On January 25, 1894, the *Sheridan Post* reprinted an interview with William F. Cody, which noted his interest in various financial opportunities available in Sheridan, Wyoming. By spring of that year, the newspaper reported that Buffalo Bill planned to invest his monies in the Sheridan Inn and to develop various mountain resorts with his son-in-law Horton Boal.[4] Miles away in Red Lodge, Montana, the local newspaper claimed Buffalo Bill was meeting with the railroad officials to establish a stagecoach line from Sheridan to Yellowstone National Park, "which would be a picturesque mode of traveling. All the drivers should wear buckskin suits, cowboy hats and big guns and occasionally a mimic holdup by Indians could add to the tenderfoot tourists' delight and Bill could keep his hand in by shooting out the coach lights."[5] A few months later the Red Lodge paper reported Buffalo Bill formed the W. F. Cody Transportation Company and the W. F. Cody Hotel Company with Horton Boal and Sheridan business leaders George and Sherman Canfield. The hotel company planned to build a $12,000 hotel in Sheridan and capitalized $25,000 to run a stagecoach line to Yellowstone National Park.[6] By September 25 it was reported Buffalo Bill would visit Sheridan and Cooke City, Montana, to establish a route for twenty-five stagecoaches from Sheridan; however, the newspapers cautioned, "there will be considerable snow in the park at that time to greet the enterprising gentlemen."[7]

During his stay in Sheridan, Buffalo Bill learned of Beck's proposal to complete a Carey Act project in the Big Horn Basin and he secured an introduction to Beck through Horton Boal. Both Beck and fellow investor Horace Alger decided Buffalo Bill would be the perfect marketing vehicle for a proposed irrigation scheme in the Big Horn Basin. Instead of visiting Cooke City, Buffalo Bill joined Beck and visited the site of the proposed irrigation project near a region the fur trappers identified as Colter's Hell, located along what was then known as the Stinking Water River (so named for the sulfurous odor produced by the geothermal springs). Both men envisioned an agricultural community emerging through their collective entrepreneurial endeavors. Not only did the region promise ranching and farming opportunities, but it also promised an extractive economy through mining and drilling. Lastly the presence of big-game and a potential transportation route to Yellowstone National Park portended a strong tourist economy.[8]

Due to the arid environment of the Big Horn Basin, a region identified as "hell" and "stinking" by past visitors, along with the lack of a railroad connection, chances of luring people to invest or settle in the project were slim—a charge that Buffalo Bill did not shirk. Even with a vocal marketing tool through Buffalo Bill's Wild West, George

Beck and his partners' chances of success were slight; especially when one considers the myriad economic, environmental, and social challenges that threatened to stunt an emerging community's growth or leave it as another ghost town. Also it did not help that the potential farm plots and town site were both located on the banks of the Stinking Water River; later renamed Shoshone River by the State of Wyoming in 1902 to provide a more appealing description of the region.

Despite great challenges, Buffalo Bill, Beck, and their fellow investors successfully completed the irrigation project. Wyoming historian T. A. Larson later noted in his *History of Wyoming* that the Cody Canal was one of the few Carey Act projects that succeeded. He noted that by 1897 only eight projects were approved in Wyoming, "of which only two in the Big Horn Basin were pushed with any vigor"; these included the Big Horn Basin Development Company under Solon Wiley, which irrigated land along the Greybull River, and the Shoshone Land and Irrigation Company.[9] Larson concluded that "Eight years after the passage of the Carey Act, Wyoming, which led the states in taking advantage of that law, had filed application for 457,500 acres of land but had been able to carry through to final patent only 11,321 acres. . . . The Carey act had fallen short of expectations."[10]

Although the Cody Canal project was a collaborative venture, Buffalo Bill received most of the credit for settling the region due to his efforts to publicize the emerging reclamation project. Publicly Buffalo Bill identified himself as the pioneer who discovered the potential economic worth of the Big Horn Basin. These tales from Buffalo Bill did generate tremendous publicity for the emerging community; however, these stories overshadowed Beck's and others' contributions to the reclamation project. In a story he told the *Big Horn River Pilot*, a Thermopolis, Wyoming, newspaper, Buffalo Bill claimed he first looked upon the Big Horn Basin after suffering from blindness caused by an eye infection. Per this fanciful account, when a friend removed his bandages and bathed his eyes with mineral water from a nearby mineral spring, Buffalo Bill witnessed the Big Horn Basin for the first time and proclaimed, "No one ever looked upon a happier, a more delightful valley . . . I chanced to be viewing one of nature's master-pieces."[11] With such dramatic tales of discovery, an authentic western-hero-turned-internationally-recognized-actor ensured the future town of Cody would not become another western ghost town.

Buffalo Bill's story of discovery was far from the truth. Buffalo Bill likely first witnessed the southern Big Horn Basin in 1874 during a military expedition commanded by Captain Anson Mills when it crossed the southern portion of the Big Horn Mountain range.[12] Beck noted in his manuscript that Buffalo Bill's first trip to the northern section of the Big Horn Basin occurred in 1894 to view the future site of the Cody Canal. Despite lacking historical accuracy, Buffalo Bill's fictional account of discovering the Big Horn Basin reflected precisely what Beck and the other investors hoped for, a dramatic tale told by a famed frontier hero that would entice potential settlers to view the Big Horn Basin, an arid region now characterized as a New Eden ripe for settling. Both Beck and Alger likely ignored any perceived slight to their financial and logistical contributions to developing the Big Horn Basin believing a mythical origin story would probably lure in potential settlers and result in higher returns from their investments.

In addition to incorporating the story of his discovery of the Big Horn Basin in his life writings, Buffalo Bill used programs from Buffalo Bill's Wild West to advertise the town of Cody, Wyoming, and lands irrigated by the Cody Canal. Covered wagon canvas tops carried the phrase "Big Horn Basin or Bust" while they circled the arena. In the 1897 program published for "Greater New York," audience members viewed an ad from the Shoshone Irrigation Company offering HOMES IN THE BIG HORN BASIN and learned the company was led by none other than Buffalo Bill as president of the company, the very hero they watched re-creating his western exploits in the arena. George Beck was listed as secretary. Images of various agricultural products and a wagon train traveling along the Cody Canal depicted the arid Big Horn Basin as potential productive farmland worthy of settlement.[13]

In 1899 the Wild West published a promotional newspaper entitled *The Rough Rider* accompanied by a two-page ad promoting the agricultural possibilities of the lands irrigated by the Shoshone Land Company. The article described Buffalo Bill's "efforts to provide cheap and fruitful homes for toiling millions [that] cover a broad area of effort and include many costly enterprises. . . . To reclaim a vast territory, establish a city, and lead whole communities to prosperity, means a fixed purpose for which Colonel Cody has long been noted, and [in] whose honor the city of Cody, Wyoming, was created."[14] Supporting these suppositions were statements from local settlers regarding the various crops produced and a letter from Elwood

Mead, state engineer of Wyoming, noting the vast possibilities of the farmland irrigated by the Cody Canal. At the turn of the century more ads appeared throughout the programs of Buffalo Bill's Wild West.[15] In addition to touting irrigated farmland, a well-illustrated article titled "The Wave of Progress at the Foothills of the Rockies" within the 1903 British tour program noted the excellent hunting possibilities, included images of Buffalo Bill's newly completed Irma Hotel named for his youngest daughter, and lauded the newly developed town, which offered a scenic starting point for visitors wanting to see Yellowstone Park.[16]

Despite the positive inferences in this vast marketing material, Beck encountered and overcame various obstacles overseeing the actual construction of the canal and the establishment of the community of Cody, Wyoming, that remained behind the scenes. When saloonkeepers established their businesses near the work camp for the Cody Canal, Beck ran them out hoping to maintain his workers' sobriety. After discovering the canal laborers would travel vast distances to secure alcohol, Beck compromised and let the saloons open near the camp so long as they did not cheat the workers and kept an orderly business. When the canal company was nearing bankruptcy, Beck called on his family friend Phoebe Hearst and convinced her to buy water bonds, an action that kept the company solvent until the canal was finished. Beck also invested in the community, developing a power plant to provide electricity and forming the Cody Club, a hunting club that evolved into a booster agency for the emerging community. After winning a considerable sum of money in a card game, Beck donated the funds to build the Episcopal church. Beck also worked with political officials to improve the road between Cody and Yellowstone. Ignoring Beck's accomplishments, Buffalo Bill's promotional accounts of discovering and developing the potential of the Big Horn Basin eclipsed much of the historical narrative of building the town of Cody.

Despite Buffalo Bill's publicity campaign and the efforts of Beck, nearby towns did not see much of a future for Beck and Buffalo Bill's new community. On March 22, 1901, an article appeared in the *Red Lodge Picket* praising the scenery surrounding the emerging town of Cody, yet also complaining that "the town is spread out a good deal over the townsite. There seems at present to be some difficulty in getting adequate water supply . . . there is no considerable ranch country adjacent to Cody to contribute of its wealth to the building of a commercial center, nor is there any mining country yet discovered that gives prospect of speedy development. . . . Even the big ditch of the irrigation company seems to have been attended with various misfortunes, so that it has not yet come within sight of the town."[17] The news article offered its prediction for Cody's future, "There are many who believe that the future town of Cody will be located several miles from its present townsite. Then there will be a good prospect of building up a good town,—never a large one—for the townsite will then be nearer to a country that offers a prospect of rich ranches under a system of irrigation through storage reservoirs."[18] The article proclaimed the community of Meeteetse, located a few miles south, had the potential to overshadow Cody as a more prosperous community.

While Beck's new town failed to impress the *Picket*

reporter, one civic institution shone brightly and warranted praise—Cody Club. From all appearances, the club formed by Beck and other community members appeared to be only a hunting club. "The club is domiciled in a commodious building. Where they have reading room facilities which are accessible at all hours of the day for all people, whether members of the club or not. Magazines and books are provided in abundance," noted the news article. Yet the membership and their work to promote the region greatly impressed the reporter, "Its members are men who have the right ideas of building up a great community if they have half a chance. They meet there to discuss matters of municipal and civic importance. Their work takes a practical form in the appointment of committees to get appropriations for roads and bridge and other things that will help build up Big Horn county. . . . Red Lodge and many other larger towns could copy the example of the Cody club with profit."[19] While the article frequently referred to Buffalo Bill Cody, it failed to mention George Beck who established this civic organization that adopted Buffalo Bill's fine art of bolstering the town of Cody to ensure its future success.

As the community expanded with the coming of the Burlington Railroad in 1901, many residents believed the success of Cody, Wyoming, was secured and would continue to flourish. John K. Rollinson, a cowboy who relocated to Cody in 1902, was struck by the arid nature of the community, "There was no vegetation, except sagebrush . . . for the few trees that had been set out were only of buggy-whip size."[20] Yet Rollinson noted the train, many saloons, and several businesses under construction, including the Irma

Hotel. That same year Boston reporter Charles Wayland Towne detailed the amenities of the "boomtown," which contained "a town hall, postoffice, railroad station, livery stable, blacksmith shop, two water wagons, two churches, three newspapers, four hotels, six saloons, a dozen stores and shops, 44 bronchos, half a hundred dwellings, 450 residents, one brothel, three chained bears, one corralled elk, and a caged eagle."[21] Rollinson noted, "I thought of the courage of the intrepid men who had faith in this new country to lay out and build this town. They had had plenty of faith in the country's future."[22] Rollinson secured three town lots to build a home; shortly after, he sold one of the lots at twice the price he paid. In 1905 James W. Hook, who served Beck as an electrician, visited Cody. Hook was more impressed by the surrounding scenery, noting the town "was interesting enough, but in the midst of the large scene it seemed markedly artificial with its low wooden buildings, many just shacks, its unpaved streets, weed-infested irrigation ditches and rickety board walks where sidewalks existed at all, the whole in a setting of treeless and rock strewn terrain."[23] Nearly fifty years after he resided in Cody, Hook noted that "the little town had grown considerably but not as much as Buffalo Bill had predicted."

Despite these lackluster accounts of early Cody, Wyoming, in 1907 the *Wyoming Stockgrower and Farmer* advertised business envelopes for sale with a promotional backing that touted the emerging community as the "Denver of Wyoming," wishfully indicating the new town's population was over 2,500! The advertisement noted Cody contained "electric lights, water works, the Bell local, and long distance telephone systems, the best flouring mill in the state, fine graded [*sic*] schools with nine teachers, three churches, two newspapers, three banks, near rich gold, silver and copper mines, the finest hotel in the state, numerous good business blocks, department stores and fine residences, a brick yard, a fire company and cavalry troop, and is surrounded by a healthful agricultural country; the best medicinal springs [and] the largest dam in the world."[24] While some of the features listed in the promotional blurb were in place, such as the electric lights, thanks to James Hook's work, others were in the early stages or would never come to fruition.

Despite Cody residents' hopes, their town would never become a new Denver; over one hundred years later, the 2010 Census reported Cody's population at 9,520 residents. Yet despite the *Picket* reporter's economic forecast for both communities, Meeteetse's 2010 population numbered 327, and Red Lodge's population totaled 2,125. If one considers the number of residents of a town as a measure of success, then Cody, Wyoming, indeed prevailed. Through Beck's ability to handle logistics and solve problems and Buffalo Bill's knack for providing a dramatic town narrative, both the Cody Canal and the town of Cody achieved success despite the tremendous logistical and environmental challenges they faced. Beck and Buffalo Bill's collaborative approach ensured they held a winning hand with Cody, Wyoming, although they did not win the large pot of poker chips they had hoped to secure. The combination of Beck's groundwork and Buffalo Bill's promotional effort safeguarded their winning hand. The emerging town of Cody, Wyoming, became Beck's new investment and home for the remainder of his life.

Eclipsing the Memory of Beck: History, Popular Culture, and an Unpublished Memoir

Buffalo Bill visited Cody, Wyoming, only a few months throughout the year, mainly to enjoy hunting trips while resting from his active performance schedule. Yet despite this limited time in the region, James W. Hook recalled in his article in *Annals of Wyoming*, "Seven Months in Cody," that the town of Cody "still basks in the reflected glory of Buffalo Bill whose spirit rises from eternity like the genii from the vase." This highly visible marketing campaign to promote Cody, based on Buffalo Bill's pioneering image, publicly overshadowed Beck's critical contributions to the developing community. This undue obscurity motivated his daughters, Betty and Jane, to attempt to publish their father's memoir after his passing in 1943 and thereby bring attention to Beck's critical role in founding Cody, Wyoming. Although Beck's memoir provided significant insight into economic investing and the town-building experience in the American West, no publisher was willing to publish his work posthumously. As noted by James McLaird, Beck's story lacked violent encounters, and although Beck peppered his memoirs with daring adventures, such as floating the Big Horn River and meeting the James Gang, it lacked a dramatic duel on the dusty streets of Cody that secured law and order to protect the innocent townspeople.

Beck's role in the founding was first eclipsed by Buffalo Bill's promotional tall tales of the founding of Cody, Wyoming. Buffalo Bill's sister, Helen Cody Wetmore, repeated her brother's story of "discovering" the Big Horn Basin in her very popular biography of her brother titled *The*

Last of the Great Scouts in 1899. According to Wetmore, her brother described to her the scene that appeared before his restored eyesight with words that would impress the most adept boosters of the American West:

> To my right stretched a towering range of snow-capped mountains, broken here and there into minarets, obelisks, and spires. Between me and this range of lofty peaks a long irregular line of stately cottonwoods told me a stream wound its way beneath. The rainbow-tinted carpet under me was formed of innumerable brilliant-hued wild flowers; it spread about me in every direction, and sloped gracefully to the stream. Game of every kind played on the turf, and bright-hued birds flitted over it. It was a scene no mortal can satisfactorily describe. At such a moment a man, no matter what his creed, sees the hand of the mighty Maker of the universe majestically displayed in the beauty of nature; he becomes sensibly conscious, too, of his own littleness. I uttered no word for very awe; I looked upon one of nature's masterpieces.[25]

Wetmore noted her brother proclaimed the region to be "the Mecca of earth, and thither he hastens the moment he is free from duty and obligation. In that enchanted region he forgets for a little season the cares and responsibilities of life."[26]

In addition to being overshadowed by these promotional tall tales elevating Buffalo Bill as the town founder, Beck also drew the wrath of journalist and fiction writer Caroline Lockhart. Lockhart modeled many of her fictional characters on the actual Cody, Wyoming, and its residents; a technique that created considerable angst and antipathy among those she targeted. Her depiction of the Becks in *Lady Doc*, published in 1912, was not a flattering portrayal.[27] Through the fictional characters Andy P. and Augusta Symes, Lockhart greatly maligned both the Becks' character and their reputations. Andy Symes is depicted as a vain and greedy developer in the town of Crowheart Butte.

Lockhart also weaves a story portraying the Becks' marriage as a sham intended to facilitate Beck's social climbing in Cody in addition to maintaining a false persona to lure investors and settlers to the community. Instead of marrying his true love, Symes marries the innocent and naive blacksmith's daughter, Augusta, due to the conspiring advice of Doc Harpe, the "Lady Doc" of the community. Harpe, whom Lockhart suggests is bisexual, was based on the Becks' friend and local female physician Dr. Frances Lane. Although fictional, the negative depiction of Doc Lane further alienated the author from the Beck family.[28] Through the machinations of Doc Harpe, Andy and Augusta become the pillars of Crowheart Butte society, at the expense of the "lower-class" characters who prove to be honest, hardworking settlers who are more dedicated to building a community than securing a place in the "high society" of the small frontier town. Lockhart jested at this slight against frontier, egalitarian society by calling the two classes "the sheep and the goats."

Lockhart's Beck-like character struggles to lure settlers to a failing reclamation project and a small frontier town for his own personal gains, mainly monetary but also for an inflated social standing. "It was necessary for him as a Symes to promote some enterprise which would give him the power and prestige in the community which belonged to him."[29] Ironically Lockhart transformed Beck, through the fictional character of Symes, into the primary "booster" of the town of Cody, instead of the Buffalo Bill–like character Colonel Pouty, whom Lockhart incorporated into her later novels. Symes became a showman like Buffalo Bill to garner power, an eastern dude pretending to be a Westerner to enhance his social standing and economic status. Lockhart wrote, "In his wide-brimmed Stetson, with his broad shoulders towering above the average man, his genial smile and jovial manners, he was the typical free, big-hearted westerner of the eastern imagination. And he liked the role; also he played it well." Lockhart argued, "Symes was essentially a poseur. He loved the limelight like a showman. To be foremost, to lead, was essential to his happiness. He demanded satellites and more satellites. His love of prominence amounted to a passion. Sycophancy was as acceptable as real regard, since each catered to his vanity."[30]

Jesting about Beck's prominent familial and eastern connections used as a tool to swindle investors, Lockhart proclaimed that Symes "never went East except to eat oysters and raise money."[31] Due to the increased manipulations of Doc Harpe and her aggressive methods to bilk money from the sheep of the Crowheart community, Symes' operation and social standing come crashing down upon him, and the fictional Ogden Van Lennop, who was modeled after Beck's fellow investor Bronson Rumsey, takes over the project. As a final insult to Symes, Doc Harpe threatens to run off with Mrs. Symes, now exposed and shamed by her disguised societal standing and the future bankruptcy and social disgrace of her husband.

Local historian Gladys Andren noted that Caroline Lockhart "probably touched more people with the tip of her pen than all the legendary gunslingers of the West combined did with their six-shooters."[32] In handwritten comments on a copy of James McLaird's article "Building the Town of Cody" written for *Annals of Wyoming,* one of Beck's daughters noted that Caroline Lockhart "wrote the book in revenge!" The comments further claimed Lockhart was welcomed in the community "until she began a great flirtation with a local rancher whose wife & children were loved by all—so they ignored Caroline," which motivated her to write a damning fictional account of the townspeople who slighted her. In his memoir Beck noted he and Buffalo Bill stranded a lady reporter as they traveled to the Black Hills in 1906 to quell a purported uprising of Ute Indians. It is possible the journalist left behind was Caroline Lockhart and she blamed Beck for giving her the slip, causing her to lose the "scoop" on a possible Buffalo Bill adventure.[33] Regardless of her motives the sting of Lockhart's pen alienated friends of the Becks and Dr. Lane, and likely motivated Beck's daughters to heavily edit the manuscript before submitting it for publication, stripping much of Beck's western vernacular and some of his anecdotes that may be considered lowbrow humor.

Throughout the twentieth century, the history of the founding of Cody, Wyoming, remained obfuscated and romanticized by a veneer of tall tales and myths, many purported as factual, historical accounts. Famed artist and Meeteetse rancher A. A. Anderson claimed he witnessed the town's founding during one of Buffalo Bill's hunting trips to the region. According to Anderson's apocryphal tale, after finishing their dinner, one member of the hunting party proclaimed the group should form a town and name it after Buffalo Bill Cody. The group appointed Beck to choose the site of the future settlement, and Anderson claimed Beck "mounted a horse and rode up on a high bluff overlooking the river. Here he threw down his hat on the ground and came back to camp, saying, 'Gentlemen, the city of Cody is founded.'"[34] This was one of many illusory accounts interpreting the founding of the town of Cody. Beck's family, knowing their father's less romanticized story as recorded in his memoir, sought to publish this work to clarify Beck's significant role in establishing the town. Unfortunately Beck's memoirs lacked the Wild West or scandalous qualities to appeal to publishers.

Since his death relatively few historians have examined Beck's role and his affiliation with Buffalo Bill in opening the Big Horn Basin to ranching and farming based on the family-edited copies of Beck's manuscripts. In 1968 James McLaird highlighted Beck's tremendous efforts building the Cody Canal, establishing the town of Cody, Wyoming, and his contributions toward its ongoing economic development. Regarding Beck's work with Buffalo Bill, McLaird characterized their personal and professional relationship as strained but long lasting: "[Buffalo Bill] was often angry at Beck, but his temper was aimed more directly at the project's turtle-pace. There is no evidence that shows [William F.] Cody ever doubted Beck's honesty and sincerity and they remained friends after the canal was finished."[35] McLaird relied on the edited version of Beck's manuscript at the American Heritage Center to complete his study of Beck's role as a rancher, canal builder, and town builder.

The same year McLaird published his two-part history of Beck in *Annals of Wyoming*, Lucille Nichols Patrick produced the first detailed history of Cody, Wyoming. Her research focused on reminiscences of early settlers and articles from the *Cody Enterprise*, which was founded by Buffalo Bill in 1899. Regarding the relationship between Buffalo Bill and Beck, Patrick relied on Charles E. Hayden's account that was published in the *Cody Enterprise* on February 20, 1946. Her notes also indicate she gleaned other information from Milward Simpson, Vernon Jensen, and the "recollections of an old timer." Patrick's history details the business dealings between Beck, Buffalo Bill, investors, and the Burlington Railroad, mainly as detailed by the local newspapers, yet it lacked many of the personal anecdotes recorded by Beck in his unpublished manuscript.

For the centennial of the founding of Cody, Wyoming, historians Paul Fees, Bob Edgar, Jeanne Cook, and Lynn Houze published a community pictorial history titled *Buffalo Bill's Town in the Rockies*. Two essays written by Paul Fees and Bob Edgar highlighted both Beck's and Buffalo Bill's contributions to establishing the community based on Hayden's brief reminiscence, correspondence exchanged between the two men, and the Beck manuscript available at the American Heritage Center. Robert E. Bonner's *William F. Cody's Wyoming Empire: The Buffalo Bill Nobody Knows*, published in 2007, contemplated the tumultuous partnership of Beck and Buffalo Bill, stressing the growing tension between the two men as they struggled to complete the Cody Canal and develop the town of Cody. Bonner noted, "Beck, in particular, can have no idea what a life-changing step he was taking to enter into this relationship. He must have thought that, as the man who would be in charge on the ground, he would be able to maintain some kind of control. . . . Although in the long run, it all worked out for him, in the next decade Beck often must have felt as if he had lassoed a whirlwind."[36] Bonner argued that while Buffalo Bill received the lion's share of credit for beginning the town of Cody, Beck and local businessman Jakie Schwoob really made the town work.

Lacking insight into Beck's puckish sense of humor, his affection for good whiskey, and his proclivity to pull practical jokes, which is clearly reflected in the unedited version of Beck's memoir, it can be argued historians have misinterpreted the tone of letters exchanged between Beck and Buffalo Bill, leading many to speculate not only on which man contributed more toward the founding of the town of Cody but also on the tension between the two founders. Regardless of questions surrounding the nature of Beck and Buffalo Bill's friendship and business dealings, along with the aspect of which man contributed the most toward the settlement of the Cody region, the most significant challenge to publishing Beck's autobiography was that it did not reflect the cliché of a town founder. Instead the American public was accustomed to stereotypical images of men who protected the innocent townspeople through retaliatory violence—not through compromise, economic development, or eastern political or social connections. Radio, literature, film, and television have praised these men who resorted to violence to build communities.

George Beck's original full-length memoir reveals a unique historical perspective of the nuanced development of a western promoter and town builder within the Amer-

ican West—one who did not "tame the West" through vig-
ilante action or by using his pistols. In many ways Beck's
memoir unromantically portrays him as the "man who *did
not shoot* Liberty Valance." Dorothy Johnson's short story
"The Man Who Shot Liberty Valance," as well as the popular film starring Jimmy Stewart as the main character Ransom Stoddard, depicted a "dude" from the East arriving in
the West where he meets the vile ruffian Liberty Valance,
played by Lee Marvin. Turning his back on his legal training, Ransom learns that only violence can suppress Liberty's intimidating hold on the townspeople and challenges
Liberty to a duel. . . . Then after years of taking credit
for the gunning down of Liberty Valance, Ransom Stoddard finally confesses that the more rugged Tom Doni-
phon, played by John Wayne, shot the desperado Valance.
The reporter notes, "This is the west, sir. When the legend becomes fact, print the legend."[37] George Beck's past
experiences, now overshadowed by the likes of Johnson's
fictional character Ransom, effectively relied on his eastern education, along with his strong political and social
connections to the East, to establish a career and build a
community within the American West—without resorting
to using violence to bring civilization to an untamed land.

Numerous western historians, writers, and filmmakers
continued to "print the legend" when it came to histories
and stories of town building throughout the twentieth cen-
tury, negating much interest in biographies like Beck's.
Silent film star William S. Hart, starring in the lead role of
Wild Bill Hickok (1923), joined forces with Wyatt Earp, Doc
Holliday, Calamity Jane, Bat Masterson, and others to tame
Dodge City. Walter Noble Burns highlighted the violent

community building in his history *Tombstone: An Iliad of the Southwest* in 1927, which popularized the actions of the Earp Brothers and Doc Holiday. Stuart N. Lake published *Wyatt Earp: Frontier Marshal* in 1931, an exaggerated, idealized interpretation of Earp's violent activities that restored law and order in Tombstone. Lake's depiction of Wyatt Earp continued to shape the widespread perception of the town tamer who ensured law and order at the point of a Colt .45, as did *The Ox-Bow Incident* (1943) based on the novel by Walter Van Tilburg Clark, *My Darling Clementine* (1946), and *Gunfight at the O.K. Corral* (1957). Hugh O'Brien portrayed the town tamer Marshal Earp from 1955–61 in the television series *The Life and Legend of Wyatt Earp*.

Fictional marshals replicated the Wyatt Earp story line. From 1955 to 1975, James Arness starred as Dodge City marshal Matt Dillon in the television series *Gunsmoke*. Louis Lamour's *The Empty Land* (1969) offered the traditional story of the taming of the fictional mining community named Confusion by lawman Matt Coburn. Later depictions criticized the use of violence to settle the American West, but violent disputes remained in many story lines, including *McCabe & Mrs. Miller* (1971), *The Life and Times of Judge Roy Bean* (1972), *High Plains Drifter* (1973), and HBO's landmark series *Deadwood* (2004–6). Although these later works represented a darker image of a town founder, violence in the form of gunfights and barroom brawls continued to present community building in the American West as a dramatic, violent affair—a characterization completely missing from Beck's memoir.

George Washington Thornton Beck's experiences in the American West were overshadowed by the legend of his famous partner Buffalo Bill Cody and the darker fictional story *Lady Doc* told by Caroline Lockhart. Legendary tales of town tamers like Wild Bill Hickok and Wyatt Earp as portrayed in historical narratives, dime novels, comics, radio programs, movies, and television shows popularized the use of violence to tame a rugged, uncivilized land, causing publishers to balk at publishing Beck's story. Later narratives depicted a darker side of the American Dream and westward expansion that ignored people from the historical record like Beck, and in some cases were even more ugly and violent than the traditional, mythical histories of the American Frontier experience. To this day visitors to Cody, Wyoming, enjoy staged Wild West gunfights next to the Irma Hotel highlighting western violence, yet one block to the south, Beck Avenue runs through a quiet residential area, indicating Buffalo Bill's renowned depiction of the American West continues to draw visitors to the region, while its year-round residents remain behind the scenes during the staging of the town's dramatic reenactment of the Wild West.

George Beck's own story of developing the Cody Canal and promulgating the city of Cody, Wyoming, in collaboration with the famed Buffalo Bill and others, significantly lacked these dramatic depictions that shaped the public's interpretation of settling the American West. Beck's memoir offers readers great insight into the building of western communities as told by an entrepreneur and town builder who deserves more renown in the historical record. As an investor, a developer, and a town founder, Beck's story dramatically differs from our perceived stereotypes. He did not rely on a pistol to shoot down the bad guys; instead he used his political and social connections to secure necessary capital. He compromised and collaborated with many others to ensure success. He knew the need of active hucksterism shored up by effective logistics to keep his projects moving forward through working with the international celebrity Buffalo Bill. Most importantly Beck's autobiography demonstrates how he used his puckish sense of humor to make light of himself and others—this skill of making others laugh, with or without offering gingersnaps, effectively assisted him throughout all his adventures and endeavors throughout the American West.

A Note on the Text

To allow George Beck an unfettered opportunity to tell his own story, in his own words, we transcribed and lightly edited the manuscript found in the Beck family collections. Handwritten edits from Beck's wife Daisy and daughters Jane and Betty, along with some others whose handwriting cannot be identified, are either referred to or reprinted in the endnotes when the editors deemed the information contributed to the story line. In some cases it appears Beck may have dictated the edits to Daisy, and she noted the recommended changes in her handwriting. Beck also tended to gloss over some anecdotes related to his mother, which the daughters expressed in their handwritten comments, and we felt this information needed to be captured in the endnotes.

Noting that Beck fully intended to publish this work, we did correct obvious misspellings and made grammatical changes, such as adding commas, in the body of the text. In some cases we broke long sentences into two or three parts to improve the readability of Beck's autobiography. Beck referred to many personal names of colleagues and celebrities throughout his manuscript; unfortunately in several cases the typist either misspelled the names or Beck provided incorrect spellings. We have corrected misspellings of names within the text and noted Beck's original spelling in an endnote. We did our best researching local resources and online databases such as Find A Grave to verify the names and information contained within Beck's account, and this information is annotated throughout this edition. After we began working on this manuscript, the Gerbers donated their collection of Beck materials to the McCracken Research Library at the Buffalo Bill Center of the West in Cody, Wyoming, including Beck's original manuscript.

Beckoning
Frontiers

THE MEMOIR OF
GEORGE WASHINGTON THORNTON BECK

CONTENTS

Preface

My children and my grandchildren have been sometimes amused, sometimes thrilled, and sometimes instructed by my recalling personal events long past and of a period which will never reoccur in our country. Thus, they have persuaded me to repeat again some of those things I have told them.

Herodotus, in writing the history of Egypt, said, "I shall tell you what the Priests said, what the common people said, and what I saw myself." My tale, quite naturally, falls in the latter category, even though the nodding introduction to my ancestors does come under the first.

And so, a short history of some of the Becks . . .

ONE

Family and Boyhood in Kentucky and Washington DC, 1856–1865

Five years before the Civil War I arrived in this world with all the annoying aggressiveness of the excessively young. It was sometime in June, in the year of 1856, and the event—with all due modesty—occurred at my father's farm which was situated two miles outside of Lexington, Kentucky.

There we continued to live until after the war began and, thus, I started life as what is so euphoniously known as "a southerner." In later years I also became, by adoption, "a westerner." And to this day those two classifications dog around after me. Out here in Wyoming, someone will explain to someone else that the old gentleman speaks the way he does because "he's a southerner." And back in Washington, they used to say on my visits there after I'd settled in Wyoming, "Great Scott, here comes that big westerner, buffalo coat and all." Perhaps one does take on the regional flavor or color of the particular adventures and excitements he has known. But I—and I should know—find in the sum total of the years one undeniable fact: I've been blessed with a succession of happy days. It's high time someone, if they have to go on classifying me, said, "There goes that damn lucky *American*, George Beck."

Occasionally I like to speculate about the day after tomorrow. And like every grandfather, I suppose, I sometimes wonder if my ten-year-old grandson, who was born in China and is now living in Australia—with suitable stop-offs in the United States—will ever have as much fun and be able to do as many things as I have done, and will he have complete freedom in which to do them?[1] Obviously, he'll see more of the places I naively refer to today as "out of the way," but will he find in his wanderings the satisfaction and romance I found in "going out West" when I was twenty-one?

Speculating, did I call it? Of course, what it really is is that fine old pastime of recapitulation, that matter of warming the heart before certain old embers and wishing that by so doing it were possible to share certain specific episodes, ventures, plans, memories with a little boy ten years old. But that can hardly be accomplished with much satisfaction for him because his fun will come from a different pattern of living. In the meantime, thanks to time and circumstance, my own period and my pattern of living have suited me superbly. All I ask is that his suits him half as well, for then I know his happiness will be guaranteed.

My father, James Burnie Beck, was a Scotsman. He was born in Dumfries, Scotland, in 1822, the eldest son of Ebenezer P. and Sophie Burnie Beck. When his parents decided to migrate to North America with the three younger children, John, Helen, and William, my father was left behind in Scotland to complete his education in business and navigation.[2] At the age of sixteen, he was considered sufficiently schooled to cross the Atlantic and join the family in the new country. By this time, Ebenezer had settled in New York State, in Wyoming County, near Attica on Tonawanda Creek, and there in the fertile Genesee River valley he had acquired a large tract of land.

James remained under the parental roof until his twentieth birthday. Then his father, ever a practical man, suggested that he should go on farther west and take up some land for himself, offering to stock it for him. Grandfather Beck, be it said for him, had lost no time in raising some of the finest cattle and sheep in western New York and had already taken several local prizes on his animals.

James began the journey in search of land where he might wish to settle by traveling up the Great Lakes as far as the extreme western tip of Lake Superior. There he stayed well over a year with the Chippewa Indians, hunting and exploring in that wild and beautiful region.[3] And there he beheld for the first time the splendid natural harbor at the head of the lake. Years later he brought a group of friends out from Kentucky, and together they laid out the town of Superior, my father surveying it. These men, among them General John C. Breckinridge, Governor Beriah Magoffin, and Edmund Rice, walked across the wilderness of Minnesota Territory with Indian guides and packers, eager to see the picturesque site my father so often referred to. The city of Duluth had not even been contemplated; it followed several years later.[4]

After his sojourn among the Chippewa, James, still footloose, trekked alone through the wilderness to a small outlying post called St. Paul, situated at the head of navigation of the Mississippi River, ten miles below the great falls. Boats occasionally came that far north to pick up loads of skins from the fur trappers, and on one of these boats he traveled down to the mouth of the Ohio River, to where Cairo is now. Then he crossed Kentucky to the city of Lexington because someone had told him that there he would find Transylvania University, then the only college located west of the Allegheny Mountains.[5]

It was not long after his arrival in Lexington that he met John C. Breckinridge, who was to become a lifelong friend. Young Breckinridge was studying law and kindled James's enthusiasm to do likewise. But when he wrote to his father informing him of his plans—and hoping to get some financial aid—he received this fine Scotch reply: "Dear Son James: The Becks have always been an honest people, never profiting from the misfortunes of others. If you wish to take up the study of law you will have to do so at your own expense, without my approval or consent."

James was nonetheless determined to see it through. To earn his tuition and expenses, he got a job working for Mr. Drummond Hunt on a large plantation on the outskirts of Lexington.[6] He soon became overseer of it over two years, and with these funds he enrolled for the two-year law course offered at the university. The exceptionally thorough education he had been given in Scotland enabled him to complete the full course in one year, and upon his graduation he and John Breckinridge became law partners, hanging out their first shingle there in Lexington. It was a congenial and successful partnership, continuing until Breckinridge went into politics and was elected to the United States Senate. Later, as we know, he was destined to become vice president under James Buchanan.

When Breckinridge went to Washington, Father and Frank Hunt formed a partnership which lasted until after the Civil War.[7] Then Father, too, "went into politics" and was elected to Congress. He eventually served four terms in the lower House—in the Fortieth, Forty-First, Forty-Second, and Forty-Third Congresses—returned to his law practice for two years, and was then elected three times to the Senate. In fact, he died in harness during his third term, and John G. Carlyle was appointed to finish it out.

Mother, Jane Augusta Washington Thornton, was born at Thornton Hill in Rappahannock County, Virginia.[8] She was the daughter of Margaret Buckner and George Washington Thornton, a nephew of General Washington.[9] Her father, going merrily to his wedding, had had to cross Bull Run Creek in mid-winter.[10] He and his best man, assuming that it was safe to drive across the ice, broke through and both were thoroughly ducked. He was a powerful young man, by some said to be the strongest man in Virginia. One of his feats, we were told, was to take a horseshoe in his bare hands and straighten it out. In spite of all his prowess, however, he caught so severe a cold from the ducking that he never recovered. He died a month before the birth of his child, Jane, my mother.

A few years later the young widow, Margaret Buckner, remarried. Her second husband was James Clark, the governor of Kentucky.[11] He and Margaret established their home at Frankfort, while Jane continued to live on one of her places in Virginia, managed for her by an uncle and guardian, Arris Buckner.[12] Mother at one time was considered a very wealthy young lady inasmuch as she owned several plantations and between two and three hundred slaves.

When she was eleven she visited her mother in Kentucky and in the fall of that year she drove from Frankfort to Washington with Henry Clay in his coach, for Senator

Clay and Governor Clark had long been good friends. But when they reached Washington, the distinguished statesman deposited Jane, her bandboxes, and her satchels on the front steps of the White House, where she was to visit with the Andrew Jackson family, without so much as pausing to hand his charge over to the president. The bitter discord between these two men had, of course, culminated in a fierce and open hatred following Jackson's election. Young Jane, jolting demurely along beside the former secretary of state on her first trip north, probably never suspected that the history books she would read to her children would record at length the struggle for political leadership between the two austere gentlemen she knew as "family friends."

Jane spent the greater part of that year at the White House while she attended school in Washington. Among her new schoolmates was Elizabeth Blair, a daughter of Francis Preston Blair, one of President Jackson's close political advisors.[13] He was also the editor of *The Globe*, a newspaper more or less noted as an organ for the Jackson administration and which later became the Congressional Record. The two girls were soon inseparable. Years later when Elizabeth had married S. Phillips Lee, afterwards Admiral Lee, they became the parents of my boyhood chum, Blair Lee.[14]

On the second visit of Jane to her mother at Frankfort, when she was eighteen or nineteen, she met the young barrister, James Burnie Beck, from nearby Lexington. They were married in Louisville in 1848, following a courtship marred by the protests of her Virginia relatives, who objected to James on the simple grounds that no Virginia woman should marry a foreigner. After the ceremony, when he was safely within the fold, his Scottish birth was amiably forgiven.

Father took his bride back to Lexington to the home he had established for her two miles out of town. It was a lovely, large place and their five children were born into the family. I was the fourth, and when I came along, I was given the maternal family names of George Washington Thornton to precede the Beck part. Father's friend, Senator Breckinridge, became my godfather. My oldest sister, Margaret Buckner Beck, had been born in 1849, and another sister, Bettie Buckner Beck, was born in 1853.[15] The two other children, Sophie and Jimmy, died in infancy.

Our life must have been exceedingly pleasant and comfortable in those years before the war. The country was rich and fertile, the tempo of our elders' daily existence seemed leisurely and thoughtful with no sense of competition nor consuming ambition, and we children knew nothing of privation or disappointment. We had, in the customary fashion, a number of colored servants and two of them were assigned to look after me: an old man called Buck and a young woman named Prim. They may have been very efficient when someone was around to look after them, but at other times I mostly had my own way. At all events, my earliest recollection is of being *catapulted* out of a baby carriage into a bush of thorns because Prim was undoubtedly thinking of something else. The impression left by those thorns has, indeed, penetrated a long, long memory.

The next thing I recall was an escapade with a pet monkey Mother owned and with which I played. Mother had made a visit to Dr. Trawl's water cure in New York State, near Buffalo, and there she had become interested in using homeopathic medicines to cure illnesses. When she came home, she had a big box of these medicines with which she dosed me, the monkey, or anyone in the household who developed obliging symptoms. One day she went to town, and I was left supposedly safe with Prim and Buck. But the minute Mother got out of sight the monkey and I took over. We got the medicine box, pulled the corks out of the bottles, poured all the pills and powders in a pile, and ate them—the contents of forty-eight bottles.

When Mother returned, found the bottles scattered around, and discovered that we were the culprits, she sent post haste for all the doctors in Lexington. When the homeopathic man arrived, he assured the group that the effects of one medicine would counteract another, ad infinitum, and that the whole thing was a stand-off. Homeopathy, after that, rather lost its reputation in our family but we, the monkey and I, as the perpetrators of this little scientific research, still had to pay the price for the anxiety we had caused. The episode was duly noted by the vigorous application of a carpet slipper.[16]

The out-of-doors was a source of infinite delight to my mother, and she was always working about the place, particularly with the trees. Her special favorites were peach trees. By building and grafting she raised some exceptionally fine peaches which were sent as far away as New York and London, for people were more than willing to pay the large sum of twenty-five cents apiece for them. She was also a splendid pistol shot, and another of her hobbies was practicing on our target range.

On one particular occasion, this stood her in good stead. Father was in town at his law office when a young buck negro got ahold of some whiskey.[17] He went on a real rampage and started a riot out in the negro quarters. Mother, hearing the rumpus and shrieks, got her six-shooter and calmly marched the rambunctious fellow straight to the smokehouse. The smokehouse was the strongest and most important building on any plantation, and there she locked him up. Another negro was dispatched to town for the sheriff, but the end was quiet enough. Mother's prisoner was allowed to sleep it off with only his headache for punishment.

Another time, however, Mother and Bettie were alone upstairs when they heard someone below trying to get in a window. Hastily Mother reached for a nearby 12-gauge shotgun of Father's, intending to shoot it out the window to scare off the intruder. Instead it "kicked" so hard that both she and Bettie were knocked down. After that Mother stuck to her own firearms.

With the coming of the Civil War, times became very unsettled in the central country of Kentucky, and Father thought it would be better if the whole family moved into town. He purchased a house on High Street in Lexington, and after we were settled there, he sold the country place to a Dr. Herr, a man who had a great fancy for trotting horses and raised some of the finest in the south.[18]

The move into urban surroundings had one immediate and desired result for me. Two houses up from us, on a side street, lived a man with long curls. His name was Bob Ferguson, and I promptly took a violent dislike to him and his hair arrangement. I sufficiently detested my own yellow curls, over which Mother and Prim took such a foolish amount of time. Each time Bob Ferguson passed with his brown ones bouncing on his shoulders, mine became a source of greater mortification. Then one day I could stand it no longer. There he was, traipsing down the walk. I burst into the house and, grabbing Mother's shears, hacked off a fistful of my sissy ornaments and threw them out the window. The regular haircut that followed, constituting a complete victory, satisfied me as nothing else had up to that point.

We lived in the house on High Street until the war was half over. Finally, when continuing there became too dangerous and difficult, Father moved us again—this time to Philadelphia—but before we were transplanted, we had a full share of wartime experiences.[19] Kentucky was not a cotton-producing state and being just south of the Mason-Dixon line did not have a large negro population. Consequently, her citizens were divided in their attitude towards the war although the majority wanted to keep out of the conflict. Eventually, the state did declare itself neutral although before the war ended, it had furnished a full quota of men to each side. The conflict of sentiment within our own family, though far from violent, was typical of the strained relationships this struggle provoked. My mother's people were, of course, Virginians and therefore loyal Confederates; my father's family were northerners. His own closest friend and former law partner, John Breckinridge, had become a general in the Confederate Army, and many of his friends and business associates were likewise lined up on the side of the South.

Shortly after the outbreak of hostilities, the Union Army

built a fort on the north side of Lexington, placing the cannon so as to command the town. On the other hand, General John Morgan, heading the opposing forces thereabouts, was a citizen of Lexington and many of our young men were volunteers in his ranks, as were seven of my Thornton cousins from Virginia. General Morgan usually made his headquarters at Richmond—a little Kentucky town some twenty-five miles south of us. But whenever he ran short of provisions or wanted to see his family, he would order a raid on Lexington, and the Union fort would then spend the night shelling the town to drive him out. These nocturnal visits became frequent affairs after he discovered a simple maneuver which he employed over and over again before the enemy saw through it. Whenever he proposed coming home for a few hours, he would have one of the many rope mills on the outskirts of the city set afire. Then the Union soldiers would expend all their energy bombarding in the direction of the fire, while the general and his men proceeded by circuitous routes to call upon their families and have a fine old time.[20]

Because our house was situated on one of the main roads leading to Richmond, we spent a good many nights with shells falling thick and fast in the neighborhood. When the houses on either side of us were struck, it seemed improbable that we would escape. Each time the thunder of firing began Mother would marshal us into the cellar where there was a big coal bin with very thick walls. She felt that there was the safest place. I did not agree with her, on the elementary theory that if a shell hit the house, we would all be buried under the coal. So, I spent these nights out in an apple tree, watching the shells come over and trying to spot those which didn't explode. The old-fashioned shell of that war had a long fuse attached. Occasionally a shell hit the soft ground, instead of a building or a target, and the fuse would get torn off. Then we would have a "dud." It was these duds I coveted from my perch in the trees, for when morning came the neighbor boys and I could gather them up and fire them off for amusement.

Living as we were between two armies, our food supply was soon cut off from the outside. The resulting short rations must have seemed even more acute to my elders because ours was a section of the rich south, a locality noted for always producing in abundance the finest beef and milk cows, south-down mutton, hams of national reputation, corn, wheat, oats, barley, turkeys, chickens, ducks, geese, and guinea fowl. Its people had truly lived on the fat of the land, and one of their greatest pleasures had been derived from entertaining one another at lavish dinner parties, courses on end. As the stores dwindled and there was no way of shipping in food—what with the few railroads and post roads alternately in the hand of one army or the other—every household became, as far as possible, a self-sustaining unit. And Southern hospitality, in its more elegant aspect, became a memory.

We had a large garden, and we kept a cow and some horses. The horses were soon confiscated, but we were allowed to keep the cow because there were children. She was a good old cow, faithfully supplying us for a long time with milk and cream for our morning mush. We had a few chickens, too, but they were a problem, for the loose negroes were as bad as the marauding soldiers when it came to stealing them. Then we had our fresh vegetables as they came along, and some of them we could dig up and bury for winter keeping. The fruit, however, was a seasonal luxury because we had nothing with which to prepare it. Sorghum had quickly replaced sugar, and with sorghum "blackstrap" molasses, that familiar standby of the colored quarters, finally made its way to our table.

With little or no exchange of money possible, many of Father's clients took to paying him for his services in sacks of corn and, very rarely, wheat. There was a mill in town where we took the corn to be ground to meal. The miller kept a percentage and returned the rest to us. On weekdays, we had cornbread and cornmeal mush. It was a steady diet relieved only by an occasional Sunday treat of wheat bread when we were lucky.

Officers of both armies ordered their men to neither raid, nor rob homes, but most of the time it was impossible to keep even a small supply of food on hand unless it was carefully hidden. Nor was food our only concern. They would take anything and everything movable from the main house, the smokehouse, or the servant quarters, considering all as fair plunder of war. One raiding party after another came along, each one claiming to be friends and maintaining that anything left behind would only fall to "the enemy."

Early in the siege Father concluded to bury what money and valuables we had so we took up some bricks in the storeroom in the cellar, dug a deep hole, and placed in it all our gold, silver, jewelry, and money, as well as the treasured George Washington's official seal—now still in my possession.[21] Then we put the dirt and bricks back. This was a solemn ceremony. We children were taken down to witness it so that if a shell got any member or members of the family, the survivors would know where to find the valuables.

We also had one storeroom upstairs which was never disturbed in all the times our house was ransacked. For years Father had been in the habit of buying five or six sacks of coffee beans at a time and keeping them there to ripen. It must have been a relief to him to have his coffee cache come through each raid unmolested. A great present in Kentucky had always been a saddle of south-down mutton. Once in a while, a farmer would be able to slip us one, or send in a pail of honey, or some neighbor would share an extra bit of salt pork. Dandelion greens were plentiful in the spring and, when cooked with chunks of salt pork, I still think they are a dish fit for a gourmet. Thus, we got by—the five of us and the four or five negroes who made up our domestic staff.

These negro servants were especially intelligent and well trained. And because they were treated as part of the family, they were always loyal to the good name and reputation of *their family*. Frequently they would go as far as to bestow upon themselves our surnames, taking great delight in being referred to as "Prim Beck," and so forth. The most severe punishment meted out to a house servant was to be sent to work in the fields, for they considered themselves different from and superior to the outside help, as indeed they were. Ours never left us, even when the soldiers had taken over everything they could find to eat and our rations were so short they would probably have fared better elsewhere. When they were eventually set free, few of them left the local families. If asked why they stuck so faithfully to their old masters, now that they were no longer bound *to them* by law, they would answer with simple logic that if they went *away* who would look after them when they were sick, or buy them the things they wanted when they were well?

As the war progressed the circulation of gold and silver money became so restricted as to be practically nonexistent. Many people had buried what they had of it, just as we had, and the rest was absorbed by the opposition governments. To ease the situation, some local banks attempted to put out paper currency, but without success. There was a general feeling that one was foolish to accept it. After all, the argument ran, you had to rush to the bank to get it changed into "solid money" anyway, so why take it?

Thus, as conditions became more straightened around Lexington, Father determined to move the family north to Philadelphia. Food could be obtained there and, more important still, we would be near my sister Maggie who was already at boarding school in nearby Norristown. Civil War travel presented its own complications. The most difficult feature was obtaining the required passports to get us as far as Cincinnati. Finally, Montgomery Blair, the postmaster general in President Lincoln's cabinet and an uncle of Mother's, interceded on our behalf and was successful in getting the permits for Father, Mother, Bettie, and me.

When we reached Washington, Father and Montgomery Blair went directly to the White House in order that Father might pay his respects to the president and thank him in person for his kindness to us. I was taken along. I was eight years old and the whole journey, tedious for the others, had been one of intense excitement for me. Eagerly

I watched from grimy train windows the many soldiers we passed, the encampments and activity. At Harper's Ferry, there had been an especially heavy concentration of men and equipment to hold my rapt attention.

Now, in his study, Mr. Lincoln drew me to his knee. Quietly and thoughtfully he asked me question after question about what I had seen on my way, realizing that I, with all a boy's natural candor, would answer him more frankly than many an adult. For these were the dark and bitter days for the president when his secretary of war and other advisors were agitating against him, and he knew full well that many of his sources of information had been unreliable. Of course, he must have talked at length with Father and shaken our hands when we left, but I only remember standing there for a long time, close beside a sad-looking man I had never seen before, trying to answer his questions as best I could.

Upon our arrival in Philadelphia Father settled us in a house at Eighteenth and Arch Streets and returned to his affairs in Lexington. The city fascinated me from my first glimpse of it, for everything was new and exciting to me, a lad from Kentucky. I enjoyed everything, that is, except the Quaker School in which Bettie and I were promptly enrolled. It held no charm for me whatsoever, and consequently I spent most of my time running away from it and, of a necessity, away from home. During these excursions, I managed to get along surprisingly well—selling newspapers, running errands, and guiding elderly strangers around, for I quickly came to know every section of the city in my wanderings. At night, I would sleep out by the boilers in the roundhouse, or by the boilers at the Baldwin Locomotive Works after I discovered that they kept fires going there all the time. True, the police would frequently catch up with me and return me home, but after a spell of being shut up, I would be out and at it again.

Two things stand out particularly in my memory of the Philadelphia visit. One was another demonstration of Mother's particular courage. In the house in which we lived there were another woman and her grown son. He was a little on the peculiar side. However, Mother and this lady became friends. Then one day the son went crazy and tried to cut his mother's throat. She ran out of her room screaming. My mother slipped on a dressing gown and, unarmed, went calmly into the room. Showing no visible fear, she was soon able to soothe him and take away his razor.

The other event was, of course, more momentous. In the early hours of an April morning, two years after our arrival in the Quaker City, word was flashed over the nation that the president had been assassinated. Many of the newspapers and bulletin sheets that day carried borders of black. A couple of days later Mr. Lincoln's body was brought to Philadelphia en route to Springfield on a great black sarcophagus. It was drawn up Arch Street to Broad Street, across and down through Market Street, and back to the depot to continue the homeward journey. Buildings were draped in mourning and crowds of intense, silent men, women, and children, black people and white people, literally packed the narrow sidewalks along the route. This, then, was good-bye to the kind gentleman who had asked me about the horses and soldiers and cannons that day back in Washington.

TWO

Post Civil War, 1865–1874

The war over, we returned to Lexington and our house on Hill Street. But the rambling habit acquired in Philadelphia was so much a part of me now that I kept it up in Kentucky, wandering around as my fancy dictated and often fairly far afield for a ten-year-old lad.[1]

Father was quite a hunter, a fine shot and president of the Lexington Gun Club. It was at this time that he made me a present of a Parker double-barrel shotgun for which he paid 110 dollars. I was highly pleased with the gift and enjoyed it immensely until I happened to go out to Dr. Herr's place, which had been our old home, to see the doctor's son, Tick. Tick had a light rifle. When he took me out to the barnyard to demonstrate his superior skill in shooting pigeons on the wing, I was so impressed I made up my mind to do the same thing. I took possession of Father's rifle and never stopped practicing until I could duplicate Tick's performance, which meant that the fine shotgun was completely neglected for quite a while. I had another great friend, Mr. Hamilton Headley, a friend of Father's. He also had a large place, five or six miles out of town.[2] It was a bluegrass farm with some heavily wooded pastures full of squirrels. A lot of my time was spent there, indulging in the great sport of barking those squirrels.

One day in the woods I saw an animal I had never seen before peeping down at me from a big limb. I shot it through the head, and when it fell, I was surprised at its size. I was standing there looking down at it when a neighbor named John Clark came riding through the woods. He realized I didn't know what the animal was and, being a great joker, he said, "Why, lad, you've killed one of Mr. Headley's imported animals," giving a strange name to it. "They're mighty expensive, and he just imported a few. Now you've killed the biggest one of the lot. You'd better bury him and make for home." I said I was sorry I couldn't do that, but I would take the animal to Mr. Headley and try to pay for it. So, I carried it up to the house, a half a mile away, and apologized to Mr. Headley. I told him I would give him my gun or anything I had to help pay him. He listened quietly to my whole story. Then he went out to the barn, saddled his horse, and, taking a heavy whip, started over to find John Clark.[3] The animal in question was a rather large 'coon.

It was also about this time that Father had a really great horse, a fine traveler named Bill. One day I took Bill and my shotgun and drove to Mud Lick Springs, over one hundred miles east of Lexington, up in the foothills.[4] Bill was such a phenomenal traveler that if you ever slackened the reins, he took his own gait. This time we made the whole distance in one day. Many a person tried to halt me on the road shouting, "That horse will get the thumps if you don't stop him."[5] I would shout back that he had nearly pulled my arms off and still I couldn't stop him.

When we got to Mud Lick, Mr. Grimes, the old man who ran the place, took care of the horse and gave me a

cabin in which to sleep.[6] The cabin was quite a little distance from the main house. After I had some supper, I
went right to bed for I was pretty tired. At daybreak, however, I was roused by the most horrible noises I had ever
heard. It seemed as though all the mountaineers must have
gone on a raid or something. I got up and, loading my shot
gun, I got into my clothes. As the noises kept getting closer
and closer I concluded I'd better see what it was that was
scaring me. Poking my tow head out the cabin door I saw
about two hundred peacocks circling overhead and landing in the yard. A peacock may be a beautiful bird, but it
certainly is cursed with a hellish voice.

There were wonderful places to hunt around Mud Lick.
Partridges and quail abounded, and I would be told on
which knob to look for them. Many of the knobs were so
infested with rattlesnakes one had to exercise great care.
The undergrowth was full of both huckleberries and blue-
berries. Small birds would feed on the berries and then
the rattlesnakes would get the birds. But I was assured,
there would be no rattlesnakes on the knobs where the
black snakes were. These black snakes were real fighters,
and many a mountain family kept tame ones around the
house and barns to ward off all other reptiles as well as
rats and mice.

This was the real thing in Kentucky mountain country,
so I spent very little time at the springs, being too eager
to roam around among the mountaineers I had heard so
much about. They were hospitable folks, all right, ready
to go hunting at the drop of a hat, even with a youth-
ful "furr'ner" like me. Although equipped with money
with which to pay my way, I was never able to spend a

cent among them. It was made clear at the start that such an offer would be highly insulting. What I did find out, though, was that you had to stick grimly to the first crowd you started running around with for the feuds in those hills were far more numerous and exciting than any stories ever made out. For two weeks, I had a perfectly wonderful time, then I went down to the springs to pay my bill and start home. Old man Grimes was not to be outdone in hospitality either. He didn't charge me a cent, except for the oats Bill had eaten.

It wasn't long after this outing that I came down with a fine case of mumps. The standard remedy in those days was to use marrow from the jowls of a hog. Mother got some and had it carefully prepared. Then she brought it up to my room in a great big dish with a nice lot of bandages and started to work applying some to each side of my face to reduce the swelling. I was very fond of marrow and could hardly restrain myself while it was being put on, especially as I was hungry as a bear, for Mother firmly believed one should have no regular meals when ill. As soon as she left me, securely tucked in and bandaged to the hilt, I listened until I thought I heard her go out of the house. Then I proceeded to tear off the bandages and eat the marrow, which made a fine meal. I had just finished this meal and was chewing the rags, which were well soaked, when Mother appeared in the doorway. Taking one look, she turned and got the old carpet slipper from her room. It was applied smartly to the opposite end of my anatomy, and that was the counter-irritant that cured the mumps.

We remained in Lexington until 1867 when Father was elected to Congress from the Ashland District, as it is called in Kentucky. The family then journeyed again to Washington, where we settled in rooms at Mrs. Chubb's house on Nineteenth and F Streets. This was my father's first political office. The Reconstruction Period was on and the Republican Party was trying to impeach Andrew Johnson, all of which made for very strenuous times.

When Father first went to Congress, he devoted a great deal of effort to the return of Confederate soldiers to their own homes, many of whom were still in Federal Prison at Columbus, Ohio. Some of these men, to show their appreciation of his work on their behalf, presented him with a handsome gold-headed cane with their names inscribed thereon. He was also on the Ways and Means Committee of the House. Later on, when he was in the Senate, he served on the Appropriations Committee, and for many years Father, Senator William B. Allison of Iowa, and Senator James G. Blaine of Maine were the Sub-Committee on Appropriations. And in 1876 he was appointed on the commission to define the boundary between Maryland and Virginia.[7]

Mother's girlhood friend Elizabeth Blair had married S. Phillips Lee and was still living in Washington, at No. 4 President Square, afterwards designated as 1653 Pennsylvania Avenue. Her son Blair Lee and I quickly became chums and for quite a while had a joint tutor, one Mrs. Towne. The close family tie was further cemented inasmuch as Montgomery Blair, brother of Elizabeth, who had helped us to get passports to travel during the war, had previously married Mother's aunt Caroline Buckner. With such a close corporation of Becks, Blairs, and Lees it was impossible for us to feel alien or uprooted.

Besides sharing our lessons, Blair and I played together constantly. President Johnson had a niece, Katie Stover, and a nephew, Andrew Patterson, living with him at the White House. We four youngsters became great friends, and the White House and its grounds became a playground. The president, occasionally, used to chase us around with a stick, but I think he must have enjoyed the chase as he never caught us. In those days, the White House grounds were not very extensive. To the south there was a stone wall capped by an iron fence and on the other side was located the dump ground of the city. One of our main amusements, when we grew tired of fighting among ourselves, was fighting rock battles across the iron fence with the rag pickers and negro scavengers.

When Congress adjourned that year we all went home to Kentucky until it reconvened in the fall. This was the last summer I spent with the family for a while. In following years, I stayed with Blair at his grandfather Francis Preston Blair's place at Silver Spring, north of Washington and just outside of the District of Columbia in Montgomery County, Maryland.

Silver Spring was already known for its part in saving the city of Washington during the war. It seems that there had been some barrels of extra fine whiskey stored there and when the Confederate troops arrived, en route to raze the capital, they decided to stop for the night and continue the march in the morning when they would be more refreshed. Naturally, the whiskey was sampled; it was sampled so liberally that by the time columns were formed the next day enough reinforcements had arrived to defend the city.

Silver Spring was a beautiful place, adjoining a great tract of wild land. Mr. Blair had been a close friend of President Lincoln's and was now a close friend of Andrew Johnson's. He knew all of the distinguished men of the period, many of whom visited him here. The clear, lovely spring which gave its name to the place was enclosed in a marble arch. Around about were large, spreading trees, grassy banks, and rose gardens. It became a favorite spot for Mr. Blair and his guests to sit, safe from prying eyes and ears while discussing political matters of great importance. Blair and I frequently joined them to listen, but then we didn't count.

President Johnson was from Tennessee, and although he was trying to carry out many of Lincoln's expressed policies, the Radical Republicans of the North had carpetbaggers appointed to offices in the South to agitate against his liberal reconstruction policies. The fight grew more and more intense as the months rolled by, culminating when the Republican faction in Congress brought charges against the president and tried to impeach him.[8] They were, of course, unsuccessful by a close margin, and he finished out his term and was then succeeded by General Grant. All of this was debated and analyzed in its many aspects under the marble arch at Silver Spring those first summers I spent with Blair Lee.

When we returned to Washington in President Grant's administration our Southern playmates had gone back to Tennessee, and Blair and I played with Jesse Grant, the general's son, and Baine Dent, a nephew.[9] We never were as close with them as we had been with the others, but the general was very kind to us. He was extremely quiet in his daily life and used to wander around the grounds and on the streets of Washington without a guard or any protection. He would have objected, I am sure, to a retinue. I once encountered him by the Treasury Building on Fifteenth Street, and he called me over to ask if I knew where a certain shop was. I told him I did and went with him two or three blocks down F Street, showed him the place, and left. That was when I observed that there was no one in attendance. It was not many years until that pleasant casualness changed and the person of the President of the United States had to be carefully guarded.

During our holidays at Silver Spring, Blair and I concluded we should occupy ourselves with marine projects, inasmuch as his father was a commodore in the navy. We were supposed to do a little work about the place, hoeing the asparagus beds and pulling weeds, but in boy fashion we always managed to get through the tasks with a surplus of energy for our own affairs. All of one summer we devoted it to the construction of a canoe. Picking out the largest poplar tree we could find we set to work peeling off fifteen feet of bark for the canoe, then we put some board ends on and hauled it a considerable distance to Rock Creek to begin our experiments in navigation. Young sailors in today's Rock Creek Park would have no such freedom, but it was all open country then, as much ours as anybody's. Our craft, however, proved to be one of the finest rotating canoes I have ever seen, and most of the time when we tried to get in it we were dumped into the creek. This fun meant the destruction of a splendid tree, but nothing was said about that because poplars were plentiful in the woods.

Soon afterwards Commodore Lee was made an admiral and was sent to Norfolk to take command of the North Atlantic Squadron assembled at Hampton Roads. He took Blair and me along for one of the biggest thrills a couple of school boys could conjure up. For the most part, we were turned loose on his barge while he spent his time inspecting the various war-ships. The ships were of the old-fashioned sailing type, the largest of their kind. When we were allowed aboard any of them we spent our time climbing the masts to determine which of the fleet had the tallest. We could get as high as the button on the main mast, but never did we get up sufficient courage to stand up on it—like some of the sailors did—the deck and the water looked much too far away. Nor did we really enjoy having our meals below deck. We fully appreciated the honor and comradery, but there was a peculiar smell to those old vessels, which they said came from bilge water, and it played hob with our young stomachs.

Commodore Phillips Lee, during the war, had been one of the outstandingly successful officers in blockading the Southern ports, having captured many a blockade-runner, a feat which brought his men large sums in prize money. All of the sailors admired him as a result, in spite of the fact he was a strict disciplinarian and had insisted that *his* ships keep to the seas during all kinds of weather, for he knew full well that it was during the worst storms that the more daring blockade-runners had managed to get through before he took command. Incidentally, here was another demonstration of rifts in a family caused by the Civil War, for Phillips Lee, sailing his ships under the Union flag, was a cousin of General Robert E. Lee.

I was about eleven when I accompanied Father on a trip to inspect some of his and General Breckinridge's business interests. Together they had invested in just about every little Iowa and Minnesota community along the Mississippi. In LaCrosse they had larger holdings, and in both St. Paul and the newer city of Duluth their real estate ventures were considerable, so we were away from home for several months.

In St. Paul a bunch of fellows with instruments and rods urged Father to go out and inspect a site, ten miles from the city, where they were surveying and planning another new and still nameless town close to the hamlet of St. Anthony and of course close to the falls. Father didn't care for the looks of these men, taking them to be wildcatters, but nevertheless we went out and looked over a barren flat. There was not a single house or farm in sight, nothing but brush. My father declined to join this project, largely because he didn't choose to be mixed up with these promoters. He gave them as his reason that, with St. Paul already established as the business center of the northwest, certainly no second city within ten miles could hope to survive the competition.

On our way back to town, however, he decided to cast an anchor to windward, like a good Scotsman, and he quietly bought up ten acres on this barren flat. The new little town was of course the forerunner of Minneapolis, and when that metropolis began to thrive Father's ten acres paid off very handsomely because they fell directly on University Avenue, the connecting link between the Twin Cities.

When I was twelve it was decided that I was too big for a governess, and I was sent off to boarding school at a place called Pen Lucy, a few miles out of Baltimore on the Tarrytown Road. The school was run by Dr. Richard Malcolm Johnston, who had formerly been a professor at the University of Georgia.[10] Consequently, most of the boys were from Georgia, or from the South. James Bayard, a son of the senator from Delaware,[11] was my roommate. Latin and Greek were the ranking studies and I had their grammars crammed into me, following the odd principles of education of the 1860s, before I even knew that English had a grammar. Later on, when I made that rude discovery, I was astonished—in fact, I still am!

Otherwise, boarding school for us was much the same as it has been for healthy boys everywhere. One gets through it and goes on to something else; but we exercised our normal rights to grumble about a few things, particularly to indulge in the old traditional kick about "the food." On the whole, it was probably decent enough, but in a minor rebellion we decided the butter was foul because it persistently tasted of garlic. One day in the dining hall we undertook to remedy the situation by slapping it all up against the tables on the underneath side. Plates and all stuck. The next day we had better butter.

After three years at preparatory school, I was ready to enter the sophomore class at either Yale or Harvard. Instead, I went back to Washington and was for a time at Mr. Young's School before returning to Kentucky. I had decided that I wanted to go to West Point, and since Father was in Congress I knew he would have an appointment to fill in the autumn. When I broached the subject he gave his consent, although he made a great point of asking me if I knew how to take care of myself—particularly, did I know how to box—for those were the days of real hazing at West Point. I told him yes, in rough and tumble fashion, but that I would go off and really learn the rudiments of self-defense.

In boarding school, we boys had held in great esteem Billy Edwards, then the light-weight champion of the world.[12] He lived in Baltimore and was a sort of local hero. So back I went and hunted him up at the Utah Hotel. When he asked if I wanted to learn to box or to fight I explained that as I was going to West Point I guessed I'd better learn to fight. He agreed to take me on at five dollars a lesson, rather a staggering amount for my allowance, but I signed up.

Edwards was an expert boxer and taught the light-weight system, which few men understood at that time. It depended largely on quickness, on never taking your eyes off those of your opponent, never using your arms for defense but instead relying on footwork to avoid serious punishment and always striking out straight without using a swing or uppercut until you were certain you could land it effectively. At the beginning, he taught me position and made me get out every morning and run slowly a few miles. Then at the end of the first week Billy announced, "Now we go at it." And he did. He knocked me down ten times in the first hour, which infuriated me. I'd get so mad I'd rush right back at him for more until he finally explained that I'd just go on mopping up the floor if I didn't learn to control my temper. Eventually I managed to get myself in hand, but not until most of my spare cash was pushed over the butcher's counter for beefsteaks to cure my bruises.

I was tall enough and heavy enough, but one day he

told me I was still too clumsy and the only thing to do was to take some dancing lessons to try to become more agile. This *was* a blow. At home, Mother and my sisters had pestered me for years wanting to teach me to dance. I had managed to hold out against them by resorting at times to prolonged absences from the house. Now all this drawing room frippery was catching up with me, advocated by a prizefighter! However, I had a goal to think of and if gyrating around would make me light on my feet or quick I figured I could afford to give it a try, off here in Baltimore. Enrolling at a large dancing academy on Utah Street I went at the thing as though it were an athletic sport.

Every evening when the doors opened I appeared and went to work wearing out all the partners the establishment provided. It was perhaps the most conscientious effort on record to master the polka, waltz, schottische, and something called the gallopade, a lively forerunner of the two-step. They were the only steps I bothered with. By the time I became proficient enough in them to suit myself, I had not only exhausted the school, but I had also worn out half the girls in Baltimore. Nor have I ever increased my so-called repertoire. It was adequate, I discovered, to get me by at balls back East as well as parlor shindigs out West.

I had been working with Billy Edwards six weeks before I had the supreme pleasure of knocking him down. That was the day he said I was ready to tackle West Point. As it was nearing the period for entrance examinations I went back to Lexington to get ready. The next morning, I walked into Father's office and he tossed a letter for me to read on a large table in the center of the room. It was from a Mr. James Mennifee, reminding Congressman Beck that he had promised some years back to appoint his son to West Point. The boy was now ready and wished to go. I handed the letter back, saying, "I suppose that's that." Father agreed. So instead of going off in high spirits to enter West Point Military Academy on the Hudson, I stayed home and went to a prosaic business school to keep myself occupied for a while.

The next spring our family went to Europe. The Thorntons of Virginia were heirs to some of the original Duke of Marlborough's land in England, but there was a proviso that the inheritance had to be claimed within one hundred years. A notice now arrived, addressed to my father as head of our family, stating that the time was about running out. When he consulted Mother, she thought it would be well to enter the claim and although Father saw no need of acquiring further real estate holdings, he agreed that it would be interesting to present the petition in order to observe at first hand the workings of the English courts of law.

We sailed from New York one fine morning, and as soon as we boarded the ship we were assigned to our places in the dining salon. All the tables had seats for ten, and I drew a place in the middle of one side of our table. The room was crowded for the first meal out. As we passed Sandy Hook we ran into a rolling sea. Soup was served, and I had finished it when suddenly I decided I didn't want it. As I was tightly wedged in with a lady on either side of me there was nothing I could do but put it back where I got it. This was the signal for a general discharge of soup. For a minute, the place seemed full of flying soup, until half the passengers fled to the deck. Father further heightened the effect by roaring at me, "Get out, you dirty dog." From then on, however, I was ready for every meal, from soup to nuts.

We landed in Ireland and crossed to England where Father set in motion the first steps of the Thornton petition. Then we proceeded to Scotland. He was naturally anxious to have his American family see the scenes of his childhood, so we spent some time in Dumfries and in Edinburgh. Then we crossed the channel to Belgium following the accepted European tour of that period. Journeying down the Rhine, we halted in Switzerland to break the trip by a long visit in Geneva. Then we went to Bern and Chamonix, in order that we men in the family might climb the Mere de Glace.[13]

One day while climbing we had one of those freak encounters which befall travelers all over the world. Resting on a big rock on the ice while we had a drink and ate our lunch, we overheard some people speaking English on the other side of the rock. We walked around and discovered neighbors from Lexington, Kentucky. Their surprise was as great as ours and the meeting led to several pleasant days together.

Then we went to Paris for a month before returning to London. In Paris Father found a great many Southern friends who, since the war, had taken up residence abroad. One day he lunched with an old acquaintance who had been the attorney general of the Confederacy.[14] He reported that life in Paris was very pleasant—far more pleasant than living under Yankee domination—but that it presented for him one insurmountable problem. He had a French cook. She was a good cook, but she gave him omelets every day. He protested vigorously and one day demanded boiled eggs for a change. The next morning another omelet appeared. When he sent for the woman her only comment was, "But, Monsieur, *ze* eggs, *zie* are so bad."

In London, we ran into an amusing hub-bub caused by the visit of the shah of Persia to Queen Victoria. The first evening at the stupendous formal dinner he was of course seated next to the dignified, stout little queen. When the entrée was served he carefully picked out a choice morsel of meat and with his fingers put it to her mouth. This was a native courtesy wholly unappreciated by his hostess and one which horrified and shocked the staid British press and public. But for us it made the few occasions when we saw either of them in public much more interesting.

During much of the long stay in London, Father was occupied with the routine of the Thornton case and I, still the roving son, found myself free to indulge in enjoyable sightseeing tours on my own or to join Mother and the girls on calm, deliberate excursions to Stratford-on-Avon, into Wales, down into Sussex, and through the countless dark, damp museums, castles, and cathedrals Mother thought every well-brought-up family should see. When autumn came it was apparent that the Marlborough-Thornton lands would eventually revert to the crown despite our petitioning, and so we, now definitely among the "enlightened," took the ss *Oceanic* from Liverpool for home.

THREE

A Student at Rensselaer Polytechnic Institute, 1874–1876

With my plans for West Point gone by the boards I decided, upon our return to the States, to study civil engineering. The Rensselaer Polytechnic Institute at Troy, New York, had a fine reputation, then as now, so Albert Fowler, a friend of mine from Washington, and I enrolled there, and for three years we were roommates.[1]

I arrived in Troy with two letters of introduction from Father. One was to Mr. Warren, whom he had known in Congress; the other was to Mr. Francis, the editor of the *Troy Times*.[2] Presenting my letter to the Warrens, they immediately invited me to dinner. It was at this meal that I first met up with that extraordinary dish, fried scallops. When the scallops were first passed I took a few; when they came around the next time, I took more. When I asked for still more, Mr. Warren instructed the butler to place the whole platter before me. At this Mrs. Warren, her motherly instincts aroused, remonstrated. "Really, you mustn't," she said to her husband, "the boy will kill himself eating." To which Mr. Warren laughingly replied, "Never mind. He'll enjoy doing it." Years later in Wyoming, I was to have a guest of mine, Frederic Remington, contemplate a gastronomic end with much the same philosophy.

I was sixteen when I entered Rensselaer. Fowler and I

took rooms at No. 4 Anthony Place, on Eighth Street. The house was owned by a Mr. and Mrs. Churchill, and we had their entire third floor. Soon it was apparent that we had room for another man, so we took in Albyn Prince Dike, of Brooklyn, and the three of us joined the Greek letter society, Theta Zi.[3]

In my freshman year, I must admit I was a diligent student, although I did go in heavily for sports, especially football and rowing. During the second year, I concluded I had simply been working for marks. It seemed to me I would be better off working for myself, so I discarded the idea of being merely book-accurate and aimed instead at a general understanding of my subjects. The third year I was even more liberal with myself and decided I could demonstrate, out of my own head, any problem put before me. I would read the headings, the topics of the day, and work out a demonstration of my own. This practice was far from popular with the professors because it entailed quite a bit of original work on their part to follow me, but I continued merrily on.

It was during my first year at Troy that sister Maggie was married in Kentucky to James W. Corcoran. He was a nephew of W. W. Corcoran, of Washington, now so widely known as the donor of the Corcoran Gallery of Art. Tragedy quickly overshadowed their happiness for Maggie was taken ill of typhoid fever while visiting in the capital and died there a few months after the wedding. It was the first break in the family and a sad blow for all of us. My brother-in-law left Washington soon afterwards and bought a ranch near Little Rock, Arkansas, where he lived, a widower, the rest of his life.

That summer instead of going home for my vacation I joined the Lees again at Silver Spring. Blair had entered Princeton, and we had much to talk over after a year's separation. The following summer I spent in Kentucky, accompanied by Albert Fowler. That summer I remember because I had to be inactive, much of it due to a sprained ankle acquired in an expedition Fowler and I made to Mammoth Cave.

At Troy, as I have said, I was fond of athletics. I boxed some, played football, and belonged to the Watervliet Gymnasium but rowing became my special enthusiasm.[4] It was when I became captain and stroke of our four-man crew that my Baltimore training came in handy, for I then undertook to build up the crew along the lines Billy Edwards had used on me as a raw boxing recruit.

We took out every man who would agree to train and walked them up a long hill east of town. Then on the comparatively level ground, we would begin to run. The rule was to jog along slowly until panting for breath, then walk until the breathing became normal, trot again, and so on, repeating as often as necessary until the heart and lungs began to work together. Our distance was ten miles. Before a month was over half the starters had dropped out, but the handful that stuck had their "bellows and pumps" synchronized, and they then began to enjoy themselves. We would end up at our boathouse, plunge into the icy Hudson and out again, rub down, rest a bit, and go to breakfast. Late in the afternoons we took the boat and rowed over the course several times. The course distance was four miles, and it lay above the Hudson River Dam, just a few miles from where the Mohawk River comes in from the west.

In the evenings, we spent an hour in the big gymnasium. It was thirty feet high, and there were rings in the center on which I always did my limbering up. Taking one of the rings I could, in three swings, touch the ceiling. The ring went through an eye spliced at the end of a rope. One evening someone put a buckled strap from the eye to the hand ring to raise it or lower it. The strap seemed strong enough when I put my weight on it. In my third pass, however, when I had just touched the ceiling, the buckle parted, and I was plunged head foremost in a long curve to the floor. I still had the ring in my hand. It struck first, then my head and shoulder. I was knocked unconscious a few moments, and when I opened my eyes a whole circle of eyes was staring down at me. My friends all figured I must be dead. The ring still in my hand and the numbness in my arm told me what had happened. I got up without any assistance, dressed, and walked home eight blocks. The next morning, I was out for the usual run with no ill effects. Few exponents of keeping fit ever had better opportunity to demonstrate their theories than I did right there.

Ten days after that we raced in our most important race. The bow oar of our four-oar shell was Willets, number two was Chadwick, number three was a fellow named Chenoworth, and I was a stroke.[5] About a week before the race Mr. Chadwick came up and refused to let his son row, so we had to put in a substitute. He was my other roommate, Albyn Prince Dike. Although he had stopped training, he was in fair shape, and he worked with us all that week. Dike was a fine student, eventually graduating at the head of his class, but as the week wore on it was clear that, for our purposes, all his brains did not take the place of those daily runs.

The big event we were shaping up for was the first meeting of the Upper Hudson Regatta Association, comprising all the clubs on and adjacent to the Hudson River as far south as Poughkeepsie. There were twenty-four entries in the four-oar class alone, as the meet was open to both professionals and amateurs. The Burden Iron Works in South Troy, for example, had a team that was champion of the Hudson way down to New York City. They were enormous, powerful men and mighty fine oarsmen.

When the day of the races arrived the captains of the twenty-four crews met in the Watervliet boathouse, a big house about a half mile above the State Dam. Most of the visiting crews were entertained there, and the finish line stretched directly west of it across the river. Our college boathouse was a few hundred yards to the north.

We agreed to race in a group of four. Numbers were given us, and duplicate numbers dropped into a box from which one of the judges drew four at a time. Those drawn had to race together. The position was indicated by the first number having the east shore side—the Burden crew drew this—an Albany crew drew next, we were third out, and another college drew the fourth place towards the west bank.

Our Rensselaer supporters were disgusted at our luck, drawing two such fine crews in the very first race, for the Albany fellows were runners-up to the Burdens. Everyone had hoped we would draw lighter crews and thus stand a chance to get into the finals. We were a glum bunch when the time came to go to our boathouse, pick up our shell, put it in the river, and head for the starting line. The other crews came out at about the same time from the big boat-house south of us, and for a few seconds, we had a good view of their backs. The mature men in the Burden boat looked even more formidable.

I didn't say a word to my crew until we were well out in the river. Then I called their attention to the heavy muscles and broad backs of our chief opponents. I pointed out that those very things would be their handicap if we could get them to follow us in the first mile, for that was where I was going to make the race. I warned my crew to be on the lookout and ready when I raised the stroke. "Our morning runs and workouts," I went on, "have put our hearts and lungs in good shape and our blood will get plenty of oxygen when theirs will fail unless they have had the same kind of training we have had. But they certainly don't look it, or they would be more trimmed down." This little pep talk put some badly needed spirit in my crew, doubly needed after our friends had assured us we would be lucky to even keep within sight of the Iron Works men.

We got to the line, turned around, and took our place third out from the home shore. The river behind us was filled with boats, tugs, yachts, and barges carrying spectators. Along both banks stretched more of the gallery, while down at the finish line we knew the river was crowded with craft of all kinds. The afternoon sun glistened on the water; flags and pennants flapped in the breeze. The starter, on a tug ahead of us, saw us lined up, said "ready," raised his gun, and fired. And we were off.

We caught the water at a twenty-eight stroke and held it a short distance. The Albany boat was between us and the Burdens. I slowly raised the stroke and pulled a little ahead. When I noticed that the crew east of us paid no attention I raised it again and pulled out two boat lengths ahead. Then I saw the stroke on the Burden boat look around as though he had missed something. He immediately raised his stroke. I raised ours to about the fastest we could do and still keep our hearts and lungs working together. In the next mile, we left the two other crews so far behind they were no longer in the race, but the Burdens were within a boat length of us.

I had slowed down a little to keep our breathing easy and so when they got that close I had a little reserve. I called on it and began pulling away again. Then we eased up a trifle but still kept gaining, for they were now really winded and had decided to slow down and make a final spurt at the finish. Luckily, I had anticipated this and, determined to have plenty of lead, had kept my stroke fairly high. We were two hundred yards from the finish line and a long way ahead when Dike fainted. His sweep fouled mine, and he sank down in the boat. I yelled to Willets to straighten him out and pull. We lost two strokes. But we crossed the finish line, three of us pulling, a boat length to the good. We felt pretty fine about it, of course, and our stock rose around the campus. But with only three men we were now disqualified. We spent the rest of the afternoon sitting on the sidelines watching the Burdens finally win over all comers in our class.

When it came to football that was a rough and tough business, in those days before they had invented the gridiron and there were still twenty men on a team. The numbers alone made for an enormous pileup, and certainly neither the costume nor the rules took much consideration of skin and bones. Padded uniforms and helmets were a dream of the future. We turned out in jerseys and breeches from our own wardrobes, the only provided equipment being the red and blue sashes identifying the opposing players.

Once the game really got going, the matter of replacements was vital. With new recruits constantly coming in on both sides, players had to be right sharp about those sashes—letting the faces take care of themselves—to avoid the blunder of knocking out one of your own men. As far as the rules were concerned, no player could carry the ball; he had to kick it or hit it. If a player caught a kick, he could drop-kick it or try to juggle the ball along in the air.

Brawn was essential. On our team, we boasted one especially big fellow, McLaren, for whom we had to carry a special stretcher, but he was worth it.[6] His father owned a foundry out in Ohio, and this chap already weighed 240 pounds. Because of his size, he was always maneuvered into the thick of the fray, whereas Willets, the bow oar on our crew, and I never attempted to handle the ball, feeling we were indispensable to the crew rather than the football team. Our contribution was to go in and harass the fastest runners on the other side. This we did very well, charging in on them with head, shoulders, and elbows. Punching with the fists was not permitted. Another big, useful player was Don Carlos Young, eighth son of Brigham Young. He came on to Troy a year after I did, and although he was an all-around good sportsman, he made out especially well on the football field.[7]

At the end of my third year, I left Rensselaer and went to

Washington to become my father's secretary in the Senate. He was on the Appropriations Committee at the time, so I met many of the distinguished men of the period. There was only one slight hitch to the setup. As Father's private secretary I was entitled to five dollars a day pay, but he wouldn't let me have it. There was a grandson of Daniel Boone's from Kentucky, he said, who wanted to study law and needed money. Father sent for him, and he came to Washington and drew the salary. After I saw him, it was all right with me. In fact, I became so interested in this law performance of Boone's that I attended the lectures for two years at Columbian University [now George Washington University] and read the complete list of books the course prescribed.

We were living in a house on Capitol Hill which we rented from Mr. Forbes Beale.[8] As it had a large yard, this seemed a good time to put in my off hours building another boat. It was a catamaran, and I spent most of that first winter making the sails and binding them. In the spring when the boat was ready, I painted a water line on it and had it taken in sections down to Robey's Ship Yard, next to the Navy Yard. It was put together there with Father and several senators on hand to see it launched. Their interest had exceeded casual politeness towards the son of a colleague, as the work progressed, and several dinners and cases of whiskey had been wagered on where the water line would finally come. My mark had been carefully calculated, but no one would accept it as official until the day of the tryout, when it proved correct.

The finished job was twenty-five feet long, four feet at the top to one foot at the bottom. I had placed two boats twenty feet apart, connecting them with five oak beams. The jib boom stuck out ten feet in front, and the mast was nearly thirty feet high. I soon found I couldn't turn her around until I took down the mainsail and put up the jib, which meant that I had to put on new rudders about one-fifth the length of the boat. Any canal boat would have been proud of those rudders. And I was proud when I got out on her and discovered she could beat nearly any small craft on the Potomac.

This catamaran was responsible for a great deal of pleasure for a couple of years as I sailed down the Potomac and the Chesapeake Bay hunting ducks to send back by the barrels full to my father and his friends. And traveling, too, over the best oyster beds in the world, it was easy enough to keep well supplied with them. Then, when the long nets were pulling in the Potomac, I would go to the places where they were cleaning the shad and get all I wanted, plus a bucket of roe at a time. Yes, there was a time when shad roe was thrown away. Today nearly all of us have the good sense and cultivated taste to appreciate it; so much so, in fact, that it is now more expensive than the shad itself. On the Virginia shore, there was good hunting for partridges and wild turkey. Diamondback terrapin was also easily found or bought for very little from the negroes. Living off the country was a lot of fun, the way I was equipped.

At other times, however, I was required to go about quite a bit socially, for Washington was a lively town in the winters. A hundred young off-shoots of the older families were members of a Bachelors' German Club who gave four dances each season. Invitations were in great demand for our dances, on the grounds that they were "exclusive." That not only made them fashionable but kept them so for a good many years.

One time, after I had been living in the West, I happened to be on a visit in Washington when Judge Joseph M. Carey of Wyoming was elected to Congress.[9] Mrs. Carey had come on with him from Cheyenne and, as I still held my membership, I thought she might enjoy attending one of these dances. The Careys were new in the capital, and she was delighted to be asked, and that night she arrived in an elaborate velvet gown, loaded down with a lot of lace. In the years that followed we often laughed together as she reminded me of her discomfiture when she realized, upon entering the ballroom, that she wasn't suitably attired. The other ladies that season were all arbitrarily wearing light chiffon creations. In addition to her depressed feelings about her appearance was the realization that her husband had said they couldn't afford this new gown and now that she had turned herself out "fit to kill" there was going to be a steep bill to explain. Nevertheless, we had a splendid time, for she was an attractive and gay partner, and Blair Lee and I had her card filled up in no time. It wasn't long, either, before she had reorganized her concepts of Washington society and had become the leader of quite a group there.

New Year's Day brought a high degree of celebration and formality. During the afternoon, between one and six o'clock, we bachelors in town were expected to call at each house where we had been entertained, and where we hoped to continue on a basis of friendship. The routine was to stay a few minutes, partake of some refreshment, and leave our cards. This was sometimes too much. My visiting list, as I recall it, numbered eighty-three. Coping with eighty-three glasses of eggnog or punch, suitably spiked, was a problem in itself, let alone the time element involved. However, we developed a system. We consumed plenty of butter before we started. Well greased on the inside we were able to put in an appearance and go through all the motions without becoming too heady; and the places we couldn't make, our friends covered for us with a few extra cards. Those were indeed the days of polite amenities.

Senator George Hearst, William Randolph Hearst's father, was a friend of Father's and also mine because in spite of the difference in our ages, Senator Hearst liked to talk about the mountains and outdoor things more than about politics, and I was a willing audience.[10] I also met Adolph Sutro, the builder of the Sutro Tunnel into the silver mining country near Virginia City, Nevada; and Hayden, whose maps I was to consult so often beyond the Mississippi; and Langley, the originator of the auto-gyro, whose work in aeronautics predates the Wright brothers and for whom Langley Field in Virginia is named. I am proud to have been shown some of his early models.[11] And I also met Alexander Graham Bell.

Mr. Bell, shortly after our first encounter, sent a card inviting me to dine with his daughter and himself. I was flattered, thinking that I had scored with the eminent physicist through my obvious interest in his inventions. We had a fine dinner in a large, ornate dining room and afterwards, alone with our cigars, he came directly to his point by announcing, "I want you to marry my daughter."

I replied that surely the young lady should have something to say about that, and then I made my escape as soon as possible. Getting involved matrimonially wasn't on my calendar at the moment. The next day I took my catamaran and went off on the Potomac, happy in the knowledge that no one would think it worthwhile to *swim* after me.

In 1876, Father was a delegate to the Democratic National Convention at St. Louis, and I went along to attend the first of a long series of political conclaves. This was the convention that nominated Governor Tilden, of New York, for the presidency.[12] Tilden was elected by the popular vote, but the election was given four months later to Rutherford B. Hayes by the Electoral Committee appointed to settle some disputed ballots.

It was President Hayes who promoted my second brother-in-law, Captain Green Clay Goodloe of the Marine Corps, to the rank of major in charge of the Paymasters Department in Washington. My sister Bettie had married the captain a few years before, and now that they were pleasantly situated in the capital, Bettie could be with Father and Mother during the rest of their lives.[13]

Our next president, James A. Garfield, had long been a close friend of Father's in Congress. There, though they were opposed in their political views, they served on many of the same committees and saw a great deal of each other socially. When President Garfield was shot in Washington's Baltimore & Potomac Station, a memorial star was placed on the spot where he fell. It seems a singular coincidence that my father should have died suddenly on the same spot from a heart attack suffered upon his return from a visit to New York, May 3, 1890.[14]

FOUR

Prospecting in Colorado, 1877–1879

In 1877, when I was twenty-one, two things happened: I received a sum of money from an inheritance of my mother's from the estate of George Washington, and I decided to go west. Mr. Greeley's famous "Go West, young man," was being widely quoted and widely heeded.[1] I believe, however, I was the only fellow lucky enough to have his first big adventure financed by the Father of Our Country. This money had been safeguarded for me by my mother and came from the sale of a grant of land situated along the banks of the Big Kanawha River—a thousand acres which the grateful State of Virginia had presented to young Washington upon his return from General Braddock's ill-fated campaign.[2]

My eagerness to get out West, already whetted by the stories I had been listening to, was further stimulated by my discovery that life in Washington as the son of a senator and a great-grandnephew of the first president involved too much social rigmarole. I wanted to go way off some-place where I would be plain George Beck, and where I would have more opportunity to indulge my enthusiasm for the outdoor life. I certainly succeeded as far as the "plain" went, nor have I any regrets about being cooped up in an office in the years that followed. I was a sensible fellow, as I look at it. I headed straight for the big, open spaces—in those days very big and very open.

Albert Fowler, my roommate at college, joined up with me and in the spring of that year we traveled out to Denver. There we met J. Sire Greene, another Troy friend, and his brother Wallace.[3] The four of us held a conference and decided to lose no time in getting on to Leadville, inasmuch as the great mining excitement was on there then.[4]

Our first stop was at a small town called Evans, Colorado, about sixty miles from Denver.[5] There we outfitted with horses to ride and donkeys to pack, as well as hiring a man named Sam Woodruff to be our packer.[6] That was a mistake, to begin with. He knew less about his business than any man I ever met. We fared better with the horses, however, for I bought them from Colonel Clopper, who had a place ten or twelve miles beyond Greeley.[7] His brand was 7UP, and his animals were of the finest strain in Colorado. He was a southerner, so we got along famously from the start. The last day I was with him I bought an extra saddle horse, and when I was ready to leave a greyhound who had become friendly wanted to follow. The colonel, seeing that the dog liked me, said I could have him, and off I started, riding one horse and leading another, with the greyhound trailing behind.

It was necessary to go back through the town of Evans to reach our camp out a ways on the banks of the South Platte River. On the main street, there was a large barn where a vicious bulldog held forth. He had whipped all the dogs in the vicinity and had a mean reputation. As we approached, he spotted my greyhound and started out after him. I thought, it's good-bye, Mr. Greyhound, fully expecting him to turn and make for home. But I didn't know my new dog. Instantly he pricked up his ears, took one look at the bulldog coming his way, and went into action on high. Rushing the bulldog, he grabbed him and threw him in the air and almost before the dog was on the ground again, repeated the performance. It was all the stable man and I could do to save the bulldog's life, for in a few minutes the greyhound would have cut down his legs and killed him.

From then on, traveling through this new, sparsely populated country, we became accustomed to having all the local dogs run out to challenge the pack outfit and our right to be passing by. But any dog foolish enough to try to interfere with our progress laid himself open to the same speedy and effective treatment from my greyhound. And before we got into the foothills, he was even more useful at killing coyotes or catching antelope for our supper.

When we were finally ready and started off in the direction of Leadville, we made only four miles the first day. The packs would come off every few hundred yards, and we would have to catch the donkeys and repack. In truth, *we* carried the packs most of the way that first day. By evening we were exhausted and disgusted, but four novices from the East had certainly learned the basic rules of loading and tying pack outfits the hard way. By the time we reached Leadville, we could each do a grade-A job of it, and that was when I finally decided to fire Woodruff. There was nothing amicable about that separation. He refused to obey orders, and we had to use a gun to make him leave our camp. Eight months later he was hanged for one of the most dastardly murders ever committed in the Rocky Mountains.

Our route led south through Georgetown and several other mining camps, over mountains and into the valley of the Arkansas River, and then up, almost straight up, until we reached Leadville. The timber around there had been burned off and, at first, we had considerable difficulty finding food for our stock. Finally, we camped on a hill just above the town and took our horses into a livery stable. The donkeys we fed a loaf of bread a day and let them fill up on burned pinecones, a diet which seemed agreeable to them.

Leadville is ten thousand feet above sea level, and the altitude alone made it a dangerous place for un-acclimated newcomers. Many of those early fortune hunters streaming in, totally unprepared for the rarified mountain air, would be stricken, after a cold night, with mountain fever— another name for rapid pneumonia—and would die within a few hours. Carts used to go around to the saloons every morning to take out the dead. The bodies which could not be readily identified were hauled out and buried in lime deposits in old, discarded placer mines, a convenient sort of potters' field arrangement. Thanks to my mother's interest in homeopathic remedies, I concluded I should buy a bottle of aconite. I lost no time in buying a bottle of aconite and always kept it with me during the rest of our stay. It was the one effective means of controlling the fever until the victim could be rushed to a lower altitude. Not a few strangers owed their lives to doses out of my bottle, whether they wanted it or not.

While still in Washington, Albert Fowler and I had considered the sartorial aspects of our trip pretty carefully and had ordered specially tailored suits of fine chamois skins. They cost us fifty dollars apiece, but we felt certain they were requisite attire for "out West." Had we not seen pictures of scouts and Pony Express riders? So, when we reached the high hills, we put them on with quite a little satisfaction.

I went for a hunt the first day I was dressed up in my chamois outfit, climbing to the top of a mountain peak. Unfortunately, I got caught in a cloudburst. My wet clothes began to stretch until the pant legs were soon down to the ground. With my hunting knife, I cut them off to what I thought was a reasonable length. Then I discovered a bear den within a large crevice in the rocks and crawled in to get out of the rain. I hadn't been there ten minutes when I was literally alive with fleas because a bear had been hibernating there all winter. So, I was back in the downpour again, and before I got back to camp, I had to trim off my excess pants again. When I got back to my tent, I hung my wet clothes up to dry. The next morning when I went to put my dry outfit on I found I had knee-breeches. My expensive suit ended cut up into strings. From then on, I swore off buckskins and wore what the other well-dressed prospectors wore—overalls and a flannel shirt.

Rather soon after that, I encountered my first forest fire. The West was not going to let a dude down. Outside of Leadville, there was a large area where charcoal was made. The trees were first signed off, then chopped down and heaped in piles which were then covered with dirt and burned to make charcoal. Frequently these fires got out of control. Two or three days after our arrival

I was out alone on horseback, sizing up the lay of the land, when I got caught in front of a sudden, raging fire. I was riding a good horse, but even so, we had a run of several miles before we came upon a sort of open park in the forest. There were about fifty acres in the clearing, well covered with grass and with a small stream running through it. Along with this stream, there was a cut bank of four or five feet. I figured that here would be a good place to escape the rapidly approaching fire inasmuch as I had to go back through the burned section to return to camp.

I backfired the grass and led my horse down to the creek bed. When the fire caught up with us, it jumped the entire park and began blazing on the other side. For a few moments, we were nearly suffocated by the hot gas and lack of air as dense smoke and great tongues of flame leaped and billowed like an inferno on all sides. Luckily it didn't take long to burn off all around us, and after waiting a while until things cooled off and some fresh air blew in, I started back to town through the charred forest. The rapidity with which a forest fire moves is remarkable and so often underestimated by the uninitiated. And to add to one's terror, pine, when heated, gives off a Venice turpentine which burns with almost explosive force, sending red-hot embers crackling high into the air. I did not soon forget that inferno of heat and flame.

We had been in Leadville a fortnight when I happened into the telegraph office one evening, and I ran into Senator John P. Jones, of Nevada. He and his family had been friends of ours in Washington, so he told me of a new gold strike in the western part of Colorado.[8] He was heading for it and advised me to do the same. I rushed back to our camp and told my companions.

Sire Greene decided to stay on in Leadville, but we found two old prospectors who were well equipped and wanted to join up with us. Their names were John Haskell and Jim Bird.[9] They had recently sold out their mining property and were already itching to be on the move again. So, the five of us, Fowler, Wallace Greene, our new friends, and I, struck out over the mountains for the Roaring Fork of the Grand River.

The road was very bad in places but all right for pack outfits. At a narrow rocky pass, along about the second morning out, we came upon a freighter who had been hauling a safe out to the mining camp of Tin Cup.[10] However, his wagon had turned over, and the safe had rolled down against some trees in a deep ravine. He was struggling with all his might and main and his ten mules to pull it up, but it looked more like the safe would pull the mules down the mountainside. The fellow begged us to stop and help him.

Here was a chance to try out some principles of mechanics. I told him certainly I could put his safe back on the wagon, but first he must remove his mules. Getting out our axes, we chopped down several trees of which we made a framework and rolled the safe over onto it. Next, we kept lifting the whole business a log at a time until, several hours later, we had the safe up on the road again and could slip it back on the wagon. The operation had taken a good half day and when we got through, the driver, out of the bigness of his heart, handed me a silver dollar— for the five of us.

This was the first dollar—or, more strictly speaking, fraction thereof—I had earned, made in Colorado, and I concluded I would leave it there. The others were thoroughly disinterested in their equities of twenty cents apiece so, emulating a young George Washington throwing a dollar across the Rappahannock River in Virginia, I pitched our reward across the Roaring Fork Canyon from where we stood. Since the terrain was about the roughest imaginable, I feel certain that that silver dollar is still there among the crags.

Underway again we traveled west towards Italian Peak, which, according to the geology in Hayden's maps, looked like a good place to prospect.[11] When we reached a stream at the base of the mountain, we agreed to separate, the main party branching off towards Tin Cup to stock up again with provisions. I was to take the rest of the pack outfit and climb up to the timberline on the eastern slope of the peak.

I had left my greyhound with Sire Greene in Leadville and had picked up a shepherd dog called Ben. Ben and I started up the mountain with our horses and donkeys while the rest of the bunch rode south to patronize the commissary at Tin Cup. At dusk when I made camp at the timberline, after a long climb, I was good and hungry. Ravenous might even be the word, and I set about getting supper. Imagine my feelings when I found, after going through every pack two or three times, that our food was with the other outfit. All the dog and I could locate to live on for a couple days was a package of prunes.

By the second day, hunger was gnawing at me, to say nothing of poor Ben, so I went out to hunt. Climbing to the top of the peak I found some interesting specimens in graphite and garnet crystal rocks, but I saw no game until late in the afternoon on my way back to camp. I had got down to a section where burned timber was lying around in all directions. When in the fallen timber I spotted a deer, I shot him, but my pleasure was a little lessened when I got up to him and found he had only three legs, a front leg having been shot off at the knee. The end of it was as hard and calloused as a hoof. However, he seemed fat enough, and I couldn't afford to be too particular. I cleaned him, put him on my back, and started for camp. It was growing late, but I was sure of my direction.

I had covered about a half a mile in the fallen timber when the wild yell of a mountain lion suddenly pierced the dusk, making goose pimples break out on me. Then he came bounding through the timber, attracted by the smell of blood and looking as though he intended to run over me. I let the deer slip from my shoulders and got my gun ready. But when the lion saw me standing ready for him, he began to circle. Around and around he went, never close enough for me to shoot, for it was now too dark to see the sights of my gun. Finally, I got tired of waiting and, hoisting the deer on my shoulders again, started on. He kept right up with me and would frequently get in front of me but still never close enough for a sure shot. When we reached the edge of the timber, I knew camp was only a quarter of a mile away. At last, I felt I could risk a shot. I fired and missed. The lion bounded back into his safe domain of darkness.

Ben and I feasted royally that night on the liver, and the next day the rest of the party arrived, loaded down with food. It was several years, however, before I again craved prunes.

In my equipment, I had an assay outfit which was put to good use as the summer wore on and we found countless specimens of interest. Other prospectors, too, drifted into camp with their rocks. I made a kiln, burning charcoal, to do our work, but the best we got was lead ore worth sixty dollars a ton. Having come from Leadville where it ran from two to three hundred dollars a ton we didn't think much of it, nor of the local deposit of graphite, although it did seem that it might be useful sometime.

As October approached, our two old prospectors, Bird and Haskell, began to talk about going to Old Mexico when the weather got cold. We had become such cronies that I had about made up my mind to go along. But "the best-laid plans of mice and men . . ."

We had worked down into the southwest corner of the Ute Reservation by this time and began wondering why we didn't see any Indians. This was suddenly explained by a messenger who, with a telegram from my father, had succeeded in locating us. He told us that the Indians had been and still were on the warpath, resulting in the deaths of several white people. The agent on the reservation, Nathan Meeker, anticipating trouble had sent for military aid.[12] Troops under the command of Major Thomas T. Thornburg had been dispatched from Fort Steele near Rawlins, Wyoming, but about two hundred miles from the reservation they were attacked by Utes in ambush, and the major and twelve of his men were killed while more than forty were wounded and all the wagons and supplies destroyed.[13] Word of this tragedy brought relief troops under Colonel Wesley Merritt from Fort Russell, but by the time they arrived at the agency, Meeker and the other white men there had been killed and the women and children carried off.[14]

All that my father's telegram said was, "Come to St. Paul at once." Because Mother had been in poor health, I supposed she must now be critically ill. Immediately I saddled my horse, took two donkeys and the dog, and, leaving everything else behind, struck out to reach the railroad as quickly as possible.

Going back over Mosquito Pass, near Leadville, towards evening, after several days and nights of almost steady riding, I met two stagecoaches bringing passengers bound for Leadville.[15] The road was narrow, and the first stage tried to push my donkeys off the edge of the road, and I shouted at the driver to stop. Jumping off my horse, I grabbed my shotgun loaded with buckshot, which was handy in one of my packs. I was successful in getting it out before the donkeys were pushed too far over. Covering the driver with it, I yelled, "Stop, or I'll blow you off that seat." That was all it took to be treated with a quick change of attitude. The lead stage stopped and the second stage, now drawing up, also stopped. All the passengers piled out. I didn't realize it right away, but I was giving them a bad minute or two while they figured that this was one more holdup. When they were reassured as to the safety of themselves and their pocketbooks, they all got solicitous enough to help me get my donkeys back on the road, and then both stages drove past me very carefully.

I traveled as fast as I could, sleeping only when fatigue got the best of me. When I finally reached Denver, I went straight to Charpiot's Hotel, elegantly advertised as "The Delmonico of the West."[16] Fowler and I had had the best rooms in the house on the way out, so I strode up to the desk to register. But an impudent clerk, after one look at my attire, announced very bluntly that I couldn't stay there. I told him it was quite all right with me but that if he would look back on the books, he would see that I had been a deluxe guest not so long before; now though, as far as I was concerned, I would just as soon sleep out in the street with my pack outfit. Striding out, I rode off across Cherry Creek to the Elephant Corral, a large livery stable sort of place without even a roof.[17] There the horse, donkeys, dog, and I put up for the night.

The next day I rode toward Evans, turned my stock loose, and got a man to look after my dog, Ben. Then I took the stage to Cheyenne where I boarded the Union Pacific train for the East. From the car windows, as we chugged our way across the plains, we could watch great moving herds of buffalo and antelope. Some of the latter would race along beside the track for miles trying to outdistance the engine. Occasionally, they even managed to cross the tracks in front of it—a slight indication of our fabulous speed. A few of the passengers, unmindful of cinders, had great sport taking potshots out of open windows in the fashion of a moving rifle range.

When we reached St. Paul, I went immediately to the hotel at which Father always stopped, only to be told that he and my mother were out fishing on Lake Superior. I was so disgusted at the breaking up of my plans, I came near turning around and going right back; but as I cooled off, I thought better of it and waited until they returned the

next day. It seemed that they had heard of the Ute uprising and Mother was worried, and anyway, they thought
it was about time for me to return to civilization. After a
day or so Father and I had a serious talk. He contended
that, although I was of age and could do what I pleased,
he nevertheless did not consider prospecting a serious
business, just wandering around the mounts looking for
minerals. He hoped that I was now ready to take up either
law or engineering. Remembering what my grandfather
had once said about the law, and being aware, too, that
my cousin Robert Thornton was taking excellent care of
Father's law practice in Kentucky, I agreed to get down to
brass-tacks as an engineer.

FIVE

Working on the Northern Pacific Railroad, 1879–1880

General Rosser, a Virginian, was head of the Engineering Department of the Northern Pacific Railroad and happened to be at their offices there in St. Paul. I went to him and asked for a job.[1] At first, he refused because it was late in the season and his men were already hired, but I talked hard and fast—like a lot of other young men before and since have done—and he finally took me on at forty dollars a month and board. Within a couple of days, I was being shipped west again, this time to Bismark, in Dakota Territory, to join an engineering party in the important work of building a railroad across the northern expanse of our continent.

We were under the supervision of a man named Keith, and my first job was taking notes and filling in topography; next, running rod.[2] Then I got promoted to running levels. By the middle of a cold and bitter winter, we had worked out through the Badlands to the Little Missouri River, erecting a permanent camp on its west bank. The government established a cantonment there to assure military protection for us, and to provide Indian guides. They, particularly, were needed in laying the roadbed through this wild, unsettled region.[3]

Our location became better known a few years later

when Theodore Roosevelt came west and located the vast Maltese Cross Cattle Ranch there. He was soon followed by the Marquis de Mores, a Frenchman with a practical idea but one which cost him a fortune.[4] In 1883, with Roosevelt's encouragement, de Mores built a slaughterhouse and packing plant in the vicinity of the Rough Rider's ranch, thus establishing the town of Medora on approximately our old campsite. The fact that de Mores' venture was aimed at breaking the monopoly of the Chicago meat-packing houses by creating packing centers for western cattle at the sources of supply focused considerable newspaper attention on the locality.

During that winter of ours, we had about seven hundred men employed on the construction gang, the contract being let to Winston Brothers of St. Paul. Leveling parties had practically all the real work to do because the location of the roadbed had been determined and most of the transit work finished. Rosser, with much of his job completed, left the Northern Pacific before the year was out and went to the Canadian Pacific as their chief engineer. He invited me to go along, which I deemed a great compliment in view of our first talk, but I declined. My heart was set upon exploring our own West.

The chief engineer who followed him was a crank on mathematics and religion.[5] He wouldn't permit any work done on Sundays, an edict that suited me to a "T," for the hunting in this country was too good to miss. I soon annexed a companion on my Sabbath forays, an Indian scout we had with us named Young-Man-Afraid-of-His-Horses. He was a Gros Ventre, and he liked to follow me around. At first, I thought he just liked to see me shoot, but before long I discovered that he also liked to share my lunch and that he was particularly partial to pie. After that, I always put an extra one in for him and let him carry the sack. We were mutually pleased with this arrangement, and I would return to camp loaded with game.[6]

However, since I had so many Sundays on my hands, I decided I ought to utilize at least some of them making a map of the Badlands of the Little Missouri. It was necessary to take our transit and locate all the hills by triangulation, then with the railroad tangents for baselines I sketched in the local topography. The paper I used was four feet by twelve feet. Inasmuch as the country was rough and full of lignite beds, many of which had burned and left red tops to the hills, it made a striking map when colored. Keith borrowed the finished job and sent it into headquarters. That was the last I ever heard of it.

The balance of my spare time that winter I put into the mathematical study of camshaft, changing rotary to vibratory motion. I wrote out a mathematical law for making these cams and sent it into the Patent Office. They refused a patent, saying that it was impossible, that the mathematical law wasn't known. I insisted, or persisted, and by paying the expenses and examination I was finally granted the patent.

When the chief engineer saw that I was well up in mathematics, he soon gave all the estimates to me to work out. The old engineers had made theirs on the average end area but our chief insisted that all work should be done by prismoidal formula. This ruling just about *threw* the work my way.

Much of the time the weather was well below zero, sometimes staying around forty below for weeks, and we had frequent heavy snows to contend with. Mail and supplies were brought out to the end of the track, then at Bligh's coal mine forty miles back of us, they were picked up by the mail carrier with a sleigh and two small ponies. The high winds of that country packed the snow so hard that he could easily drive on the icy crust over the deepest snow banks. Once I traveled in with him to experience the novelty of riding over the telegraph lines.

Sometimes I get a little amusement now, sitting in a plush comfort of a lounge car on the *North Coast Limited*, of the Northern Pacific, trying to tell some incredulous traveling man, as we speed east over the shining rails, about how damned cold it was laying out those rails.

As the winter progressed, an order came out from headquarters to cut the salaries of all the men twenty-five percent. This made us indignant because we were trapped there. When spring came, and we could get out, a number of us sent in our resignations. Finally, when the weather permitted, I took my time and went into Mandan and from there on to St. Paul to collect my accumulated pay.[7] As soon as I stepped into the home office, I was asked to go in and see the chief engineer. He announced that he was prepared to give me a month's leave on salary, and at the end of that time I was to report back and take charge of the party that would locate the road from Rosser Creek west.[8] This was a flattering jump. I was almost tempted to accept, but when I mentioned that I would expect the men who had resigned with me to be taken back on my party, the answer was an emphatic no. There could be no such wholesale reinstatement; so, I declined the offer with equal emphasis.

My mind was already made up, anyway, about getting back West and I had invited three friends to meet me in St. Paul: Hamilton Headley from Kentucky; Albyn Prince Dike, my college roommate from Brooklyn; and Sedgwick Rice, whose father was lieutenant governor of Minnesota.[9] They were as enthusiastic as I was about making a real expedition into the Rocky Mountains. Moreover, there were five men still out at the railroad camp on the Little Missouri who were eager to join us, and I had left some money with one of them, Billy Powell, to buy a team of mares the engineer corps wanted to sell.[10] From St. Paul I shipped out a wagon, harness, and complete outfit for the party, including provisions. Then Headley, Dike, Rice, and I went on out to our starting point at the end of the tracks. There we annexed still another recruit, one Rudy Heinselman who had been among the early settlers on the Little Missouri.[11] He was well equipped with a team, another wagon, and some riding horses and was willing to pool his outfit with ours. When the party of ten was all assembled, they voted that I should be captain of the expedition and that we would go out to the Rockies via the Yellowstone River.

Crossing the Little Missouri at our old camp we followed the last of the Northern Pacific's location stakes for fifteen or twenty miles, and then headed boldly off in a general westerly direction. It was early summer, but day after day as we rode on into the high country the problem of water became more serious. It was neither plentiful, as we had expected after the heavy snows, nor very good. Then came a day when our kegs ran dry, and we were without any water. We, humans, quenched our thirst with tins of tomatoes from the supplies, but the horses were beginning to suffer. It was in that bleak moment that someone in the party, searching the horizon through the field glasses, spotted a welcome telltale sign off in the distance—a long, thin, winding line of green trees. There was our water. We figured we could reach it by nightfall. Midway we began to hear heavy firing, but this we attributed to buffalo hunters in the vicinity. As this firing kept moving north of our line of travel, it didn't even faze us, and about an hour before sunset we reached the stream.

As we rode up, we noticed that the ground all around was pretty well cut up by horses' hooves. We dismounted, and leading our horses through the brush to the water we suddenly came upon three dead Indians in a small clearing. One was lying practically at my feet with his head resting on a log. He was the handsomest red man I had seen and superbly dressed for an Indian. In other words, he had on a lot of paint and a pair of buckskin pants elaborately beaded. A heavy, old Sharps bullet had torn its way from his left shoulder down through his ribs, exposing the heart. Upon closer examination, we found that all three bodies were still warm.

I blithely suggested we camp there and wait until their friends came back, but somehow this did not meet with the approval of my companions. We hurriedly watered our horses and filled our kegs while a couple of the old-timers in the party took a split second to strip the Indians of their valuables. My young brave had three scalps hanging from his belt. They were not fresh ones, and I figured they no longer belonged to him anyway, so I "lifted" them for a souvenir.

Then we struck a course due west and traveled steadily

all night, nor did we stop long for breakfast the next morning. After another day of hard riding, we reached the Yellowstone River and that night made camp on its banks.

No sooner had we built our fire than we discovered through the glasses that there was an unusually large Indian encampment on the opposite side of the river. The Yellowstone, fortunately for us, was at high water but we took no chances. All night we kept a lookout posted, relieving one another at the job every two hours. It was impossible to sleep much anyway, for our neighbors were having a fine old time, beating their drums, yelling, and dancing until dawn. A few days later we learned that that night there had been six thousand Sioux engaged in a bona fide war dance just across that swollen stream from us. They had sent out a war party to steal the horses of the Gros Ventre because the latter, although belonging to the Sioux Nation, had refused to join with the others in the general uprising. In revenge these Sioux had concluded, as they were riding back down from Canada to surrender to Colonel Nelson A. Miles, to take the Gros Ventre horses first before surrendering—sort of a final rebuke.[12] It was part of that fight we had all but stumbled into the day we listened to the heavy firing as we approached Cabin Creek.[13]

When we broke camp in the morning, we decided to follow the course of the river to Miles City, situated at the juncture of the Yellowstone and Tongue Rivers.[14] On the west side of the Tongue, near Miles City, was Fort Keogh where Colonel Miles was then in command.[15] Mrs. Miles had been a Miss Sherman, and I had known her, as well as her husband, back East.[16] They welcomed us cordially and took us in for a fortnight.

Here we lost Sedgwick Rice. He became so enthusiastic about army life he elected to stay on at the fort and enter the service. My father, in Washington at the time, proved helpful in obtaining a commission for him as a lieutenant in the infantry. Some years afterwards Rice got tired of being a foot soldier and transferred to the cavalry, remaining in that branch of the service the rest of his life. Here, also, we lost another member of the expedition, for Hamilton Headley was called back to Kentucky. He departed by boat for Bismarck and from there he took a train on home.

Before the rest of us left the fort, a large band of the Sioux rode in and officially surrendered to Colonel Miles. It was an impressive sight to witness, but the colonel was still to encounter plenty of rebellion and trouble in moving various tribes onto reservations. Two Moons, chief of the Northern Cheyenne, objected so vigorously to being confined within a restricted area of his own country that he and his Indians struck off up the Tongue River and settled themselves at the foot of the Wolf Mountains. They were left alone for a long time while the other tribes were being moved into the Dakotas.[17]

In one of the many talks we had at the fort, the subject of ranching came up, and Colonel Miles advised me to have a look at the Goose Creek country east of the Big Horn Mountains in Wyoming Territory.[18] He was convinced it was the best ranch country and grassland he had seen in all his many years in the West. He became so eloquent about it that when we took our leave and pulled out of Miles City, we again moved west along the Yellowstone River, this time en route to the Big Horns.

We had heard a great deal about the buffalo hunters

on the northern plains, and now we began to encounter them along the way. These itinerant hunters, who followed in the wake of the early fur trappers, were making huge stakes killing the bison for their hides. Frequently, we were told, they averaged from three to five thousand dollars a season. The hides, after being dried and stacked, were sold to steamboat crews who managed to navigate way up the Yellowstone River in the summer months of high water, and as far west as Fort Benton on the Missouri River. The valuable cargoes were then shipped back down to St. Louis to the leather factories.

As we rode along, we saw huge buffalo herds, one numbering possibly forty thousand animals, moving north to fresh pastures. The buffalo, with its small eyes set far apart in the large head, cannot see directly forward and consequently travels a trifle on the bias, and in herds, they move in a long, winding line. Our party, therefore, was held up quite awhile letting them pass, for a buffalo stampede was a far more serious matter to encounter than a cattle stampede. Not only is the brute strength of the full-grown animal to be considered; there is that matter of power of numbers. When the animals scatter out to feed, they become a lot more shy and vulnerable, and that is when the killing is easier. I say "easier" with due regard for those hardheaded beasts. Once I shot one ten times in the forehead. Each time he would rear and charge. Then I finally got him with a bullet through the shoulder.

As a source of nourishment, the bison was more useful to the red man than to his white brother. All we considered edible was the tongue and hump, slitting the animal down the back to get at the hump. The Indian ate all of the meat, some of which they dried and smoked and, mixing it with crushed wild berries, made into pemmican. The carcasses also were utilized in a number of ways. The skulls were battered in so that they could extract the brains, which they used in tanning; the sinews they used in sewing; the hides for their tepees. Then they would boil up the feet and make a glue, after which they took a stick, shaped it and dipped it into this glue and then into a silica substance, and set it out to dry. In a few days, they had as fine a file as they needed for smoothing bone or wooden implements.

Now that we were meeting up with one band of hunters after another, some of the men with me, particularly those who had been on the railroad crew, began to argue in favor of abandoning the expedition and going into the buffalo hunting business. My vetoes were long and loud, and gradually I worked my party southward and then up the Big Horn River to Fort Custer. General Hatch was in command there, and the post adjutant was young Lieutenant William Francis Roe, from New York. Four short years before he and his company, scouting ahead of General Terry, had been the first men to find General Custer.[19]

Roe and I struck up a friendship, and he took me out to the battlefield, pointing out the places where the different officers and men had been found. Inasmuch as I had met Custer, Lieutenant Crittenden, and several other officers of this doomed command around Washington several years before, I was keenly interested in hearing Roe's theories and reconstruction of the tragedy over which the nation still shuddered.[20]

From Fort Custer, we moved on along the Little Big

Horn, following the road used by the Star Route Stages which the Patrick brothers operated. The Patricks had the government mail contract into this vast district, otherwise I doubt there would have been any road. It was a mighty sketchy affair at that, and I never ceased to marvel that the stages got through on any kind of schedule, but they did.[21] When we reached Wyoming Territory, we willingly deserted this feeble excuse for a road building to skirt along the foothills of the Big Horn Mountains. We crossed Wolf Creek and Soldier Creek and then about noon one day towards the end of June, of this year 1880, a companion and I scouting ahead on foot came to a bluff that looked down into the beautiful valley of Big Goose Creek.[22]

At this point, I shot a deer among the willows of a small stream flowing into the creek. I left the man with me to see that the deer got loaded onto a wagon. The wagon followed the stream down into the valley. I wanted to walk on alone. It was a perfect summer day; the sky above was brilliantly blue with only a few white clouds drifting idly across; the air was clear and cool even though the sun was warm on my back. The range of the Big Horns stretched out ahead of me to the west, the brown ruggedness of the valley about me was softened by all the varying greens of the sage, the wild chokecherry, the quakin' aspen, the willows, and the cottonwoods. Only the infrequent song of the meadowlark or the occasional rustling of a sage hen in the long grass broke the stillness. By the time I had reached the creek I knew I had found all the things I was looking for—good water, plenty of grass, wood for my fires, and wild game. So, with my hunting knife, I cut a stake from a cottonwood tree by the creek, wrote my name on it, and drove it into the ground. There I lived for eighteen years.[23]

The wagons and party soon caught up with me. We crossed the creek and followed it up a mile to make our first camp that night. As we ate our supper, I told the men that I was planning to settle down where I had driven in my marker, and I tried my level best to get them to join me. They were unwilling to commit themselves to so permanent a decision, but because it was a tantalizingly rich game country and the streams were so full of fish, they were agreeable to staying around awhile anyway. The next day I set about cutting poles, and with one or two of the men helping I made a chain survey of the whole section from the mountains down to the creek. Still confident that they would all come around to their senses in time, I located a claim for each man, dividing the location so that each member of the party would have a mile of creek frontage.

The last day of survey work I shot a deer as I was coming back into camp. The deer was slung across the saddle of the horse I was leading and Ben, my old shepherd dog, was trotting along beside me. I had had Ben shipped from Evans to St. Paul and then had brought him on the westward trip with us. Rudy Heinselman also had a large dog along, and it had had many fights with Ben. Rudy had declared that the next time they fought, they must fight it out, to which I agreed. As I came into camp Rudy's dog attacked Ben again, but Ben was quick. He got his opponent by the foot and was getting so much the best of the fight that Rudy couldn't stand it and ran in and kicked my dog. With that, I knocked Rudy down, and for a short time, we had a general melee with man, dog, and dust pretty-well mixed.

That was the first incident to mar the serenity of things. The next day there was a recurring agitation among the men who wanted to go back to the buffalo range. Rudy became a ringleader of this faction, and as he owned a team and wagon, as well as the riding horses, they were equipped to go, but the hitch was that they wanted me to go along and do the shooting for the outfit. Their proposition was that I should shoot and the rest of them would do all the skinning and then haul the hides to the Yellowstone River where the selling would be handled. Again, I refused. I didn't want to be a party to the buffalo traffic, and I didn't propose to leave my newly found home on the Goose Creek. After a while, they thought up a scheme whereby they figured I would be forced to go with them. They laid claim to their pair of mares I had bought, through Billy Powell, from the engineer corps, which of course meant I would be left stranded without horses. This conniving came near ending in a shooting scrape, but more sensibly we decided upon a sort of al fresco lawsuit.

We chose the oldest man in the party to be the judge. He was a real old-time pioneer. Sitting around the campfire I stated my case: that I had given Billy Powell 275 dollars to buy the team. This Billy acknowledged. But as he had taken the bill of sale out in his own name, the judge declared that alone gave him the ownership. I said, "All right, pay me back my money."

I had no idea they could do it, but they managed to raise the 275 dollars among them and brought it over to me. Again, they thought they had me in a spot and that I would have to string along, but I said that inasmuch as I had always considered the team mine, I was going to claim it for a few hours and then I would return it. I harnessed up the horses and hitched them to the wagon I had bought in St. Paul and which was still well stocked with supplies. Then I drove down the creek, crossed it, and went back to the spot where I had driven my stake. There I pulled the wagon into the brush along the banks of smaller Park Creek, stripped the horses of everything except a rope apiece, rode them back to camp, and handed one of the men the ropes. Then I walked down and waded the creek and, walking back to my claim stake, I made camp for myself.

Early next morning the party pulled out and crossed the creek, going north through the valley that I had laid claim to. As they passed by, my friend Dike, who had no horses either, jumped off their wagon and came over saying that he would stay with me.[24] I told him all right if he really wanted to, but to consider it well. He ran and caught up with the wagon, which had not so much as slowed down, and threw off his bed and war bag. By this time the outfit was fully half a mile away from where I stood, and they kept right on going. Then I saw a heart-warming sight. Dike was dragging his belongings across the sagebrush. I went out to meet him, and together we packed his bed and bag back to camp.

There seemed to be enough provisions in the wagon, so we took the next few days off to kill some game. A lot of this wild meat we cooked up hard and dry to eat in lieu of bread with fresh meat as we killed it. But in short time we came to the irrevocable conclusion that it was horses we *must* have and that, if necessary, we would walk the 150 miles back to Miles City to get them. Aware that Goose

Creek ran into the Tongue River and that the Tongue, in turn, would take us into Miles City, we knew we had merely to follow downstream all the way. After taking all the nuts off the wagon wheels so no one could run away with that, we made caches around of various other items we thought would be valuable. Then early one morning we took a blanket apiece, a small sack of food, and our guns and set off east down the creek.

Unexpected good luck was in store for us. When we got to where the city of Sheridan now is, and where General Crook had made his headquarters during the early Sioux Campaign, we found a shack and a man named George Mandell living there. He had a four-horse team, the leaders being a pair of bays.[25] These we promptly offered to buy. True, we didn't look as though we had any money, but both of us happened to be fairly well supplied. Mandell scratched his head a long time before announcing that he guessed he'd sell 'em for 175 dollars, confident that he had hit on a price that would stump us. We went off a little way to apparently talk it over, but in reality, not to let him see how much money we had. Picking out our oldest bills we handed them over. Old George then became very friendly and gave us some rope, gratis, to make hackamores so that we could ride the horses home.

Dike and I drew straws for the nags. One was definitely sway-backed, and Dike got it. He got on, and everything seemed to be all right. Handing him my gun I vaulted onto my steed, but no sooner had I hit his back than he tossed me about five feet in the air. I kept on trying and kept on being thrown until I happened to remember how the boys down in Kentucky used to break horses by putting what they called a jockey strap around them. Mandell supplied another piece of rope, and I put it around my horse so that when I got on, I could get my knees under it. Then I turned him loose and stuck until he bucked himself out; then Dike handed back my gun, and we rode off up the creek, the proud owners of two horses.

Mandell told us that there was an empty cabin on the other side of Goose Creek, about a mile from where we were, that had belonged to his brother, Phillip Mandell.[26] We found it on the way back, and a year or two afterwards Phillip sent out a man named Tony Yeltzer to live there.[27] Tony was not only my first neighbor, and only close one for a number of years, but he also helped me out on a good many occasions by looking after my place during my absences.

When Dike and I got back, nothing had been disturbed so the next day we decided to have ourselves a joy-ride in the wagon. After all, as landed gentry, we felt we should survey our domain in comfort. We put the harness on the bays expecting to start merrily off. But we didn't budge. No amount of giddy-yap, flicking the reins, or applying the switch helped. Dike's sway-back was bent on displaying a prize case of the balks. It took two full weeks of persever-ance and human strategy to get him to cooperate under this new setup, which he apparently didn't approve of *at all*.

But man can be a match for stubbornness, so day after day we hitched the two horses together. Old sway-back would throw himself on the ground, and no amount of pulling would get him up. When our patience ran out, we'd build a fire under him. That always got him to his feet so that we could unhitch him and go into the second part of the routine. This consisted of taking the wagon up a long, sloping hill, my horse and I doing the pulling while Dike walked the balker up. At the top we would turn the wagon around, facing it downhill, and quickly hitch the second horse in. My horse, Billy, was a good puller, and eventually with the weight of the wagon crowding him from the rear, Billy pulling faithfully, and Dike and I alternately pulling and pushing, we'd get down the hill. We did this over and over, going up the grade three and four times a day. At last the fool horse was bright enough to realize that he might as well operate under his own power as to be pulled and shoved by us, and so at the end of two weeks, as I said, he came around. Then we took our ride.

Our next major undertaking was the building of a cabin. We chose a clearing down near the creek and set to work digging a trench in the shape we wanted the cabin to be. Into this trench we set *upright* posts, this being the first log work either of us had ever tangled with. Then we hewed out plates to put on top of the posts, driving wooden pegs through the plates into the posts. Nails were so scarce that our two augers came in very handy, what with all the dozens of wooden pegs we had to make and use. The next step was putting on a heavy dirt and sod roof over split poles. A short distance away we found some rock which we hauled in and used to build a fine big fireplace and chimney at one end of our one room. It was to be the sole means of heating as well as where we cooked. Luckily, we knew enough not to use the more ornamental boulders, which were conveniently around, for they would have popped as soon as heated and then we would have been living in something resembling an active popcorn popper.

We had allowed for two windows and, of course, the door, but when we came to seal the building, we found that the mud chinking wouldn't stick to upright logs, so we had to put in place a lot of small split logs and then pack the mud in between them and the uprights. It was a fierce amount of extra work, but it did give us good thick walls. The floor was made of hard-packed mud. Then with four bunks built into the end opposite the fireplace, we were all fixed. We were glad to move into this somewhat bare but neat interior from our sleeping bags under the stars.

SIX

Homesteading in Wyoming, 1880s

With a roof over our heads and Indian summer in the air, it seemed we should be getting into some kind of industry. Dike maintained that we could make money in the sheep business because he had an uncle in Brooklyn who had made a fortune as a wool commission man. I said all right, if he knew so much about it, he should go and get some sheep. "Oh, no," said he, "*you're* the countryman. You come from Kentucky." Right then and there I told him that Kentucky was a more highly civilized place than Brooklyn would ever be. To settle the dispute, we again drew straws. It fell to me to go after the sheep.

South of us about fifty miles was Fort McKinney.[1] I set out for the fort on foot and from there took the Star Route stage on still farther south to Rock Creek, Wyoming Territory.[2] It was a four-horse stage, and on that trip, I ended up doing most of the driving because the regular driver got so infernally drunk, thanks to the adequate number of bottles concealed on his person, that someone had to spell him. At one point, just after we got onto some good level country with the road stretching invitingly ahead and I had handed back the reins, for the umpteenth time, the driver spied a wolverine. That was too much for the crazy fellow. Off we went in mad pursuit across the flat prairie. The wolverine, however, was in no mood for a chase. Instantly, he wheeled about, snarling and charging the stage. Then we really covered the ground, for almost a mile, trying to outdistance him while some of the well-jolted passengers inside hung out between the canvas flaps brandishing canes and umbrellas. Not one of us had a loaded gun— about the only trip I ever made in the unarmed company.

From Rock Springs I caught the Union Pacific into Cheyenne. Governor M. E. Post, of Cheyenne, had a band of sheep and he made me a price on them, but I was the big businessman from Kentucky, and I thought I ought to look around a little.[3] When trips into Colorado and New Mexico failed to show a better price I went back to Cheyenne and closed the deal with Post for a thousand head.

My old friend Wallace Greene joined me, and with my horse and donkeys sent up from Evans, Colorado, I began to feel like a going concern. To make things even rosier, I bought another wagon and another horse. On a late September day, Greene and I started our homeward trip by going out to Post's sheep camp on Horse Creek and cutting out of the flock one thousand ewes and about thirty bucks. All told, I bought $3,200 worth of sheep. The governor had guaranteed that all were without scab, so we started north, Greene driving the wagon and following the stage road, while I went on foot driving the sheep and avoiding the road as much as possible. With no dog along this time I bought two dozen bells and put them on some of the animals so that if they stampeded at night, I could follow them by the sound—which, incidentally, I had to do a number of times.

Even though I was a novice, I soon learned how to get

the considerable distance in driving my band because sheep always keep moving as they feed. Early in the morning, I'd make them feed in the direction I wanted to go. By noon they would want to rest, and when they started in the afternoon, I repeated the process. In that way, I got nearly twenty miles a day covered, which was a lot better than one could do with cattle.

On the way down, I had picked out three points to the north to guide me. The first was Laramie Peak. When I lost sight of it, I could see Pumpkin Buttes. After leaving them, I watched for Clouds Peak, the highest point in the Big Horn Mountains being over thirteen thousand feet. When I reached there, I knew I wasn't far from home. But long before we got there, we had to cross Powder River.[4]

We came to the crossing at about noon one day. Stopping to rest on the bank I received an unexpected delegation of rough and typical cowboys who were working for the Englishman Sir Moreton Frewen, Clare Sheridan's father.[5] Frewen had established a huge ranch on the west bank of the river, on the site of old Fort Reno. His was the powerful Powder River Cattle Company and thousands of head of cattle bearing the 76 brand roamed his acres. His foreman demanded to know what I was doing there with those sheep—didn't I know that this was cattle country? In short, he forbade me to take the sheep across the river. Undaunted, I stretched a point or two and told him that I had been living in the country before there were any cattle and that I was going north to my own place on Big Goose Creek, and that I fully intended to cross right there. His reply was a terse, "Well, I'm warnin' you *not* to."

Wallace Greene caught up with me, and as we ate our

lunch alone on the bank, I told him not to hitch up the wagon but instead to saddle the best horse and be ready to strike out south down the trail if I got into trouble, and to be sure and not get caught. I had a shotgun along with me, which I loaded with buckshot. Then I started my sheep down to the river.

The two donkeys were a great help as the sheep had grown used to them and would follow them. I drove the whole bunch into the river, and as I did so eight or ten cowboys appeared on the bank opposite, making a lot of big noise. I had succeeded in getting most of the herd across when a bunch of them split and started back into the middle. One of the most disagreeable experiences of my life was when I had to turn away from those rowdies and go back after my blamed, recalcitrant beasts. As long as I was facing the bank, I didn't worry because I had made up my mind that the first fellow to raise a gun would find himself filled with buckshot. But when I had to turn my back, so strong is the effect of imagination, I could almost feel their bullets going through me thick and fast. And yet nothing happened.

When all my sheep were safely across, the foreman sauntered over and said that he had seen Mr. Frewen who had told him to let me go on to my place but that absolutely no more "damn sheep" were ever going to cross the river. And for some years none did, the cattlemen soon gaining control of that whole section.

When I got home, I had lost only one animal. That one I killed because I suspected it had scab, a disease of which I knew little beyond hearsay, but that I was to learn much about during the ensuing winter when we lost four hundred head from the ravages of it. The sheep that got blighted shed practically all their wool and died of cold. At first, I carefully retrieved a sack-full from sagebrush and ground, hoping to salvage something from the disaster, but even as an inferior grade of wool the stuff turned out to be worthless.

During my absence Dike had been very industrious and had built a big sheep shed and corral. His was the kind of industry that extended on into the winter, for he was always making something. When it was too cold to work outside, he made baskets, at which he was a wonder. He had cut bunches of red and yellow willows, bound them and had them hanging around where he could get at them easily. Then he would draw a pattern and make the basket to the drawing. In a few months, we had a generous supply, of various sizes and shapes.

But as spring came on, Dike began to feel that he had better quit the sheep business and go home. This necessitated some paperwork trying to figure out the value of our concern. When we failed to reach an exact figure, I told him I would reimburse him for all he had put into the deal and take over the sheep, land, and so-called—though hardly perceptible—improvements. It was a settlement that suited us both. Dike went home to Brooklyn to rest up awhile from the rigors of homesteading, but he did not go into engineering as he expected and for which he was highly trained. The bug of the West had got him. When his uncle agreed to let him have a large sum of money to loan out on property in the West, he established himself in Omaha and became a very successful note-broker. It is my impression that he got about three hundred thousand dollars from his uncle at two percent. He loaned this out at eight and ten percent, the legal rate of interest in those lusty days being as high as twelve and fourteen percent.

At the ranch it was now up to me, the proprietor, to do something about scab on my sheep, Post's guarantee notwithstanding. This infection, resembling mange, is too contagious to monkey with. So off I rode to Fort McKinney to buy up all the chewing tobacco, cigars, and "making" I could get ahold of. In fact, I was accused of creating tobacco famine around the fort for a while. Home again, I chopped it all up, put it in barrels, and poured gallons of hot water over it; with this solution, I washed all the angry spots on the afflicted animals. But this proved a slow and tedious process, so I ordered a wagon-load of sulfur shipped out from St. Paul. Then I went to the foot of the mountain back of my place and built a kiln in which I burned some lime. When warm weather and the sulfur arrived, I built a dipping vat and filled it with hot lime and sulfur water. I treated the flock three times that summer and again the following year until I was satisfied I had the thing completely eradicated.

After Dike left, Wallace Greene stayed on a couple of years, helping out as sheepherder while I tried to fix my place up. He was a fine herder, too, disproving the theory that intelligence and education were a hazard to the job. But of course, that was just a case of beginner's luck for me. I never again had the opportunity to hire an erudite wool tender to spell me. And spell me, Greene did; for the while he was with me, I could go off on occasional exploring trips into the Big Horn Mountains with a couple of donkeys, a horse, and a dog. More often, however, these respites snatched from wool growing were made on foot. Somehow horses and donkeys didn't enjoy each other's company out in the hills, and the donkeys were definitely a nuisance at night if any mountain lions were around. It took me a long time to get over my surprises at how timorous those obstinate animals could be. Time after time I had to make a corral around my own bed to ensure myself some privacy when the wild shrieks of mountain nightlife got too close to suit them. It was never necessary to fence in those donkeys to keep them from straying.

How enjoyable those trips were though. The country was alive with game. Everything was fresh, unsullied, practically untouched. Also, these solo prospecting trips helped keep my hand in and my hopes high against the day I would eventually strike something worthwhile.

When Greene had to go, this fun was substantially cut off, and I got right down to being boss, herder, and handyman all in one, with no wasted motion. To help with the sheep, I sent for some goats and turned them all together. In the mornings I headed the herd towards the mountains. Late in the afternoon, going out after them, I would meet them all returning to the ranch thanks to the unsuspectingly cooperative goats who just naturally had a hankering to sleep in the same place night after night. One big billy goat assumed the leadership. He enjoyed a fight as much as any dog, but that never seemed to interfere with the real business of heading his charges back to their bedding ground at the right time every day.

While I was "batching" alone, an occasional stranger would come riding through and stop. I'd take fine care of him for a day and then inquire how long he intended to stay. If he replied a week or so, or even a few days, I'd say, "Fine. Stay as long as you like, only *you* do the cooking." Some of them did very well, others almost gave me indigestion. But risky or not it was a welcome break from the monotony of my own cooking. And I had one other rule—we cleaned up after each meal. The cabin was small; it would have become intolerable year in and year out if it hadn't been kept in shipshape order. Because lanterns and kerosene lamps were unknown luxuries in our part of the hills, and candles were darn hard to come by unless I took time out and made a few, we'd eat our evening meal while there was still a little daylight and then clear it away and wash up by the firelight from the hearth. If there was any reading or letter writing to do, that also was done by the firelight, and it wasn't exactly unpleasant, either, close to the fireplace on a cold winter evening, with the snow whirling around outside and a hungry coyote howling not so far off. But for the most part, once the dishpan had been put back on its nail and the final chores attended to, the weary, lonely homesteader and his guest, if any, headed for the bunks. The dawn came all too soon, for winter or summer we got up with the first rays of light.

The supply of fresh game and fish was inexhaustible. When a transient fellow did drift by I could make flourish asking at once what kind of meat he preferred and in half a day, without even going up into the mountains, I could have any of the big game animals of the Rockies killed and hung up at the cabin door. The nearby creeks were full of trout; pinnated grouse and sage hens were thick in the long grass.

By far the most congenial guests were the officers from

Fort McKinney who rode up once in a while to return my combined business and social calls down their way. I looked forward to their visits chiefly because there were several good chess players among them, and chess was a game my mother had taught me to enjoy as a little shaver back in Kentucky.

One young chap from the fort with whom I played fairly often was Captain Charles Rockefeller, a nephew of the oil man.[6] One day he made a hurried trip to the ranch. He had had a letter from his uncle asking him to go to St. Louis and take charge of the family oil interests there. The captain said he simply couldn't bring himself to give up his commission in the army and so he had thought the matter over and had decided to give the job to me. I countered right off that I simply couldn't bring myself to give up my sheep . . . "so let's let the darn job go." We did. His uncle, need I say, went right on prospering mightily without us. Years afterwards I heard that the dashing captain had been killed or went missing in the Philippines.

Most of the time, in the early stages, before I got acquainted with the Crow Indians, I was alone weeks and weeks on end, with only my dog Ben and a couple of other pets. There was plenty of dumb, stupid sheep "bah-ing" around in an unrelenting orchestration to every move I made, but only the dottiest of shepherds would try to tell you that sheep are companionable. Dogs, yes. Sheep, *never*. And so, I had no other company unless I rode off the place to find it.

There was the time, about a year after Dike left, that I did encounter a little untoward sociability off the premises. I was needing supplies badly, so I started down the trail to

Fort McKinney to stock up at the post exchange. About halfway to the fort, an old mountain man named Elisha Terrill had a cabin by an aspen grove.[7] He was originally a Kentuckian, but by the time I knew him he passed for a true old western character, fearless, cautious, shrewd, and observing. Believe me, it took those characteristics to exist in his day, when often the white men were more dangerous than the Indians. We had become great cronies, and I usually stopped off with him en route to and from the fort. He had a magnificent repertoire of hunting and fishing stories and tales of the good old times before so many settlers had got in and made the country overcrowded. He had arrived some twenty-five years before, and he thought that now, with forty of us living between the fort and the Montana line, the country had gone to the dogs.

On this trip, I planned to spend the night with him. I shot a deer and took it along to hang up at his cabin, but when I got there, he already had one. After picketing my horses, I set about fulfilling the guest's obligation of cooking the supper while the old man worked around at his evening chores. We were just ready to eat when somebody called at the door. The old fellow went out and was followed back in by eight men, a real mob for that section. I put some more meat in the frying pan and cooked supper for the bunch. Our host had a big chunk of sourdough bread on hand and some coffee so we had quite a meal. The newcomers seemed friendly and pleasant enough and they spoke with a sort of Southern accent. I got along with them all right, only no names were mentioned.

When it came time to turn in, one of them pointed to the far corner of the room and told me to make down over there. I remarked that it was none of his "d—— business," but Elisha said I had better make down as indicated, so I did. This run-in made me a little suspicious of my company, and although I apparently fell asleep right away, I watched what was going on through half-closed eyes. The last two men to lay down shut the cabin door, put their feet against it, and placed their rifles, cocked, on each side of them. Then I knew I was staying in peculiar company.

The next morning while I was getting breakfast they told me they would look after my horses, water them, and change their pickets. Their final instructions were that I was not to leave for half an hour. After their departure, Elisha, who had come to know them pretty well from previous visits, enlightened me. Our house guests had been Jesse James, his brother Frank, and their bunch from northwestern Missouri; and furthermore, they were currently among our neighbors for they were building a cabin on Little Goose Creek.[8] That cabin is now within the town site of Big Horn, Wyoming. It was well constructed, and back of it they dug a cellar, a very special cellar, on the upper edge of which—about two logs above the ground—was a series of good openings for loopholes.

As this cabin was on the road I had to travel between my ranch and the fort, we got fairly well acquainted, and for a while, they dropped in at my place quite frequently to visit. Their conduct was quiet and friendly, and they interfered with none of the civilians in that section except one man, some twenty miles to the north on the Tongue River. He got excited when he heard they had taken up a place among us and wanted to drive them out. Suddenly about half his horses disappeared. Then he made a stable right adjoining his house and kept his remaining horses in it. As he became more bitter and more active in his attempts to rouse the rest of the landowners, the other horses were removed one dark night from the barn next to his sleeping room. All of his horses were driven south. He traced them and followed them as far as the North Platte River, and that was the last we ever heard of him. Suspicion naturally rested on the James Gang, but as there were other bad men in the country, there could be no certainty about just who was responsible for his removal.

Nine white men and a negro cook made up their party and not long after their arrival they asserted their stand against *the law* in more typical James Gang fashion.[9] The only law enforcement agency in that whole region to bother them was Frank Grouard, a scout from the fort.[10] So they set to work to make clear to Mr. Grouard that they proposed to be left alone in their activities, personal and professional, and that they were completely devoid of respect from government scouts anyway. It was an illustrated lecture they delivered, and it worked like a charm.

They set out some tents on a point on the west bank of Lake DeSmet, not far from the fort, where a small stream flowed into the lake from the mountains.[11] Then they went up this stream a mile or more and concealed themselves around in the bushes close to the water's edge while one of their men rode into the town of Buffalo.[12] Buffalo consisted then of two or three frame saloon buildings on the banks of Clear Creek. Their man got a fellow out of one of the saloons to go to the fort and tell the officers where the James crowd were camped. Pronto, a troop of cavalry, with Frank Grouard leading, was sent out to trap them. Skirting carefully along the hills to the west, the soldiers on horse-back then started slowly down the creek bed toward the decoy tents. When they got to the spot where the James boys were in ambush on the banks, the outlaws rose and covered the completely surprised party with their guns. To a man, the soldiers knew that if they offered any resistance, they would all be killed. Not a shot was fired. Jesse and Frank then issued their ultimatum. They stated that they had arranged this meeting; that they were living on Little Goose Creek and that they expected to be left alone, and that if Frank Grouard ever came over Massacre Hill, he would never go back.[13] When they had had their say the soldiers turned and rode back to the fort while the James crowd adjourned to move their fake camp. Then they came on up to their cabin site, and for the year and a half they lived there they remained undisturbed. Exactly when they pulled out from our country, or where they went, none of us ever knew, but it was presumed that they drifted back towards Missouri.

I must have been away when they left for at about that time I went to Iowa to buy a lot of bucks for my sheep, and when I came home, I came in style—a style I have never forgotten. After purchasing the bucks, I found that the shipping charges would be very high. While I was thinking it over a fellow in the railroad office came forward with a helpful suggestion. "Why don't you," said he, "buy some furniture and then you can take advantage of the 'emigrant moveables' rate?" When the government opened up the vast tracts of ranching land in the West the problems of colonization were numerous. Foremost was that of getting the would-be homesteaders out to their new home.

The railroads, equally anxious to see the new country populated as soon as possible, came forward with the inducement of special rates, known as "emigrant moveable rates,"
whereby whole families could be transplanted intact at a
financial outlay within their means.

To get the rates one had to travel by boxcar instead of
a coach and had to be accompanied en route by one's
household goods and livestock. Hundreds of families came
West in that manner, with a couple of horses, a cow, dog,
chickens, furniture, and crockery all crowded in together.
Sometimes there would be whole trains made up of emigrant cars, but more often two or three would be hitched
onto a passenger train or slow freight. So that was the way
I came home with my bucks. Knowing a little about jerky
transportation by this time, I realized there would be many
sudden stops, that we would be shunted onto frequent sid-
ings and generally knocked around. There were no air
brakes then, mind you, and every time those early trains
ground to a stop, everything loose in the car slid from one
end to the other. In anticipation of this, I bought some
heavy two-by-six boards and penned off my animals from
my new furniture and the furniture from my "quarters."

Then the matter of feeding the human freight as well as
the animals had to be considered. The railroads, mindful
of the livestock, saw to it that we stopped at about every
water tower along the way. With a barrel and several buck-
ets, we managed that part well enough. Hay and grain,
we brought along, of course. But a single man not wishing to cook on a little oil stove along the way, thus adding to the democratic aromas of the trip, had to be right
quick about jumping off at the occasional station stops

and grabbing some hot food at lunchroom counters. I figured I would be on the safe side by bringing along a picnic basket big enough to last me. I also carted along a barrel of apples. Those apples made me quite popular for word of them soon spread, and at every stop, I'd have a few callers from the other cars. When we arrived at Junction City, Montana, my car was detached, and from there I drove the bucks home on foot while the extra stuff I had bought was freighted up by wagon. For quite a while after *that* trip, the cabin seemed more comfortable to me than any Ritz Hotel.

SEVEN

Sheepherding and Crow Indians

Work with the sheep soon made me realize that I needed more dogs. That I was eventually to end up with a hundred about the place didn't matter at the outset. All I considered important was to get a good strain started. Fortunately, I had an officer friend up north at Fort Keogh who was in command after General Miles left, and when he himself left he gave me some greyhounds he had brought west from Fort Totten.[1] They and their progeny started me off with a fine pack of hounds. Then a Scotch shepherd bitch was shipped out to me from Kentucky and from her and my original Ben I raised some extraordinary pups. At any rate, I have a story to substantiate that claim.

One of these shepherd pups I sent to my friend Dike in Omaha. He couldn't keep it and sent it on to his brother who had a store in Iowa. A few years later I received a sworn statement as to the reasoning powers of that dog. It claimed that he had watched his master very closely and observed that every evening the man put his money away in a safe in a back office of the store. The dog made it his business to always be on hand when this was done. But one evening when Mr. Dike was gathering up the day's receipts the dog suddenly dashed out of the store, ran two blocks down the street, picked something up, and returned to the store just as his master was about to close the safe. You've guessed it, he laid down a five-cent piece.

The other pups, his brothers, were equally intelligent. The one I kept with the sheep usually knew more about the flock than any herder. As long as he could see you, he could be directed by a mere wave of the hand. When he was in doubt, he would stand on his legs and watch intently. That was the signal for further instructions.

In the foothills, there were countless mountain lions, far too many for the good of the sheep. Now that I had dogs I began hunting the lions, but I soon found they were a cinch to get that way, for once treed, it was a simple matter to shoot them. It would be more sporting, I concluded, to outwit a lion on foot. There was an Indian scout named One Eye Riley who was a good hunter, and one time when he came to the ranch with a party of officers from Fort Custer I asked them to leave Riley with me a fortnight.[2] Then we located a place where a fine mountain lion ran and proceeded to spend practically a whole week trying to get him without dogs. We finally gave up when we discovered, on back-tracking ourselves, that he had frequently been behind us instead of in front, and probably enjoying the sport more than we were.

Since I have started talking on dogs, I ought to tell how old Ben saved my life once. The elk used to come out of the Big Horn Mountains by the thousands in the autumn. Sometimes they would penetrate down into the valley near my cabin; at other times they were content to lie on the high slopes running up into the foothills. One day I spotted a bunch on one of these slopes and, needing meat, I took my Springfield needle gun and started towards them.

Ben followed me. Climbing the first slope, perhaps a mile and a half from the cabin, I found that the animals were still quite a distance away. While I stood there surveying the situation a big bull elk, hidden in a swale at my right, stood up. I didn't want him, but I knew if he whistled the entire bunch would run so I took a snap shot at him. He plunged forward on his head. Then I ran quickly towards the herd to pick out the animal I did want. I fired and dropped a yearling, but as I did so, I heard a sharp bark behind me. Turning, I saw the bull I had supposed was killed charging me with head lowered. I hastily slipped another cartridge into the needle gun and this time really finished him. It was in the nick of time, too—when he fell his head was right at my feet. If Ben hadn't given me that warning, I never would have known what hit me.

It was now ten years after the Custer fight, and the Crow Indians were settled on a reservation about thirty miles north of me, across the Montana line. Their land lay on both sides of the Big Horn River, bounded on the north by the Yellowstone River, on the west by Pryor Creek, on the south—in my direction—by the Wyoming Territorial boundary, and on the east by the Wolf Mountains.[3] They were content there because it had been part of their former home and also because their very presence kept certain of the Sioux tribes from returning to a favorite hunting ground.

Some of these Crows, knowing the terrain so thoroughly, made hunting expeditions down my way and that is how I came to make friends among them. They took a shine to me on account of my rifle shooting. The fact that I could kill birds on the wing as easily as game on the ground pleased them. Their shooting lacked any such free, easy scope because they always carried along an improvised gun rest. This was made by tying two sticks together at the top with a piece of buckskin. When they got close up on their game, the sticks were spread apart and stuck into the ground so that the gun rested in the notch. Such a rest, though bothersome, was essential inasmuch as they had great difficulty in obtaining ammunition and therefore couldn't afford to waste even a bullet. Naturally, being this careful, they were extremely slow shots, and I became a sort of wonder man among them.

From the start, our relations were friendly and enlightening on both sides. Their moral and mental stamina hadn't been exactly improved by association with the white man, but I found that the older Indians still held firmly to certain of their ancient traditions. For instance, not one of them could look you straight in the eye and tell a lie. Therefore, certain respect was due to them. Plenty of their white brothers around our way accomplished this feat with bland indifference. And if an Indian was angry with you, he would not look you in the face at all. It was singular, too, how easily their feelings could be hurt. If one wanted to joke with them, it had to be made clear at once that it was a joke. But then I *have* seen other people equally obtuse.

After a bit, my new friends indicated that they still liked my shooting but that they also liked my stories. Only a few Indians spoke English, and they were usually secretive about it because they wanted to hear what the white man said without his knowing they understood. My vocabulary in Crow was never very large, but I became tolerably proficient in the sign language, and in that medium I managed to tell most of my yarns. But it wasn't hunting sto-ries they wanted. They knew better ones than I did. Their main curiosity was to know how the white man lived and what he did in the country where he was thick. The sim-plest little detail of life in cities was of absorbing interest to them, and it was quite by accident I happened to hit upon one successful item in my repertoire.

I was alone cooking supper at the fireplace one evening when, out of the tail of my eye, I became aware of being watched. There at the window were a half-dozen Indian faces peering in. I waved and went right ahead with my meal. After I finished, they were still hanging around, so I asked them in to share the luxury of a smoke.

They squatted down in a semi-circle around the fire-place, and I joined them. Cigars were running low with me, so I lit a cigarette, took a puff, and handed it to the next man. Solemnly each took a puff and passed it along. In the course of the visit we smoked two cigarettes, and to entertain them further I began to rack my brain for a new topic. I have forgotten what brought it up, but I casually mentioned horse-cars and how people in cities rode from one place to another. "Horse-car," grunt, "what thing?"

So, I explained, with gestures, about a long covered box-like affair set on tracks in the middle of the road, like tracks for the Iron Horse only not so big. One man stands on a platform in front and drives two horses to pull it. Another man stands outdoors at the back. When white man, or squaw, wishes to get on and ride he waves to the driver to stop, climbs up the little ladder, and gives the rear man a little piece of money (holding up the tip of my finger to indicate a small amount: the whole hand would have signified a very large sum). He then goes inside and sits down. When he wants to get off, he rings the bell, and the driver stops the horses. All day many horse-cars filled with white man and his family ride around.

This was a fine story. When I had strung it out as far as it would go, and it was getting dark, my guests got up and silently filed out into the night. But I knew I had scored a hit when some of their friends began coming down asking to hear about that incredible invention, the horse-car.

On another occasion, after I had been there a few years, I did a little disciplining first and entertained afterwards.

A large band of Indians was camped down the creek about a mile below me on one of their trips out for game. A boy herding sheep for me came and reported that the Indians' dogs had attacked the sheep and killed eight or ten. I sent for the head man and told him they would have to pay for the sheep and move off with their dogs. This was declined to do, so I took my Winchester and a pocket full of shells and went down to their village and shot every dog I saw, some twelve or fifteen. Then I started home. One old Indian followed me. After we had gone quite a distance, I stopped and asked what he wanted. He said he was very poor, and so was his squaw, and he asked me if I would give him some of the dogs. In his mind, the dogs all became mine after I had killed them. I told him all right, to gather them up and I would give him half. After that, the Indians were very apologetic and wanted to pay me and be friends again, so I concluded to give them a dance and food.

To make the occasion more festive, I also invited the handful of neighbors around the countryside and their wives. When the appointed day came, having recently killed a number of hogs, I chopped up the heads and put them in a big vat I used for scalding. This was to be a special mulligan, the pièce de resistance for my red friends. While I was stirring away at it with a big stick, some of the white guests arrived. Immediately the ladies, always inquisitive—even pioneer ladies—wanted to see what I was cooking for the Indians. Down they trooped to where I had the fire going and the big stew simmering. When they inquired what kind of stew it was, I told them, "Dog, of course." Thereupon two of those hardy souls got sick at the stomach, and all of them departed. If the truth of it were known, dog is probably better eating than pig's head, but anyway everyone, including the guests of honor, had a successful all-night dance and party and ended up in a fine state of good will.

There were more encounters with the Indians, but first I got out of the sheep business. In the eight years I stayed in the game I studied the wool markets closely and consigned my shipments to a responsible firm in Boston. Once, in my second or third year, I indulged in a flyer and sent the entire lot to Liverpool, but I realized when the check came in that the Atlantic crossing didn't enhance its value any. The price was identical with the Boston quotations, showing that the English market controlled or set our prices. But the point is when I finally sold off all my sheep I had cleaned up 32,500 dollars—which wasn't bad in view of the original investment of 3,200 dollars. But what a stretch those eight years had been. Being nurse-maid to a bunch of muttonheads was clearly not my dish. The last two or three years rooted to the job, without any Dike or Wallace Greene, were more trouble than I thought it was worth.

Struggling along with an ever-increasing flock through blizzards, scab, lambing, shearing, and shipping I began to feel I could talk the sheep language better than they could, a clear indication, I knew, that I had better get out of the business while I was still reasonably sane. Even a record I established, hand-shearing 115 animals in one day, didn't make me think I was suited to a lifetime spent getting rich via the wool route.

So, with that out of my system, I decided to try farming seriously. It seemed to me, having acquired all the public land I could, that I should begin to improve it. It was good soil but still in the virgin state, boasting plenty of rocks and covered with sagebrush and wild grass.

Down at the fort, they had a heavy road plow, which I borrowed, but after it was hauled up, it proved too large for my team to pull. While I was struggling with it, a freighter came along with a small outfit consisting of four yokes of oxen. He was agreeable to working a little, so we made a deal to plow some of the land. But here again was a complication. Although he could pull the plow he did not know how to hold it, and besides he couldn't do that and drive his bulls, too. Then I remembered a fellow over on Tongue River, called White Horse George, who had once told me he had been a farmer somewhere. Off I went after him.[4]

When I reached his cabin, well hidden in the timber, I could find no one. Ten miles down the river was a stage station where I guessed he might be hanging out, so I rode on. Sure enough, he was there, and he would come and plow for me, but first, he had to go back to his cabin to get his cat. He said if he left her, the bobcats would get her. His concern was reasonable enough. Field mice and pack rats were active enough around some sections to eat a man out of house and home, and thus the prevailing price for a domestic cat, out our way, was five dollars per.

It was now late, so we decided to stay the night at his place. He made a bed on the floor of buffalo robes and a few old army blankets. There was the customary stone fireplace in one corner where we cooked our supper. After the meal, he went out and found his cat and brought her in, but she bolted right out again. That didn't bother him. He said we'd catch her all right in the morning.

I slept next to the door, and when daylight came, I sat up. The first thing I saw was a rattlesnake crawling out of our bed. I nudged George in the ribs with my elbow. When he woke, I suggested we throw the robes off the top of us and get up together as there might be another snake. We did, *and* there was. When we had cleaned out the snakes, we breakfasted, caught the cat, put it in a gunny sack, and started for my place.

My contract with the bull-whacker was that he had to pull the plow to the beam all the way through, and when the three of us got through we had ten acres plowed as deep as any ground was ever plowed west of Missouri. It proved a very productive piece of land and taught me a fundamental lesson in farming. Afterwards when I plowed over four hundred acres, I got a sub-soil plow and used it on a number of fields. The crops invariably showed up where the sub-soiling had been done, paying more than double for the added labor.

Along with the plowing it was necessary, of course, to start digging irrigation ditches. As a result of this pioneer experiment, I received the number one water right on Big

Goose Creek and in Sheridan County, when Wyoming was organized as a state and required a recording of all water rights, as well as the number one right on seven other recorded ditches. Mr. Forbes, the present owner, says he's eternally grateful for this fine water supply.

Now with a good crop of oats coming along for the horses my next job was to plant ten acres of corn to help feed the dogs. Then I decided to try raising wheat because flour, of all our essential imported commodities, was the most expensive.

The wheat did so well it was soon obvious I should build myself a mill. Just as I was adding up the benefits to be derived from supplying flour to Fort McKinney and the whole district, a covered wagon came through the valley from Kansas. It was driven by a woman and her elderly father-in-law. Inside was her husband, a consumptive fellow named John Rummel.[5] They were looking for a place in the high country in order that he might regain his health, and so they settled in the foothills not far from me. Rummel occupied himself chopping wood, and within a year the outdoor life had so agreed with him he was thoroughly well. In the course of various talks, he told me of mills he had built back East in Kansas and that he was a mill-wright by trade. Now that he was able to work again I hired him right off the bat to build my mill.

In order to construct the building, I had to erect a sawmill up Goose Creek Canyon to get out the lumber we needed, so I decided at the same time to build myself a two-story frame house down the creek among the cottonwood and box elders, and within a hundred yards of the cabin. I suppose I felt I should suitably indicate my increasing prosperity, from homesteader to rancher in ten hard years.

For both projects, we cut the logs in the mountains and ran them down Big Goose Creek to our sawmill at the foot of the canyon. It was a hazardous undertaking because the handful of local men available knew nothing about running logs, and at times we found ourselves with sizeable jams in that racing mountain stream. When we broke the jams, the logs moved with such rapidity that it was exceedingly dangerous to be caught on one, so each time I swung a cable over the jam in order that the man on the logs could be lifted to it and hauled ashore immediately when the timber began to move. We were lucky, indeed, to get through without any accidents, for there were no doctors, or first aid stations, or rescue parties within a great many miles.

When it came to harnessing sufficient power to operate the mill, I ran a ditch out of the canyon so that I had a sixteen-to-eighteen-foot drop. Next, we put in a Leffel water wheel.[6] With this construction underway I went to Minneapolis and bought the rest of the machinery we needed, shipping it out to the Northern Pacific Junction on the Yellowstone River, 135 miles north of the ranch. From there we had to haul it in by bull team. This last lap of the freighting, using eight oxen, was the most economical part of the whole transaction because the oxen could rustle their own feed along the way and still make somewhere between twelve and fifteen miles a day.

My mill was the first one built in Wyoming and was finished along about 1885. I heard later that some of the folks in the district thought I was too far ahead of the times and the needs of our people, and that it was just another one of my extravagant ideas. Into it, besides the Leffel turbine, went two burrs and six sets of rolls, all as good equipment as I could get. I was determined it should be thoroughly automatic so that, once set, all one had to do was keep it oiled and clean, and it would stay in condition. I knew if a single bearing got hot and stuck everything would go wrong, an especially bad feature in a mill where the feed is continuous, and all the parts would have to be cleaned out each time an unintentional stoppage occurred.

As it neared completion, Rummel was anxious to stay on and run it. Inasmuch as he had built it, it seemed logical that he could operate it, so I gave him the job—a mighty costly error in judgment, as I soon found out. I lost nine thousand dollars the first year because being able to build a mill and having a knowledge of wheat are two entirely different things.

In accordance with my original plan, I took on a contract to furnish Fort McKinney with all its flour. This was a huge order for us, and to meet it Rummel bought up every bit of wheat in the country. When our first shipment was ready, I engaged a big bull outfit and had it hauled, wonderfully sacked in brand-new sacks, down to the fort. The stuff was no sooner delivered than I was ordered to come and get it.

We had had an early frost through the basin and Rummel, not knowing any better, had bought both the frosted wheat, which had a peculiar sweet taste, and the earlier grain, which was ripe and all right. By mixing the two together, he had ruined the entire output of flour, for when the cooks at the fort tried to bake bread with it they discovered that all it was good for was making biscuits. As soon as yeast was added to the mixture and heat applied, the dough turned to a liquid mass, or mess, and ran all over the ovens without rising even a fraction of an inch. Of course, the cooks reported to the head of the commissary, and he certainly reported to me. In order to retain my contract, I had to hustle up and import from outside their full order of grade-A flour, making up the difference in its cost as well as the shipping.

The only way I could salvage anything out of the fiasco was to raise a lot of hogs. Some years before I had acquired two pigs named Pete and Lucy. They had become pets around the place and produced quite a family. Now I went out and bought up all the pigs in the neighborhood and turned my frosted flour, mixed with bran, into pig food. They throve on it, and this started me in the pig business as a sideline. I was right pleased when eventually a few old fellows tipped the scales at 450 pounds even though it did mean we had to prop them up at the feed trough. They looked so fine I thought I'd try supplying the fort with pork, too. Again, I ran into trouble. The personnel down there liked its pork lean, and once more I had to haul back what I had delivered, render the fat into lard, and return it in that form to my fussy clientele.

Naturally, after the wheat deal, I was disgusted and discharged Rummel. Then I pulled all the machinery out of the mill, laid it out on the sagebrush, and re-set it myself, piece by piece. This taught me every step of the operation. Then I turned miller, with the help of a bright young boy who had drifted onto the place. He ran the day shift, and I ran it at night, catching what little sleep I could by lying against the curb of the warm millstones. The slightest change of motion in the burrs would waken me, and every hour through the night I made an inspection tour from the cellar to the third and top floor. The rest of the time, from sunrise to sundown, I gave my undivided attention to keeping the ranch going.

In working the mill, I was again extremely careful of our safety. In all the years I ran it we had only one accident, and that one happened to me, and during a daytime shift at that.

One hot morning I was dressing a burr with a mill pick. Pausing a moment to wipe the perspiration away I raised my glasses up, and a piece of steel popped off and embedded itself in the center of my right eye. I tried to get it out with a strong magnet. When that failed, I tried pulling a horse hair over the surface of the eye to dislodge it. I only succeeded in making it more inflamed. There was nothing to do but saddle up and ride to the fort. There at the hospital, the surgeons starved me a day before they would put me under anesthetic to operate. Even at that, I was so full of oxygen and vigor that the first quart of ether had absolutely no effect. Finally, they chloroformed me and cut out the piece of steel.

This bit of surgery roughened the surface of the eye so that when it healed, I found it had ruined my fancy rifle shooting. I could distinctly see two notches in the hindsight. This was maddening because I had been so proud of my ability to bring down hawks, prairie chickens, and curlew on the wing. Then, too, I had my Crow Indian "public" to consider. But that is the way we are—I forgot to count my blessings.

Going back to the Indians, as soon as the mill was functioning they came down in numbers from the reservation to inspect it. I would take a group through and explain the workings in detail. Within a month, back they would come with some of their friends, and then they would conduct the tours and do the explaining, usually very well. When some of them took to buying flour from me, I got further insight into their character and some amusement out of it.

As a race they were close with money, haggling over every purchase they made with the storekeepers on the reservations or in small crossroads communities. They were adept at barter among themselves and consequently must have relished trying to best the white merchant. But they had one scruple which unfortunately laid them open to a little victimizing from the other side of the counter. An Indian would always pay, without dispute or bickering, for any article his child got ahold of during the time spent in the store, whether he wanted it or not. As they nearly always brought along the whole family, many a frontier storekeeper took advantage of this by hanging up lines of brightly colored objects, baubles for the most part useless, within easy reach of the papoose on the squaw's back or the small children tagging around her skirt. It was a petty form of retaliation, but it was worked for many years.

In my business, there wasn't much room for haggling. I had but one thing to sell, and I was completely indifferent about selling it to them. Every time they came, however, we went through a routine. My flour was put up in fifty-pound sacks, but not one of them would buy a whole sack the first day. Instead, they paid for a smaller amount and took it off, returning within twenty-four hours for more. In some obscure way, they figured that this was being thrifty.

Fundamentally, they were right because every tradesman knows that fifty-pound sacks actually weigh only forty-eight pounds, the difference being considered legitimate to cover the cost of sacking, etc. Not only did they come out on top, but they got extra sacks out of me to boot.

Only once in my personal experience did I ever catch an Indian in an act of dishonesty. That time three squaws were involved. One day a buck came up, the squaws trailing behind him. There was always a lot of mixed bran and wheat germ which had come off one of the centrifugal reels, and I sold it cheap. This buck said he would like some of it but that he wanted it in good flour sacks. He was very poor, he explained, and couldn't afford flour, but he didn't want to be ashamed of his purchase in front of the other Indians. To humor him I took him up to the third floor, and we sacked up eight sacks of the mixture. The squaws then came up and carried the sacks down to the loading platform at the side of the mill. The Indian and I lingered a little while upstairs, and when we came down the women picked up their load, and they all went away.

Later in the afternoon, I told Johnny we'd better take our regular filled sacks away from the sacking machine on the first floor and cut them up in the second-floor storeroom. The first armful I picked up seemed unusually light, so I opened up a sack and beheld the bran shorts. Down I rode to their camp to tell the buck to bring back the good flour and get the stuff he'd bought. He listened like a graven image, then, picking up a stick, he beat each squaw in turn. That accomplished, he made them trail back to the mill with my flour and carry away the bran.

Perhaps it was a put-up job, but I prefer to think it was just one time when the womenfolk were a little too sharp for their own good.

Speaking of the bran, the dogs soon learned to lick it up from the cracks in the flooring with the result that their coats were in fine shape. I was raising quite a bunch of greyhounds by this time, and they were animals to be proud of on a hunt.

A group of officers from Fort Keogh came down to see me one autumn bringing all the equipment for a real hunting expedition. They had a troop of soldiers, army wagons, and a big outfit generally and were all primed to go antelope hunting in the Powder River region. I was busy with the mill and couldn't leave, but I loaned them sixteen of these dogs. They stayed out ten days and upon their return had nearly a hundred antelope. The wagons were certainly loaded with meat and skins—that is, all the wagons except the ambulance. The ambulance was full of my poor dogs whose feet were so sore they had to be hauled home. The supply of meat I was given was poor compensation for the extra miles the greyhounds had been allowed to run in getting it.

Pronghorn antelope were plentiful in our country, and in the morning when the dogs were fresh, it was a great sight to see them run. They would start a large bunch of two or three hundred pronghorn and then outdistance the entire bunch until they caught up with the leader, threw him, and killed him. The antelope would then scatter, and the dogs would pick up the individual ones. In those days it certainly didn't look like the antelope on Powder River could ever be killed off, but in later years sheep with scab penetrated that section, too, and gave the infection to these graceful wild creatures, practically wiping them out. The hunter cannot be blamed on that score.

After the sheep were gone, I bought a hundred head of cows from a friend, Matt Murphy.[7] Murphy was the owner of the Flying E brand and a really great cattleman. The animals he first brought into Wyoming were Texas long-horns and they were a wild bunch, but he kept improving them with good bulls. My cows were of this improved stock, but even so, they were by no means first-class milkers. So, I thought it would be right smart of me to buy some extra Hereford bulls from another fellow, Sam Hardin.[8] Part of the agreement was that Hardin was to deliver them, and following the contract to the letter his boys drove them over and turned them loose in the pasture close to the house. That night when I came in from the field, I thought I never would reach the inside of my house. They charged everybody and everything in sight. They belonged, undoubtedly, to the bullring and not to a ranch, and after several days during which the men and I dodged them frantically, I opened the gate, turned my greyhounds loose, and told them to take the bulls away. This was just what the hounds wanted, and they happily tore off a few tails driving them into the mountains. That was my new brand for a while—any bull without a tail was mine. I later developed and registered as my brand the quarter-circle T.

Along with the cows, I added more horses to the ranch stock. One was a thoroughbred I purchased from my old friend Hamilton Headley, and at the same time he was shipped from Kentucky I shipped along a number of fine mares. Then I built a race track on the ranch and kept a few boys around working on my "stable."

One of the first colts I raised I didn't run until he was three years old. We had named him WYO, and when a trainer came along and wanted him pretty badly, I let him go to California. Out there he turned into a fair money-maker, winning a number of races and never disgracing us by running unplaced.

With all this going on, operating the mill and the expanding ranch got to be a little strenuous, so when I heard of a good miller named Billy Moline I was quick to hire him. This arrangement gave me a little time for prospecting again.[9] Along with Moline I hired an Austrian named Ben Schneider who was a good worker and, more important to me, liked nothing better in the world than prospecting.[10] Together we dug a good many holes in the Big Horn Mountains in the course of the next few years. The success we had was negligible, but the fun was worth it. The only time I ever succeeded in making enough money prospecting to pay expenses was the year I put in a hydraulic plant east of Bald Mountain on what was called Dayton Gulch.[11] My second summer there I took out enough gold to pay for my plant costs, but when we couldn't find another place to work we quit.

Returning to the ranch after one of these prospecting trips some of my Crow friends said they noticed that I frequently went into the mountains and dug holes. They asked for what? Gold and silver, I told them. Oh, they said, they knew where there was plenty of silver because the old Indians of their tribe used to melt it and make bullets. When I asked for explicit information, they said *they* didn't know where the silver was, but they would find out.

Not long after, some of them came back and told me that the mother of Yellow Crane remembered seeing her buck get the silver but that she was too old to guide us.[12] However, she would tell her son, and he could conduct me to the place. This seemed uncertain to me, but inasmuch as Yellow Crane maintained he knew exactly where the place was I concluded to take a chance. It promised an adventure with the Indians besides the long odds of really finding silver.

My four-horse pack outfit was soon ready and, choosing Elisha Terrill and Ben Schneider for companions, I rode north to meet the Indian party on the Little Big Horn River. I had obtained a permit to take six Indians with me, and when we met as arranged, I assumed everything was under control. Together we rode down the river and then struck off up Lodge Grass Creek several miles to a fine camping ground where we knew wood, grass, and water were plentiful as well as the game.[13] There I was surprised to find more than thirty Indians waiting in camp and determined to go along on the trip. The next two or three days were spent trying to make the outsiders go home, but it was a waste of time. They were all related to my six and would not leave. After sending a messenger to the agency for permission to take them all and being refused, I told them they would have to take their chances as I would not be responsible for them. Then my six objected. They would not go without their kinfolk. It looked as though things had reached an impasse, but I was in no mood to abandon the expedition now, so I capitulated and announced that I'd take them all anyway because after all, I was as good a man as their agent. That was true, they said, for I was much bigger and a much better shot. But I had to write them out each a piece of paper to satisfy them about the coveted permit. Not one of them could read, and what I scribbled on those thirty slips of paper was far from complimentary, being what I thought about them at the moment, but the recipients were pleased and grateful.

Then we packed up and started northwest until we reached the old mission crossing on the Big Horn River. It was the only ford we could make during high water. We got over all right and turning southward traveled through a large Indian camp, of which Dancing Woman was chief.[14] I thought my Indians would want to stop and visit a bit, inasmuch as they were all Crows and we were still on the reservation, but they showed no inclination to tarry. When I asked what was the matter, they replied that Dancing Woman was no good. Probing further the trouble seemed to be that he was despised because he was the richest of all the Indians, having over two thousand horses, but he would not give any horses to the poor Indians who needed them. He was so unpopular with my gang it was obvious that we'd better move on up the Big Horn farther before making camp.

That evening and the next morning I hunted but had no luck. This was serious because we were dependent now on game, and as I was the one member of the party equipped with sufficient ammunition it was up to me to be the provider. However, the Indians didn't hold my luck against me. As far as they were concerned it was just one more black mark against old Dancing Woman, for they were sure he had killed everything around and driven the other animals into the high mountains. Hurriedly we broke camp and went on south to the Pryor Mountains.

I was in the lead by several miles, accompanied by Yellow Crane and White Horse, when a big doe jumped out of some brush. I shot her. Much to my disgust, two fawns ran out from another thicket. The Indians yelled, "Shoot, shoot." I realized that I had killed the mother of these young ones and that coyotes would certainly get them if I didn't, so I shot both of them.

My companions went to look after the fawns while I bled and dressed the old one—for I had a hungry bunch to feed—but I noticed that as they worked, they kept arguing a little between themselves. Finally, they came over to me each carrying a fawn's paunch. Holding them out they said, "Eat." I said, "No eat." Again they said, "Eat." And again I refused. Then one of them said, "Of all the things we know this is the best." "Well, then," I said, "you eat." The words were hardly out of my mouth when they fell to with gusto, eating curd, grass and all.

By the time the rest of the party caught up with us the paunches were practically gone. Then I nearly had a riot on my hands. Obviously, this delicacy was a rare treat and should have been shared generally. In order to end the disturbance, I had to assure the others that I had *ordered* my friends to eat the paunches and they had obeyed me. When all was quiet again, and everyone had been fed on heart, liver, and intestines of the doe, we moved on up the mountain.

Pryor Mountain certainly did not look like prospecting ground to me, starting in with the Cretaceous Formation, slowly going into the Carboniferous Formation and Devonian Formation, but much at my surprise before nightfall we were on a patch of granite halfway up the east side of the mountain and extending over five hundred acres. That night we camped by a stream on the outer edge of this granite.

For two days we did nothing about prospecting. I hunted, and the Indians packed the game into camp. I was giving Yellow Crane time to locate the place his mother had described. Then on the afternoon of the third day, he made the long-awaited sign for me to follow him. Together we went out of sight of camp. Going first southward and then turning west we climbed to the top of the granite outcropping. Continuing north we next came upon an outcropping of serpentine, dark green, and rather inclined to be crystalline. Yellow Crane pretended to be pleased. Handing me a piece of it he said, "Heap good." I said, "No." He tried me out with two or three other samples, and I repeated my sentiments about the stuff. We walked some distance along that dike before he was satisfied that I would not accept his find. Then we went back to camp.

Those in camp were very watchful, but we said nothing. Sometime during the night Yellow Crane got his horse and left. He could not or would not stand the disgrace before his tribesmen of failing in his mission. All that day the other Indians were restless, but I kept them with me in order to give him time to make a safe distance, for it was apparent his friends and relatives resented the wild goose chase far more than I did. When I finally let the others start, I supplied them with sufficient game to eat on the long ride home.

The next morning Ben, Terrill, and I packed up and headed south, following the course of the Big Horn Basin. Above the river's canyon, we found the country very dry with no grass to speak of. But the river was high. Camping that night three miles above its magnificent canyon we decided to cross it next morning. First, however, we had to make a raft in order to get Terrill, who could not swim, across along with such supplies as we wished to keep safe and dry.

We had two axes and plenty of rope, so we went upstream until we found some dry logs in a drift, and there we made the raft and ran it down to within a quarter of a mile of our camp. When morning came Schneider and I swam our seven horses across to the east bank and then—because my horse and I worked well together in water—I went back and started Terrill on his ride across. Very carefully I turned the raft slightly sidewise to the current so that it would help navigate him. We had provided the old man with a paddle to steer with, but he had not gone far before it was evident he was rapidly going downstream. I put my horse into the water again and caught the raft in midstream. Leaning out of the saddle I secured my lariat to one of the logs. Swimming hard and pulling with all the combined strength of horse and rider we all finally landed on the far bank only a half mile below where we expected to.

The canyon was just below us now, and though impressive to view it would have been dangerous for a person to negotiate with the best equipment. Poor old Terrill on his raft wouldn't have had a chance, and I don't know whether he was more relieved or I was when we climbed up on the dry bank.

After repacking the horses, we started a long climb up the west slope of the Big Horn Mountains, south of Devil's Canyon.[15] The ground about us now was rough and dry. We saw some tracks but no game. By late afternoon we reached a better country and found a spring creek flowing into the canyon. There was plenty of grass there for the horses, so after making camp I went out alone to hunt our evening meal.

A mile away I discovered a meadow which appeared to have been an old lake bed. The grass was coarse and high, and through the center, there was a line of willows and brush. On the hill opposite me I spotted three deer grazing. They were too far away for a fair shot, so I concluded, inasmuch as the wind was from them toward me, to crawl or snake it through the heavy grass until I got to the brush where I would have a better chance at them.

Dusk was beginning to gather, and I had no time to lose. Taking a sight on a mountain behind the deer I got down in the grass and put my gun—a one-shot needle gun .45 caliber Springfield—out in front of me in line with the mountain. Keeping a straight line that way without once raising my body, I had nearly reached the willows when, putting my gun ahead again, I struck a cinnamon bear in the back. He was in a wallow and had been asleep, I suppose, but in an instant, he was standing up and snarling. There I was stretched out on my stomach with nothing between us but the gun. Believe me, it is truly remarkable how many things you can think of in a second. Of all the ideas that raced through my brain, the one practical one was that I must have that gun. Partially rising, I sprang forward to grab it. That surprise move was too much for a bruin. He turned, dropped on all fours, and ran towards the willows. Before he reached them, I was on my feet and had him covered, but as quickly as the idea to get the gun had come to me, another idea came. It was, simply, that he had had me in his power and let me go. Now that I had *him* on the spot it would be unfair to shoot. I grounded my gun and with my right hand saluted his retreating rear. The deer were also gone. In the early dark, I walked back to the campfire with nothing for the skillet.

Soon after daybreak Terrill went out and got us a deer. With that in the larder, Schneider and I felt free to go prospecting down in the bottom of Devil's Canyon. We found nothing to warrant all our efforts, but during the course of a long, pleasant day we caught a dozen fine trout. It was a good stiff climb before we got back to camp for supper that night. A few days later we pulled in at our own ranch gate again.

EIGHT

Return to the East

After several years of this free, open life I went east for a short visit with the family. My clothes were about worn out, but I did have one thing I was proud of—my wheat. Putting a bushel of it into the bottom of a seamless sack I tied a string around the middle and, putting a change of linen in the other end, I took my buffalo coat and started for Washington. *En route* I admit I was regarded with some interest, but I didn't give the matter much thought. When I reached Washington, I threw the sack over my arm and started to stretch my legs by walking out to where the family lived. A block from the house I met Father on the street. He took one look at me and said, "My God, George, is that you?"

That salutation made me feel that I perhaps wasn't properly attired. "Yes," I said, "it's me, and if you don't like it I'll go on back."

When we reached the house, I turned my wheat out on a table to show him. He admired it, but he still couldn't get his attention off my clothes, and without further ado, he telegraphed his tailor in Baltimore to come at once. It was a rush job egged on by Father, but it produced four good new suits, three of which I still have around somewhere. (You see, there's just a wee bit of Scot in me.)

The other one I eventually gave to a Wyoming neighbor, the Englishman Oliver H. Wallop, to be married in.[1] In 1925, Wallop was called back to England as heir to the title of Earl of Portsmouth. He came back to Wyoming, and a few weeks ago when he died and was buried from the Episcopal Church in Sheridan the papers all over the nation carried tributes to this old friend of mine and of the West.

When Father felt I was presentable again, I started renewing associations around the capital. John Chamberlain, among others, entertained me at several dinners, providing me once more with the opportunity of enjoying the finest food in the world.[2] I mean that literally; for Chamberlain thought nothing of sending all over the globe for choice things, and for years he kept me supplied way off out in Wyoming, with curry from India and paprika from Hungary.

I stayed East only a short time because an expanding ranch is something you can't leave too long unless you are lucky enough to have a real foreman. Up to that time, I hadn't been able to hire or train one.

In Chicago, on the return trip, a telegram arrived telling me to wait at the Palmer House until a package arrived from Kentucky.[3] The second day it came—a box containing a fox terrier from the Belmont Kennels near Lexington. Fox terriers were not in my line, but because the Belmont people raised the best breed in the United States, I was properly pleased and named him Tuck, an abbreviation for Kentucky. Then I boarded the Union Pacific out of Chicago with my new duds and the new dog. At Rock Creek, Wyoming, we left the train and took the Star Route stage up to Buffalo where I planned to spend the night at the Occidental Hotel.[4]

I walked into the bar only to be greeted by the bartender with "For gosh sakes, take that little dog out of here." He added that he had a big tomcat that had whipped every dog in town and that he'd kill anything as insignificant looking as my terrier right *now*. Almost immediately the cat walked in. But the fox terrier saw it first, and before the cat knew what had happened the terrier had it nailed against a wall. They hit the wall so hard that the dog lost his grip and the cat fled, running out of the hotel and up a long flight of outside stairs. When it reached the roof, it decided to take to the chimney. My pursuing Tuck couldn't quite make that, and I retrieved him still full of plenty of fight.

When we got home, he elected right off to clean the skunks out of the neighborhood. There were plenty of them, and within a year he had them practically eliminated. My only objection to this was that he also insisted on sleeping under my bed. For years I was never sure whether I had Tuck or a skunk in my house.

Hearing about my one terrier Major Thomas, a friend in Louisville, sent out a fine bitch as a present.[5] Her name was Becky, and her mother had been champion ratter of the country, killing ten rats in twenty-two seconds as I recall it. Along about the third year Tuck and Becky raised a family of six pups. From sucklings up the pups spent the entire time fighting. One morning, long before they were full grown, I heard a fight going on but paid no attention. When I went out, however, I discovered that the six pups had set to and killed their father. That was the end of Tuck. My feelings were so hurt I gave his offspring away as fast as I could.

Mother and Father made two visits to the ranch in different summers and seemed to enjoy the country very much. Both times they came on the Northern Pacific from St. Paul and were met by a group of officers from Fort Custer who, with soldiers and an army ambulance, formed an escort for the 135-mile trip to the ranch. Officers and men alike enjoyed this detail because it involved a pleasant excursion for them, and they always returned to the fort with a bountiful supply of game and fish.

At the ranch, Father claimed a big gray mare and an old foxhound and had a fine time grouse hunting by himself. That mare was an obliging old girl; she'd let you shoot from her back or get down to let you shoot around or over her if necessary, and she was completely indifferent about what kind of game was loaded on her. Frequently Father and his hound would be so successful they would come back laden with all the horse and hunter could carry. Then Father would carefully clean the grouse, stuff them with fresh grass, box them up, and send them to the stage station to go, with his compliments, to the officers up to Fort Custer.

I might tell how I came by this foxhound. Colonel Alexander at Fort Custer had brought out a bunch of finely bred foxhounds with which to run coyotes, wolves, and game around the fort.[6] When he was ordered to an eastern post, he decided to make me a present of them without my knowing it. An army wagon came into the ranch one day loaded with these dogs together with a note from the colonel, presenting them to me. They were beautiful dogs but useless in our country because western game runs straight away from the hunter for great distances, instead of doubling on its tracks and circling, as game does elsewhere. These dogs were so persistent that once in pursuit of an animal there was no stopping them. They would eventually disappear from view on the chase and most of the men and horses on the ranch would be worn out trying to catch them and bring them back. When it was apparent there was no hope of training them otherwise, I had to let them all go. But this one dog called Dick, which Father liked, I succeeded in keeping, and a singular thing happened to him.

He associated with my greyhounds after a bit and hunted rabbits with them. The greyhounds always caught their rabbits, while he never got one. Then one day he seemed to suddenly realize that it was his barking on the trail that attracted the greyhounds' attention to quarry they would otherwise miss. From that day on he became absolutely silent while hunting and at last had some fun of his own with the rabbits. This was before Father succeeded in turning him into a first-class bird dog.

My boyhood chum Blair Lee came along with the family on one of their trips. He enjoyed the immediate neighborhood around the ranch where he would hunt for sage chickens or go fishing but didn't care at all for my mountains. They were too strange, bare, and wild for his taste. I was disappointed, but I confess the formation of the country differed radically from the beautiful region around Silver Spring, Maryland, where he has spent his life.

Lieutenant Roe, the young officer who had shown me around the Custer battlefield a few years before, escorted

Father and Mother to the ranch on their last trip to visit me.[7] It was a large party and a gay one. At the time, I had a pet deer who followed me everywhere, or if he wasn't with *me*, he was out running with the dogs. One of his stunts was to come into the dining room and stand by me while I ate dinner. He had quickly learned that this attention netted interesting scraps from the table. When my parents, the lieutenant, and the others arrived, I had all the china and best stuff I owned put on the table for a big dinner party, issuing strict instructions to the boys to keep Prince out of the house. Everything went all right until we sat down at the festive board. Then Prince managed to get in through the living room and as far as the dining room door. All the strangers and confusion excited him. He gave one buck jump into the room and a second which landed him plumb in the center of the table, scattering the dinner and my best possessions in every direction. In an instant, everyone hurled or yelled something at poor Prince; after that evening dishes were a scarce item on my ranch.

Mother had heard that the fur of angora goats was much more valuable than wool, but she put even more faith in the rumor that these animals were good to have around other stock because they smelled so strong they just naturally combatted any and all barnyard germs. When an immigrant came through with a big billy goat, I bought him for fifteen dollars to please her. Upon her arrival the second summer, she was highly pleased to find it and, although she was a dainty and fastidious person, a friendship grew between them. Every day she took him bread from the house, until one day she forgot. When he saw her outside, he nosed around and, finding nothing, he stood on his hind legs and glowered at her threateningly. She became a little alarmed and retreated towards the house. At that point, the goat charged and with one powerful butt bowled her over, as much as to say, "Madame, you'd better remember the bread the next time."

I had finished my new house the year before their first trip to see me. Mother seemed to enjoy the visit to the ranch, and she kept herself and a local fellow, who was a fine carpenter, very well occupied doing things to the new home.

The country I had settled in was now known as Carbon County, and our county seat was Rawlins.[8] The population was slowly increasing, but from one year's end to the next we saw neither our sheriff nor the tax collector. My few neighbors were kindly and extremely helpful with one another in domestic emergencies. And rough language, as one imagines it liberally used in the West, was strictly taboo, for everyone went about armed, and too many "unkind" words, or a careless name, meant an instant fight. So we had none—well, hardly ever.

Among the newcomers was the future Earl of Portsmouth, Oliver Wallop, the only Englishman to ever get a suit away from me and probably the only Englishman to hold out for years against accepting an inherited title. Wallop, when he first landed from England, had settled in Montana near Miles City. Then he came down into our section and traded a bunch of horses for a log cabin in an aspen thicket up Little Goose Creek, twelve miles from me.

The Wallop place originally belonged to a fellow named Davis, a character in his own right.[9] Davis was especially good at drawing the longbow when he told stories. Once I stopped by and listened to him tell how he had killed seven deer all in one place. He said he saw the deer on a hill and getting up close on them he shot two before they started to run. As they got in motion, he stopped another. When they started to circle the hill, he got two more. The rest ran for the top of the hill, and again he got two more before they reached the summit. When as noted the deer turned to go around the hill, his little daughter interfered with, "Stop, Dad, you've got 'em all."

We boasted another character along the creek in the person of old John Coates.[10] So far as we knew he never drew a sober breath, but when he died at the ripe and happy age of 104, the women around the countryside all tut-tutted and said wasn't it too bad for poor old John to go and drink himself to death. But that was what liquor did to one.

After Wallop settled on Goose Creek, he expanded his place. A few more Englishmen followed in his wake, attracted as always by a title, or more correctly, a title-to-be. We made quite a mixed society what with the assortment of local characters, the bona fide old-timers, British remittance chaps, the staid folk of the earnest ranching type, cattlemen, and the promoters who foresaw wealth in every kind of a scheme.

Along about this time John H. Conrad, who had been a post sutler at Fort McKinney, built a store in the little town of Buffalo.[11] When that prospered, he built another in Sheridan, which a man named J. M. Lobban came up and ran for him.[12] Sheridan itself came into existence when John D. Loucks bought George Mandell's old cabin—the place where Dike and I had purchased our first team of horses.[13] Shortly after, Ken Burkitt, George Brundage, and Dudley Thurmond went in with Loucks and built a town on the site, which they first called Mandell and later rechristened Sheridan.[14]

Before Conrad built the Sheridan store, he came and asked me to move my mill to Sheridan, offering me as an inducement half the town site. I told him the mill cost more than the town did; therefore, why not move the town up to the mill and I would be pleased to give them forty acres. That's as far as the matter got.

My next trip east resulted from Blair Lee's invitation to be his best man when he married Miss Anne Brooke, of Birdsborough, Pennsylvania.[15] When Blair and I arrived there, we found the whole town had declared a virtual holiday for the event. The Brooke family owned the iron and nail mills there and were remarkably popular with the townsfolk. It was an elaborate wedding. I particularly recall that Margaret Blaine, a daughter of James G. Blaine, was the first bridesmaid and it was my pleasant duty to escort her about. Not long afterwards, she married Victor Herbert.[16] Blair and Anne spent some of their wedding trip in New York where I saw a little more of them before returning west. They then made their permanent home at Silver Spring. That was my first wedding experience, but the next year I had to repeat it when Albert Fowler married Mamie Ferguson in St. Louis. She was the daughter of a prominent banker there, and again I served as best man.[17]

While in St. Louis, I became acquainted with William J. Thom who was working in Ferguson's bank.[18] He had a yen to get out West and asked me many questions about the country. Not long after the wedding, he arrived at my ranch; he bought some sheep and went into the sheep game. It was soon evident that he was more of a banker than a sheep man. As John Conrad had also established a bank in the town of Buffalo, I decided to get Thom a job in his proper environment. Conrad's cashier wanted to sell out, so I helped Thom raise five thousand dollars to buy his stock, and then he took charge of the bank. That was one time when minding someone else's business benefited everyone. Thom became a successful banker, married, and settled happily in Buffalo.

Also, while in St. Louis at the Fowler-Ferguson wedding I saw a good deal of Mrs. J. Sire, who was an aunt of Wallace Greene, a friend from my Colorado prospecting days and my early sheep experiences in Wyoming.[19] She was devoted to her nephew and very proud of a bearskin that Wallace sent her. It was an unusually large cinnamon bear, which she had tanned and then shipped to the New Orleans Exposition where it took a special blue-ribbon award.

I remembered well Wallace killing the bear. He was herding my sheep close to the foot of the mountains when he thought he'd like to get a little game on the side. He hadn't walked far up Rabbit Creek Canyon when he encountered this cinnamon bear and got fairly close—within a hundred feet—and then he had to shoot three times before the animal dropped. He came tearing back to the ranch to get me to take a team and wagon and go back with him, all the time telling me what a huge bear it was. I figured it probably seemed large to him because it was his first bear, but when we got to the place it was all my team could do to drag the animal out of the timber. We skinned him carefully and carted the hide to the scales to weigh it. The skin, perfectly clean, weighed ninety-five pounds. On this basis, we figured the live animal at something over 1,600 pounds, so I was not surprised when the hide drew a prize. It was really as large as a buffalo hide.

After those pleasant days in St. Louis, I concluded I had had enough holiday and should get back to my ranch but had a slightly longer stopover in Denver than expected. The train to Wyoming did not leave until the following day. So, I registered at the Brown Palace.[20] While walking through the lobby, I noticed two ladies and suddenly recognized them as Mrs. Ames and her daughter Mary whom I had met in Washington. Mrs. Mary was a sparkling brunette with a charming voice and manner, and I was pleased to run into them. When they told me this was their first visit to Colorado, I suggested that they accompany me on a picnic up on Pikes Peak to get a view of the country.

NINE

Trips to the South and to Cuba, 1889

Snowstorms started in earnest in October 1886 and seldom let up. An occasional slight thaw would quickly turn
the snow to ice and then more snow would come down,
so the animals could not get food. My dear mother died
in March of 1887, one of the worst months of a terrible
winter in the West. Stages and mail were often weeks late,
and I did not get the sad news in time to get to Washington for her funeral.

In the next few years, I made several trips to Washington and various places with my father. His health was a
matter of concern to all of us, and it seemed I could be
most helpful by being with him in the capacity of secretary-
companion. On our last trip together, we spent the winter in the south.[1]

We stayed awhile in Savannah and went from there
on several hunting trips. Stopping off at Brunswick,
we put up at a place known as Tyson's Pasture. It was
owned by a friend of Father's, and in preparation for
the visit we had gathered up some dogs in Brunswick
to take along. Among them was one dog we had to be
very careful with. The owner told us that if on the first
run of deer out of the brush we failed to get our deer,
the dog would in sheer disgust go to the railroad sta-

tion and get on a train and go home. Fortunately for us, Father saved our face.

The manner in which these small deer were hunted was of particular interest to me after my recent experiences with larger game in the Rockies. The hunters took their stand on the passes, or run-ways, near a swamp and waited while the beaters took the dogs around several miles in order to drive them into the swamp from the opposite end. The hunter could then get his deer as it came on the run out of the swamp.

One day I chose to remain at the plantation while Father went out. I was sitting on the veranda reading when a fierce racket broke out down on the bayou a hundred yards east of the house. Walking down to investigate I saw a bunch of twenty-five or more porpoises come up the bayou pursued by a boatload of negroes beating the water and making a great commotion in an effort to drive the porpoises on up into the shallow part of the bayou. There was a narrow place, ten or twelve feet long, where the negroes could turn the boat sideways and block the quarry in. They accomplished this much of the maneuverer, but the porpoises objected. Having gone to the end of the inlet they turned around and swam back for the broader part. The negroes continued shouting and beating at the water with oars and poles, but the porpoise in the lead was too smart. He leaped into the air and struck the boat amidships, breaking it to pieces. Negroes and boat flew in all directions. Each porpoise that followed jumped, like so many sheep, in the air at the identical spot. It was quite a sight. Had the negroes been quick enough to drive their poles into the shallow water before their quarry got turned around, they would have helped them in and eventually, of course, realized a little money for their effort; now all they got was a bath.

From Brunswick, we went out to Senator Norwood's place.[2] It was a beautiful plantation on the Ogeechee River. Unfortunately for me, however, he had hundreds of magnolia trees around the place, and the perfume was more than I could stand. After the first evening, I concluded I would have to spend the rest of my nights off hunting opossum if I was going to stick out the visit.

Getting ahold of a mule and an old buckboard I drove up the river a few miles to a place where there was a colony of truly primitive negroes. A few of them had their teeth filed to point, and some of them had seldom seen a white man. They stared at me, and I certainly thought they were a curiosity, but we got acquainted, and I discovered that they liked nothing better than to hunt 'possum and raccoons. So, I proposed paying a dollar a night to the negro whose dog spotted the most 'possum. That was fine with them.

There was one good-sized cabin in their village, and an old negro woman there was a very good cook. That place became my headquarters, and each night we started out from there. I must have cut quite a figure dressed up in hip boots, a hunting coat, and carrying a shotgun, while my retinue of eight or ten negroes wore hardly any clothes and carried only an ax and a sack. After branches of fat pine had been cut to use as torches, we headed into the swamps.

When we caught up with the barking dogs, the 'possum would usually be up a tree. If it was a small tree, we cut it down, killed the 'possum, and put him in the sack. If it was a large tree, I would tell all the negroes to put out their torches, except one. After retiring about a hundred feet from the tree, the one negro with the torch would then take his stance behind me and slowly wave the torch back and forth. The foolish old 'possum's curiosity would be his undoing. He would look out to see what was going on, the light of the torch reflecting from his eyes, shining like stars. Then it was an easy matter to shoot him.

It was a remarkable thing that during the time I hunted with those negroes we never had a dispute about whose dog had started the most 'possum. The master always knew that when his dog's voice changed it meant he had struck a trail, and the decision was left on that.

Towards daylight, we'd start back with our sacks full, and ready for a meal. The old cook always had two or three 'possum ready for us along with sweet potatoes baked in the ashes, and an enormous lot of corn pone.

Our raccoon hunting, on the other hand, was not so easy. They frequently gave us a long run and many times got away. The 'coons could elude the dogs by getting to the tops of the trees, many of which were 120 feet high. They could outdistance the dogs easily once they started jumping about from one treetop to another.

In this way, I avoided the magnolia trees and had a very good time doing it. Snipe and quail were plentiful, and Father and Senator Norwood amused themselves shooting them. I also recall that during our stay south that winter a package of butter would come to us by express every day as a present from Colonel Andrew Jackson III.[3] Colonel Jackson's dairy on his Tennessee plantation, the Hermitage, was the finest in the South for his cows lived on bluegrass pastures. He milked one hundred Jerseys and a hundred short horns daily, and his butter was so exceptional that it used to bring a dollar a pound in New Orleans and other Southern cities. We were more than gratified for it because the general run of butter in the South in those days invariably tasted of garlic and other weeds.

Leaving the senator's plantation, we went to Jacksonville and then to St. Augustine and stopped off at the well-known Ponce de Leon Hotel. We were shown to a large room, nicely located, with twin beds, a big bath, and closets. No sooner had our luggage been put away than I happened to see a notice on the door which read, THIS ROOM $50 A DAY. I suggested to Father that we had been there too long already. I was for moving right out, but he thought I'd better go down and see the clerk. When I found that fellow he didn't seem at all perturbed and announced in the most matter-of-fact way that the room was ten dollars a day for the two of us. "We put the notice up," he said, "to keep the Jews out. Once they get started at a hotel here in the South, the hotel loses all its other patronage."

Shortly after our arrival Bishop Spalding, the Catholic bishop in Illinois, came and when he found that we were going to Cuba, he asked to join us.[4] Together we went to Tampa and from there took a boat to Havana. The bishop cheerfully discarded his clerical robes and everything else that might indicate he was a priest, in favor of being an ordinary layman on his holiday. He was a pleasant, entertaining person and we enjoyed his company. The boat was the *Olivette*, and the captain was a Scotsman so that Father also got chummy with him.[5]

I had taken a .22 rifle with me and when I found, on docking at Havana, that the duty would be more than the rifle was worth I decided to send it back with the captain. As I was about to leave the customs, one of the revenue men asked me which hotel we would be stopping at. I told him the Pasachi. He said, "Give me one dollar and your gun will be there tonight." I didn't need the gun, but I was interested in the performance. I handed him the dollar, and sure enough, the gun was delivered as he had said.

The Pasachi was not the largest hotel in Havana, but it was reported to be one of the best. Father and I were assigned to a room on the second floor, with big windows opening down a long veranda. The door had no lock on it, which seemed unusual to us, but we figured that if any-one broke in, we could throw them out through the win-dows. The next morning, before daylight, two native boys rushed in on us carrying two little tables, which they set by our beds. On the tables were peeled oranges and a pot of coffee. My father asked what this might be, but the boys spoke no English except "breakfast." As breakfast it cer-tainly did not suit us, nor did we approve of the hour. We finally got a clerk up to find out about this monkey business.

He informed us that it was the custom; that the regu-lar breakfast would be at ten o'clock and that it would be a hearty meal, but at daylight, when one got up, one had one's oranges and coffee. We arranged a compromise by announcing that hereafter they must send along rolls and butter with the number one breakfast.

Of course, business in Havana is attended to early in the morning or late in the afternoon. From eleven until two o'clock the town is quieter than it is at midnight because the inhabitants have their siestas. We were not prepared for this until we walked into a shop around noon a day or so after landing and found the clerks asleep on the counters. They objected to being disturbed, and after we got onto this custom, too, we got along very well.

Father, as a United States senator, had special passports from the State Department. We had not been in Cuba twenty-four hours, therefore, before we were called upon by special delegations and invited to dine the following day with General Valeriano Weyler, the governor general whom Cubans referred to as "the Butcher" because of the severity of his administration.[6] All of our activities included the bishop and dinners and receptions kept up for a week or more. I soon got tired of that phase of our visit and left Father and the bishop to do the social things while I went off to see Havana on my own.

I could read a little Spanish, and looking over the newspapers I noticed that there was a big chess tournament about to start between Tschigorian, the Russian champion, and Steinitz, the American champion.[7] The announcements said that d'Hadres, the chess club, would be the headquarters but that the official games would be played at the casino, the city of Havana having put up ten thousand dollars for the tournament.[8]

At the club, I found I couldn't make the doorkeeper understand my Spanish, so I walked past him into a large hall. Some fifty or sixty people were inside, and I looked around for someone to interpret for me. I noticed one gentleman sitting at a small table. I thought I recognized him, so I walked over and said, "I'm sure you speak English." He smiled and said, "I wish I spoke Spanish half as well."

Then I explained that I was interested in chess and would like to see some of the games. He invited me to sit down while a boy was sent to fetch the secretary of the club. While we waited, he asked me where I was from, and I told him Wyoming. He immediately wanted to know if I knew Horace Plunkett.[9] I said, yes, that we had played a good deal of chess together.

Sir Horace Plunkett was an Irishman who had a cattle ranch at the head of Nowood.[10] Before his father died and he was recalled to England to become Lord Plunkett, he used to come over to Buffalo every so often, and there we would play chess for a straight week at a time, often without a board. He was a brilliant player. I've seen him take on twenty men at once. He had just one idiosyncrasy which I never would understand. He invariably carried with him on these trips a satchel in which there was nothing but paper, pen, and ink.

My knowing Plunkett delighted my companion. "Why," said he, "Horace Plunkett is my greatest friend. When he was in Parliament, as secretary of agriculture for Ireland, he was the Parliament chess champion." And then he introduced himself as Captain George Henry MacKenzie, the English chess champion.[11] When the secretary arrived MacKenzie introduced me as a friend, and I was presented with complimentary tickets for the entire session of ten games at the casino.

Through this connection with the club, I also met some of the young Spanish set with whom I had a few interesting games of my own. One evening, before the tournament began, I was there with two young Spaniards. We walked over and stood by a table where a couple of men were playing and attracting considerable attention. As we watched one of the players, a Frenchman made a false move in my opinion. I commented on it to my friends. The other player looked up, and when he had finished with the Frenchman in three more moves, he motioned me to take the place opposite him. We played a little while, but he got me. It was only then that I found out I was playing with none other than Tschigorian himself.

Several of the Spanish men my age offered to take me around and show me Havana. On this trip, I had with me a very fine detective camera, borrowed from Professor Smiley, the head photographer at the Smithsonian Institute in Washington. It took pictures at right angles to the line at which it was pointed and was, therefore, most convenient in photographing strangers without their knowledge. I had shipped five hundred glass plates down, and this camera amused my Spanish friends so much they insisted I take it with me on all our trips around the city.

One afternoon five of us were going out to see the Jean Alvarez tobacco factory. It was in the suburbs, and a streetcar was the easiest way to reach it. There was an elderly woman and an extremely pretty girl sitting on the car we boarded. My friends immediately commented in enthusiastic English on the girl's beauty, and all wanted me to take her picture. They were so insistent I finally turned the camera around, caught her reflection in the finder, and pressed the button. It made a little click, and my group asked if I had it. I replied I thought so. Whereupon the girl turned around to the old lady and said in perfect English, "Well, that *was* cheeky." We got out at the next corner and walked several blocks in the sand to cool off our red faces.

Before I got through with it, I had photographed most of the wives and sweethearts of my new cronies. In this way, I certainly got to see much more of Spanish life than did either Father or the bishop. In the homes, I discovered that there was a great deal of formality when visitors came. The ladies sat in a dignified manner on one side of the room, the gentlemen on the other side. Occasionally a lady lit a cigarette or cigar, puffed on it a few seconds, and handed it graciously to some gentleman she wished to favor. On the whole, I wasn't much attracted by the señoritas as nearly all of them were too fat for my American taste.

There was one especially handsome showplace on the edge of Havana, a house that was practically a palace. Some real estate men got in touch with Father and tried to persuade him to buy it. It must have cost a quarter of a million dollars originally, but the price asked was a very tempting ten thousand dollars in gold. It was so tempting we concluded there must be something wrong, so we looked into the matter. The taxes, we found were so heavy one could not afford to take it on even as a gift. They were taxing about everything in Havana and to have one window in a house was a luxury, in itself, costing two cents per pane per annum. After counting the windows in the castle, we declined the bargain.

We drove about the country a good deal and spent a short time in Matanzas, going there by train. But when the spring came on, we felt it was high time to start back to the States. In Havana we engaged passage on the *Olivette* again, sailing the next day. But that night a northerner came up. In the morning I went down to look at the ocean. The waves were so huge I felt certain we could never get out of the harbor. A wave, striking the rocky point of Moro Castle, where the great lighthouse stands, would succeed in throwing several hundred tons of water completely over the top of the light. It was a beautiful thing to see, but I was more convinced than before that we would be wise to stay where we were. However, Father had great faith in his Scottish captain and determined that if he sailed, we'd go, too. And go we did. Until then I had no idea a boat could stand tossing around like that boat did. One old Spaniard and I were the only two passengers to stick it out in the smoking room. Everyone else on board took to their cabins.

Safe at Key West we spent a few days resting up before taking another boat to Tampa. From the mainland, we proceeded north by slow stages.

My sister Bettie and her husband, Colonel Goodloe, had a country place called Woodreve, just outside the District of Columbia in Maryland. The post office was in Brookland. My father went out there to stay, and I spent a few days with them before taking the train west again.

My sister's next-door neighbors were Jerry and Mrs. Johnson who had a son named Nelson and a daughter named Betty. They were close friends, and my sister became young Nelson's god-mother. These children afterwards became friends with my children, Jane, Betty, and Thornton. In 1931 Jane went out to China and married Nelson Johnson who was stationed there as our United States minister. Shortly afterwards, in 1935, he was elevated to ambassador. As I write this, he is currently serving his country as United States Minister to Australia (1941–45) and is living "down under" in Canberra with my daughter and their two children, Nelson Beck and Betty Jane.

TEN

Wyoming Territorial Legislator, 1889–1890

When I got back to Wyoming from that trip things were badly disorganized, but what upset me most was that all my dogs had been poisoned. When I left I had had some of the finest greyhounds and staghounds in the territory, the latter acquired as a result of one of my previous trips east.

One visit to Washington I had been dining one evening at Admiral Lee's and had taken Mrs. Andrew Gratz to dinner.[1] She and her husband were fellow Kentuckians from Lexington but had moved to St. Louis. There Andrew had become president of a rope and bagging trust. In the course of his business, he had encountered difficulties in lining up some important Scotch interests which were vital to him because they controlled the Manila [rope] trade from the Philippines. Andrew had therefore gone to Scotland to see the old lord who was the head of that branch of the business and had eventually gone out to his castle to visit him. He was making no progress until he happened to notice that this old Scotsman was very proud of his staghounds. Andrew immediately began to praise them and insisted on buying two. The old man finally sold him two prize dogs for five hundred pounds. Andrew had had them shipped home to St. Louis, and then the jute and Manila trade went through.

Mrs. Gratz was telling me this story at dinner. But, she said, she did not have a friend left in St. Louis because of the dogs, and so she was going to have them killed before Andrew got back from another business trip. I asked her to give them to me instead, assuring her I would have them removed before either she or her husband got home. She was delighted and said, "They're yours." I scribbled off a message to Andrew in New York and gave it to the butler, and before we had finished dinner, an answer came confirming the gift.

I had frequently stayed at the Southern Hotel in St. Louis, and there was a porter there named Tom who used to look after my affairs around the hotel.[2] I telegraphed him to go to the Gratz place, get the dogs, and keep them at the hotel until I arrived. When I got there about a month later, they had become one of the attractions around town. They were enormous in size and people seeing them would wonder what they were. Tom was very proud of displaying them.

When I got them out to Wyoming, my greyhounds didn't like their looks, and we had trouble saving their lives. When I wanted to let them out I had to keep the greyhounds shut up, or the other way around. This problem was eventually solved by trading one of the dogs off to an officer friend who owned General Custer's favorite staghound bitch, a dog named Mada Custer. After the trade, peace reigned and all my dogs ran together. But these and their progeny were among the dogs killed. Cattlemen, I was informed, had put out poison for them claiming they had destroyed too many head of cattle.

Politics was at last beginning to take up the attention

of the country, and I got interested, along with my neighbors. The town of Sheridan had grown, and the county
of Sheridan was being cut off from Johnson County.[3] Perhaps I got interested largely because the town of Buffalo
was in Johnson County and I had been buying up some
land around and in Buffalo. The two counties, however,
were to have one territorial senator, so I decided to run
for that office on the Independent ticket.

Henry Asa Coffeen, whom I ran against, was a Sheridan
resident and quite a booster for the town inasmuch as he
owned a store there.[4] His one brother-in-law was in business in Buffalo, and when the votes were counted I was
amused to find that I had every vote in Johnson County
except that one, and as I had more than half of those of
Sheridan County, I found myself elected.

Thus, I went to Cheyenne to attend our last legislature
as a territory. There I was elected president of the Senate, or Council as it was then called. We had a Democratic
majority of one, while the House was strongly Republican
with Mortimer Jesurun the Speaker. Francis E. Warren,
whose daughter later married General John J. Pershing,
was governor.[5]

When I was about to appoint my officers for the Senate, the Republicans—thinking to get me in trouble with
the Catholics—proposed that the Catholic bishop be a
chaplain. They surmised, of course, that I would react by
appointing a preacher of another denomination. I didn't
commit myself. Instead, I quietly went to call on Father
Nugent, the acting Catholic bishop, and told him that I
intended to appoint him chaplain but on one condition:
that all of his prayers must be in Latin.[6] When our first

session opened, and the reverend father appeared, it was a great surprise, and when his prayers were delivered in Latin there was a considerable relief. Chaplains, as we all knew, had more than once become active politicians by the simple expedient of slipping a few extra phrases into their prayers for or against some bill or measure. Father Nugent and I became good friends that winter although I never became more Catholic than I always had been. Later on, I had hopes that the worthy churchman might become bishop of Wyoming, but these hopes were dashed when, largely through the counterefforts of my friend Janie Riggs, he became bishop of Missouri.[7]

The Council members, for the most part, knew little of parliamentary procedure and the Council rules seemed actually primitive. Because of my earlier training as Father's secretary in Washington, this all bothered me, and so I set about rewriting some of the rules and making the changes required to get the body in good running order. As this was the last Territorial Legislature, we worked largely on unfinished business in preparing for the change to statehood. On the final day of the session, I was presented with a fine ivory gavel by all the Council members. They made the presentation at four o'clock. At eight o'clock that evening when I closed the doors and kept them all at work, they tried to take the gavel away from me, but I held on to it and had the pleasure of pounding the desk repeatedly for order during a very unruly session.

I had, of course, become a member of the old Cheyenne Club.[8] In those days when the cattle business was booming, more than half its members were English stockmen, and it was an interesting meeting ground. A week after we convened Mortimer Jesurun, the Speaker of the House, gave a dinner there to the members of the legislature.[9] When dinner was over, he suggested a game of cards to some of us. As I had been an honored guest, I could hardly decline, but when I saw the room that had been prepared, I was somewhat suspicious of what I had let myself in for. I had never played poker for money; in fact, I knew very little about the game. Jesurun, on the other hand, had quite a reputation as a poker whiz.

Five men were invited to play, three from the House, and my friend Charley Campbell and myself from the Senate.[10] That made the game take on an added political aspect, we thought. Each player took one hundred dollars' worth of chips. I figured I would lose mine and be able to withdraw gracefully from the game, but I lost so quickly that I had to re-invest. Before midnight both my salary and my mileage allowance were gone. In one of my pockets, I had a draft for one thousand dollars. This I gave to the secretary of the club with instructions to bring it to me in chips. I lost half of that before four o'clock. As the game was limited to eight o'clock, when the winner was to buy breakfast, I thought I might as well stick it out. Suddenly my luck changed. Everyone was calling me every time I made a bet, and I found the change of cards so beneficial that it was I who had to buy the breakfast. I not only won all that I had put up, but each man at the table had to draw me a check. I was glad when I found my friend Campbell's was the smallest; it was for 250 dollars.

All this did not make me believe, however, that I was a born poker player, and after that, I studiously avoided the game for the rest of the session. But I did give a return dinner the next week, which I managed very easily with my profits.

On the 10th of July 1890, Wyoming became the forty-fourth state admitted to the Union. Its citizens were justly proud of the new state and of the fact that, new as it was, Wyoming was the first state in the Union to grant women the right to vote.

Having got into politics, I went on to our Democratic State Convention. I had no intention of running for office again, but I did feel I could help perfect some sort of organization. The Democrats could find no one to run against Clarence D. Clark for the House of Representatives, and they insisted that I should oppose him, so I finally agreed to do so.[11] I still maintain that I did it to help our organization.

It was a foregone conclusion on all sides that I would lose because Clark was the attorney for the Union Pacific Railroad and a great friend of the Mormon Church. The railroad and the Mormons were both powerful in our state politics. The Mormon towns along the Union Pacific boasted most of the state's population and any move the railroad dictated was law with them. Early in the game, I was requested to meet with some of the brethren and was asked what my stand would be if anything pertaining to the Mormon Church should come before Congress. I replied that I would be strictly impartial, which did not seem to be the answer they wished. There wasn't a prayer for me, and I knew it.

I proceeded to hitch up my best team to the buckboard, threw my bedroll in the back with a sack of oats for the horses, and started out. Campaigning by buggy was a strictly one-man affair, a matter of driving weary miles from one isolated ranch to another, of pulling up beside the fence and talking to the rancher in the field, or the cowboy in the saddle; of hoping to reach a clean, comfortable farmhouse at dinner time, and sitting down with the whole family, youngsters, hired men, and all—and trying to judiciously count the votes along with some conversation about the price of hay and the threat of hail. Only on rare occasions did we have any report of a crowd collected in one place long enough to hear a set speech.

It was while I was campaigning this way, off in the far western part of the state and a long way from any railroad, or telegraph line, that my father died in Washington and was buried in Kentucky before I even heard the news.

I was later told that he had been so popular in Kentucky that when the train bearing his body from the capital to Lexington crossed the state line, the track was lined with people showing their respect. He was laid to rest in Ashland Cemetery beside my mother, who had died nearly three years before. Many of his old friends including General Breckinridge, his closest friend, were buried close by, and the monument to Henry Clay, erected by the people of Kentucky, stands not far from his grave.

My sister later sent me the memorial volume put out by the U.S. Senate with the speeches made in Congress after his death. As I read of his efforts to defend the South during Reconstruction, to gain lower tariffs, and to help Confederate prisoners to return home, I relived the years when he had had no help in his senatorial office except me at various times. Twelve to fifteen hours a day were common to him, and his reply when my mother remonstrated was, "I'd rather wear out than rust out."

ELEVEN

Another Trip Back East and to California, 1890

I did not go east until after the election. Of course, I lost, as I had expected. Then I went on to help settle Father's estate in which my sister, Bettie Goodloe, and I shared equally. When these matters were attended to I somehow did not feel like returning immediately to the ranch, so I hit upon the idea of going on out to California.

On the way, I stopped over in Chicago for the Christmas holidays and put up at the Auditorium Annex. It was pleasant seeing some of my Chicago friends, L. Z. Leiter, his son Joe, and several others.[1]

Jim Corbett, too, was around town doing exhibition boxing on the stage with another man.[2] I had seen him and was satisfied I could lick him, so when I met him, I asked him to box with me. He declined on the grounds that as a professional he could not afford to risk his reputation inasmuch as I was just boxing for fun. But he agreed to put on a special sparring match with his partner, and he gave me a couple of boxes. I took old man Leiter and Joe and others, and afterwards we all repaired with Corbett to a Turkish bath. Then Corbett left Chicago.

I was still hanging around when one evening Horton Boal, a Chicagoan whom I had met in Wyoming, and several other western fellows I was running around with, came in to see me late one evening and insisted that we all go across the street to the Congress Hotel bar.[3] We were sitting there having our drinks when a fellow we called Pony Express Bob came in. He had with him Fitzsimmons, the Australian heavyweight.[4] Bob brought Fitzsimmons to our table and introduced him. The boxer turned to me and said, "I understand you box, Mr. Beck." I said I did a little. Right away he said he would take me on. I pointed out that he was in training and I wasn't, but I agreed to box him three three-minute rounds, instead of the customary two-minute ones.

We sat around talking until very late. Fitzsimmons, it seemed, had hit his sparring partner Reardon too hard a month before in Buffalo and had killed him.[5] Since then he had had a tough time finding anyone to take his place. Finally, when we broke up, we had arranged to meet the next morning at ten o'clock at the Chicago Athletic Club for our match.[6] As I went up to my room, I left word to be called at nine o'clock. However, when I awoke, it was already ten. I rang for a bellboy to bring me a gin fizz as quickly as possible. He hadn't arrived with it by the time I was dressed so I started for the elevator. In the hall, I met him and drank the thing down while I was pushing the bell. It was a cold, snowy day. I dashed out of the hotel and ran the four blocks down Michigan Boulevard, dodging pedestrians right and left.

There must have been two hundred men on hand when I arrived at the club. Fitzsimmons had begun to get discouraged and had decided I was joking and didn't intend to come. He was so pleased when I showed up that he helped me find trunks and shoes to fit, and then we went up to the gymnasium. He announced that he wanted to warm up, and the first thing he did was hit the punching bag such a blow he burst it and sent it flying across the gym. Then he told an attendant to bring one for me, but I assured him I didn't need any warming up as I had already done some fast sprinting.

The boxing floor was of good maple, cut diagonally with very fine lines so that no resin was needed. Selecting the athletic instructor as a referee, we decided to begin without further delay. As we walked up to the ring, Horton Boal took my arm and said, "Don't box with that fellow, George. He thinks you're a friend of Corbett's and he'll kill you." I tried to reassure Horton by telling him that Fitzsimmons only weighed 178 pounds whereas I weighed 205 and that if things got going badly for me, I'd just sit on him for nine minutes. Then I gave Boal a ring I was wearing, and we donned our gloves, shook hands, and listened to the usual referee spiel about breaking on the clinches, and so forth.

The bell rang, and we met in the middle of the ring. I led with my left and surprised him right off with a good jolt from my right. I never swung an uppercut; I just kept straight right and left, which kept him from getting in his dangerous swing. I was in touch, and I never stopped going. Soon he got on to this business of leading with my left and punching with my right, and he took to ducking under my arm and punching me in the waist, not realizing that my muscles were stronger there than they were in my arms. He was to knock out Corbett by this method, but with all his tries it didn't bother me at all. The crowd was getting excited and yelling like mad. Even the timekeeper got excited. Suddenly he called four minutes; we had gone a minute over.

After one minute to rest we started again, I with my straight arm blows, leading away with the left. That time he expected my right to follow straight, and he ducked under to hit me in the solar plexus. I undercut him and lifted him clear off his feet, and when he fell, he was several feet away on his hands and knees. He was pretty well jolted and stayed there for a few seconds. I walked to my corner. The crowd was going wild. Then when Fitz got up, we met in the middle and belted each other for a solid minute. He hit me a glancing blow on the shoulder and head, and my shoulder hit my head in a hard blow.

In the final round, I repeated my straight blow strategy. I, being heavier and taller, had the same reach so he really couldn't get the best of me. We finished without a knockout, and as fine friends in the bargain.

This was on the 24th of December. That afternoon he went down to a blacksmith shop and turned smithy again for a few minutes to make a special racing horseshoe. This was something he knew all about, having been a champion horseshoe maker in Australia before his ring career. Christmas morning, he arrived in my room before I was up. Jumping on the bed, he slapped this thing, all done up in a lot of ribbon, down on top of me, yelling "Merry Christmas" like a boy. In the next few days, we had a great time together, fighting, wrestling, and playing pool—both of us being equally punk at the pool.

That next summer he fought Corbett out at Reno. This time Fitz wrested the title, in the thirteenth round, by going after Corbett in the solar plexus, just where he'd hit me a few times. The following winter I was stopping at the Hoffman House in New York, and Fitz showed up at the hotel every day while I was there. He must have been about twenty-eight at the time. Anyway, he kept his title for five or six years and then finally lost it to a fellow who weighed 230 pounds.

When I finally reached San Francisco after my stop-off in Chicago, I again saw a good deal of Senator George Hearst. He had been ill and was living at the old Occidental Hotel, having closed his house on Nob Hill. The senator really seemed more lonesome than sick, and when I came along, he insisted that I spend every afternoon with him. We soon established a routine that appeared to benefit him as well as being pleasant for both of us.

When I arrived after luncheon Hearst would get me to send his attendant out of the room, then he would toss me a bunch of keys. These opened a cupboard in which were several cases of Old Crow whiskey. We would each have a bottle, and then he would say, "Now send for that worthless valet and have him order my carriage."

Then we'd drive out through Golden Gate Park to the Cliff House and have our dinner, along with a bottle or two of champagne.[7] After dinner, we'd sit out on the deck watching the sunset over the Pacific, and Hearst would talk for hours of his early prospecting and mining days in the Feather River country, of his start and of how he made his fortune. Because I, too, had been bitten by the prospecting bug we were very congenial, and frequently we'd talk about going back to prospecting together. He'd invariably tell me that whenever I found anything that looked good to telegraph him and he'd come. The old senator didn't know much about books, perhaps, but he certainly knew his rocks. Then we'd drive back to the hotel.

This regime had been going on for about a week when

one day a boy came from Mrs. Hearst's apartment with the request that I stop in and see her.[8] I went expecting to receive a lecture for leading the senator astray, but to my surprise, Mrs. Hearst announced that she had ordered their yacht put in commission, that it was ready to sail at any time, and that she had ordered it turned over to me. I thanked her and said I would go down and look at it. I found that it was a great oceangoing steamer, the largest private yacht on the Pacific. Declining the offer with many thanks, I explained to her that I couldn't even afford to buy the fuel for such a ship. "Oh," said she, "just charge the bills back to the home office." When I couldn't get out of it that way, I concluded I had better leave San Francisco and head for Los Angeles.

I was sitting in the smoker in the Pullman, Los Angeles bound, when two gentlemen came in, one a man in the Alaska fur business and the other an old French merchant from San Francisco. They were lively and full of fun, so I joined them in disposing of several bottles of their California wine. The Frenchman began telling us about his place west of Fresno. His stories were so large I concluded he was loaded and began to make fun of him. As we neared Fresno, he said, "You're coming with me. I shall show you I am telling the truth."

"All right," I said. "I'm used to sleeping out-of-doors, so I'll go along provided I get my trunk taken off."

He sent for the conductor and had it arranged, and at Fresno, we got off. I left all my belongings in the checkroom, and then we boarded a side train going west toward the mountains. After riding not more than fifteen miles the old man asked the conductor to let us off. The train stopped, and there we were in open country. There was no station, and no house, and it was growing dark. The old man said something about striking the path and going north. Again, I assured him I would follow. About fifty feet from the track we both fell in an irrigation ditch full of water. When we climbed out on the far side, he announced matter-of-factly that he had missed the trail. "Oh," I said, "I thought this was the regular route."

We finally found a road and walked along a half mile to a beautiful place with a lot of magnificent trees around it. I suggested that we better go to sleep under one of them. "No," he said, "this is my place."

"You go up there," I told him, "and they'll sic their dogs on you, or you'll get shot—one or the other."

But we kept on going, and when we reached the house, we walked up the front steps. "By the way," he said, "my stepson is down here running the place. What is your name?" I said, "George Beck. What is yours?" Then he introduced himself as Frank Locan, and we shook hands. But I still didn't believe it was his house.[9] When he beat on the front door a fine-looking young man finally came and let us in. Only when he called my host Dad, did I at last decide everything was all right.

Locan introduced me as his great friend who had come to spend the month. Then he asked where the cook was. When he was told that the Chinamen had all gone to bed, I reminded him that he had said on the train that he was the best cook in California and that I could cook eggs myself, so why didn't we get our own dinner? We did, and we made out very well.

Charley, the stepson, went off to bed, but before leaving, he mentioned that he had a schoolmate, Bert Thornton, staying with him.[10] When our meal was finished, we went into the wine cellar, and each of us took an armful of wine bottles and repaired to the great porch that surrounded the building. After smoking a cigar and finishing a bottle or two, we decided to go to bed. We went up to Locan's room and there found someone asleep in his bed. We agreed that the thing to do was toss him out, so we took ahold of the blanket on either side of the bed and made an attempt to throw whoever it might be up in the air. The little Frenchman, however, wasn't very tall and I was six feet two, so I ended by tossing the sleeper over onto the Frenchman, and together they rolled on the floor. This was the way I got acquainted with young Bert Thornton, who happened to be a distant cousin of mine and the son of Judge Thornton of San Francisco.

Instead of a month I spent a week with Frank Locan and had a very fine time. He had a mile square of raisin grapes, and in another vineyard close to the house he raised every variety of grape he could find. Some of the bunches were two and three feet long. I had never before seen such grapes. In addition, he raised every species of fruit that grows in California, including a large tract of fine figs. All the roads through the place were lined with Bartlett pear trees, and he even had a factory where the raisins were taken care of and boxed. Those that got too heavy with a dew on them and turned dark were sent to his private distillery to be made into brandy. The little Frenchman really had quite a place.

Leaving him with some reluctance, I went on to Los Angeles and from there took the train to Omaha and then came back to my ranch, fresh from quite a vacation.

TWELVE

Beckton, Wyoming

A family named Wilkerson had been running the ranch in my absence and stayed on another year. They had a daughter, Anna May "Fannie" Wilkerson. Fannie became a great attraction to one Frank Canton, a detective for the stockmen's association.[1] Later he was one of the leaders of the stockmen's expedition against the cattle rustlers, the expedition which ended in the Johnson County Rustlers War and the big fight at the TA Ranch were the army intervened and took the cattlemen into protective custody. Thanks to Fannie I got well acquainted with Canton as he stayed around the ranch quite a bit. Eventually, when things got hot in Johnson County, I wasn't so sure whether knowing him helped or hindered my position.

In the meantime, I went on running the mill, farming on a larger scale each year, gardening, and prospecting some more in the Big Horns.

When I began real farming operations, I had to hire a number of men, and as we were now a small colony there, we figured we ought to have a post office. I applied and was told I had to give the place a name, so I called it Beckton and I used a Beckton cancellation stamp on letters for some time. This seemed official enough and out came a lot of paper and stamps, and I forwarded my check. Then

I just let anyone around the place who wanted stamps or envelopes help themselves. It was all very convenient, but at the end of the first year when an inspector came around, he was horrified down to the soles of his boots. I found out that this was not the way the government wanted a post office run, even a minute one way off on a ranch and even if I did pay all the bills. When he explained about the reports he wanted in the future and about keeping track of every little one-cent stamp, I washed my hands of it and let someone else take on the red tape.[2]

The gardening phase worked out a lot better, probably because I recalled the trials of my first garden. When I had built the cabin, I had spaded up a half acre for potatoes. Then I rode down to Fort McKinney and bought a sackful of them. These I carefully cut so as to have two eyes in each piece, and with the greatest pains I laid out nice rows and planted them. The next morning, I went out to look at my crop. There were all up. . . . The most remarkable potatoes I had ever known. My friends the cinnamon bears had visited me during the night and left not a single piece of spud in the ground. Those bears and I were no longer friends. I declared war and some of their hides soon decorated my cabin. Then I turned that garden into a sheep corral, which years later paid agreeable dividends. The strawberries grown there were larger than my thumb while the rhubarb leaves were as big as tabletops.

The year I started real farming I went to northwestern Missouri and southern Iowa and shipped a carload of mares out to the Rock Creek station on the Union Pacific. There I bought another wagon and some farming tools and started to drive north. Before I had reached the first stage station, my new horses began contracting pink eye, and I again found myself turned veterinarian. I'd take the well horses and haul the wagon from one stage stop to the next, then go back on foot and drive the sick nags up, treating them all along the way with a solution of warm water and aconite. When I finally arrived under my own roof, I must have walked that road three times. At all events, I was a lot more weary than when I'd driven the sheep to my ranch.

That year I also acquired two self-binders and a thrashing machine, the first implements of their kind in the country. They were good investments for in one year I produced over fifteen thousand bushels of wheat, necessitating the building of a granary next to the mill to hold it. This hardy, red wheat ran about sixty-two pounds to the bushel, and the oats we raised ran nearly forty pounds to the bushel. It was good earth, indeed.

Not only was I doing well, so were my few neighbor farmers. There was a German boy, named Alfred "Alph" Lambrigger, who had a little place nearby.[3] He got some seed from me and put in twelve acres of wheat. It was such nice-looking wheat he brought it over to the mill and had me put it through the cleaning machine. We were standing there admiring it when the idea struck me that we might as well send some of it to the Chicago World's Fair—the biggest fair I could think of! Alph didn't care, so we put enough in a seamless sack, wrote his name on it, and nonchalantly sent it off. That little German boy was mighty surprised in the fall to receive first prize in competition with the entire world. It tied in looks with the best Russian wheat, but when analyzed, it showed a much higher percentage of protein. Alph was also surprised when a delegation of salesmen from seed houses all over the country beat a path to his door to buy seed from him. They offered a dollar a pound for his crop, but as the poor fellow had already fed it to his chickens and pigs and had the rest ground into flour, he didn't have much left to get rich on.

Still another local record was established by a woman near Big Piney Creek. *The American Agriculturist,* a magazine, had offered a prize for the best acre of potatoes. The contest rules were strict as to measurement and certificates of production. She raised something over one thousand bushels to the acre and won first prize in the United States. A neighbor of hers, a man, won the next year of this contest, producing just a few bushels under her mark.

The two self-binders were busy night and day until I wore them out. And the J. I. Case threshing machine, in the end, made me about twelve thousand dollars. There was a great demand for it for years because I allowed the farmers around to use it and pay me in wheat. Any other machines they subsequently could get ahold of required cash on the line.

Among the men I hired was one fellow I've never forgotten. His name was Simon Kearn, and I first heard about him around Fort McKinney.[4] He was a powerful man, an Austrian, and a wonderful man with an ax. When I wanted to do some more building, I looked him up. Finally, I found him in a little cabin on the banks of Clear Creek, so drunk he was helpless. I broke in and took care of him several days until he was in shape to talk to. He said he'd come and work for me after he finished a job at the fort. I suggested that in the meantime I would haul his things up to the ranch. He said no, he'd bring them. Sometime later we were properly startled to see him walk in with a pack on his back weighing over four hundred pounds, a pack that a stalwart horse would have staggered under. In it were his grindstone, three axes, his bed, and his war bag full of clothing and stuff. He was strong, and he was good natured. Nothing made him angry except when someone took one of his axes.

With a broad ax alone, he could hew a log smoother than it could be down with a plane. He built me several cabins of cottonwood. He would fell a tree, hew it to the shape he wanted, and then carry the log on his shoulders down to where he was building. No assistance from any horses for Simon, thanks. All his contracted work for me had been finished when, observing my increasing problems running the ranch, he said, "Mr. Beck, I'm going to stay and work for you." Highly gratified, I said, "Fine, Simon. What do you want to do?" He announced he would cook, which seemed an astonishing proposition, but knowing him I said to go ahead, and he could name his own wages.

The next morning breakfast was ready at daylight. When he rang the bell, a few fellows failed to appear. With that, he marched to the bunkhouse and dragged them laggards to the table. He never had to pull a man out of bed the second time. Of all the ten or twelve hired hands about the place, Simon did more outside work, in addition to cooking, than any other person. Such good fortune couldn't last, of course. After two years with me, he took up a piece of land for himself, bought a team of horses, and built himself a cabin. The horses, incidentally, were just pets for he continued to do all his own hauling, *personally*. Finally, he went to Montana, near Billings, and took up a section of land under the Desert Land Act.[5] When it was sufficiently developed, he sent for me to come up and see the place because, he said, he was getting it ready to give to me. He was a great friend to have.

In order not to neglect my first love, prospecting, I figured that the time was about ripe to build a supply town for prospectors. In these excursions, I was working largely around Bald Mountain, and I built myself a cabin there for an official residence. We had managed to locate quite a little gold around a gulch, known as Dayton Gulch, and I put in a hydraulic plant and worked away at it for two years. The returns the first year were negligible, but the second year we did make enough to pay expenses—and then the gravel bar played out.

On one of these excursions into the hills, I took my friend Horace Alger[6] and a Mr. James Robinson, who had built a cabin near me on Goose Creek.[7] We took a good pack outfit of donkeys but only two guns—a .45–90 and a .22, the latter for prairie chickens. We had reached the divide and were going north along it when at the top of a ridge a short distance away we saw a bunch of elk. It seemed advisable to take some meat into Bald Mountain, where a number of men were living at the time, so we stopped.

Robinson said he would like to try something. He took the .22, and I took the other gun. When we were within shooting distance we each picked an animal and fired simultaneously. Two elk fell. That was the one time I ever saw an elk killed with a .22. Robinson was a splendid marksman and had been keen enough to hit the animal in the backbone just back of the skull so that it died instantly. Aiming for the backbone is, of course, the secret in killing big game for then everything below is immediately paralyzed. The hunter must then quickly bleed the animal by cutting its throat; otherwise, the meat spoils.

Some years later I took a large party, including George Holdrege, C. H. Grinnell, Charley Dietz, Harry Fulmer, Mike Elmore, Alger, and others up Big Goose Creek trail until we neared the same divide.[8] There we came upon a number of beautiful small lakes. They were delighted and wanted to organize a club, to be called the Dome Lake Club. I joined temporarily, but when they wanted to do too much work on the place I dropped out. My idea of enjoying the country was wandering around instead of being tied down to one spot. That was, however, the first of several deluxe hunting clubs I got mixed up with in the formative period.

The most elaborate of these was suggested a few years later by John Mackay of New York.[9] Mackay's fortune came, of course, from his tremendous mining interests in Idaho and he never lost his fondness for the West. After he was transplanted to New York, he bought a mansion where he maintained a special apartment. During the years his wife was living in London, he entertained his western friends at dinner when we came to town. Wednesday nights were the big nights. The crowd would be nearly all from the plains with seldom a New York man in the group. There would be everything: soup, oysters, champagne, but the main course was always a great mulligan. Four footmen would carry this masterpiece into the dining room, and in the center of the enormous platter, there would be a boar's head surrounded by all manner of vegetables. With it, we'd have burgundy, whiskey, and brandy, and plenty of good talk and tall tales.

But to get on with Mackay's club. On one of these visits, he gave me a check for two hundred thousand dollars to start a sportsmen's club in Wyoming. It was designed for a small, select group—notable hunters who had been in Africa, and so forth. The site we chose was a lot of land adjoining Yellowstone Park before the state forest reserve had been created. We really thought we had something, and I even went over to Philadelphia, at Mackay's suggestion, to urge the president of the Pennsylvania Railroad to come in with us. When the matter of dues came up, Mackay said, "We'll make the membership fifty thousand dollars." Here I interrupted to the effect that that was a little rich for my blood. I added that I'd help organize it but that I didn't see how I'd get in. "Oh," said John Mackay, "I'll pay your dues along with those of both my boys, John and Clarence." Right then and there he gave me the check for all four memberships. But Wyoming was a jump ahead of us. The state had already passed laws prohibiting individuals from buying more than one section of land. We fought for a year trying to put the scheme over, and finally I just handed Mr. Mackay back his checks.

In the course of these negotiations, I was in Washington for one of the Presidential Balls. Mackay senior sent the younger son, Clarence, over with a guardian and turned him over to me. We went to the ball, and I introduced him to the young Leiter girls. They presented him to a friend of theirs, Miss Katherine Duer, and that was how he met the first Mrs. Clarence Mackay.[10]

On another occasion, I was enthusiastically telling John Mackay about a friend of mine in Troy who had developed a system of sending one message over the wire at a time—a method not then perfected. He said for me to come down to his office tomorrow and he'd have some men there to listen to my story. I was all for helping make my friend famous, so I went. About twenty men were present, including a number of important electrical wizards, [Nicola] Tesla among them.[11] With such an audience I told in detail about the progress my friend was making. Then one man spoke up, "It's a great idea, Mr. Beck, and one we have already patented although we'll not be ready to use it for a long time." That was old John Mackay's sense of humor.

THIRTEEN

The Johnson County War, 1892

Along in January 1892, I was in the East, and George Pullman invited me to join the party in his private car and go
down to St. Augustine, Florida.[1] Father and I had been
there, and I thought it would be pleasant to revisit the
place. We had a lively time, and I met some more interesting men of the day, among them William Lyman, the inventor of the Lyman sight for guns.[2] Two or three younger
men my age were along, and in the evenings we frequently
sat out on the grass talking, an innocent but eventually
expensive pastime. Four of us contracted typho-malaria
fever.[3] None of us died, but while we had it, we definitely
wished we would.

Going home from Florida, I went by way of Louisville
and bought a thoroughbred horse from Mr. Lewis Clark,
the head of the Louisville Racing Association.[4] The horse's
name was Dalgetty, and his pedigree extended back twenty-
three generations to the importations of Queen Anne.
When the sale was completed I got a boxcar and shipped
him west via St. Louis with a Kentucky negro boy. I arrived
there ahead of the horse, and then I began to feel the
effects of malaria. Nevertheless, I started the horse and
boy on their way again and went on to a little frontier town
in Wyoming called Newcastle to await them.[5]

When I got there, I *was* sick. I engaged a room in what passed for a hotel and sent for the doctor. The Patrick brothers, of the Star Route Stage line, were friends and exceedingly kind about looking after me. The local doctor said I had typhoid fever. I disagreed with his diagnosis having heard that a typhoid patient cannot bear even so much as the weight of a sheet on his back. I fired that doctor and had a man come down from Deadwood in the Dakotas. He said the same thing, so I fired him. Finally, Bill Patrick brought his family doctor up from Beatrice. I took a good look at him and was satisfied I had a medical man at last. Then I went to sleep for the first time in ten days. That was the beginning of my recovery. All this while the horse and negro stayed on with me, the negro taking care of me as well as of Dalgetty.

When I was feeling better, the same Frank Canton who had been courting Fannie stopped in to see me. He was full of the raid the cattlemen were going to make to drive the rustlers out of Johnson County.[6] Major Walcott was to head the expedition, and nearly all the cattlemen in the party were friends of mine.[7] I begged Canton to advise them against the move, for I was convinced it would end in disaster. As an emissary, he had no effect. They proceeded according to plan and brought on the now famous Johnson County Rustlers' War, one of the great feuds in the state's history.

The wealth realized from cattle grazing on the open ranges had naturally produced bands of marauders and petty thieves who made depredations on the herds, changed the brands on the animals, and drove them out of the district to be sold elsewhere. Cattlemen in Wyoming had banded together, as they had in other western states, to control these cattle rustlers, but the monetary returns were too enticing for the rustlers to give up easily. Now the situation in Johnson County, one of many strife-ridden centers, had come to a head. The local stockmen had elected to arm and resort to a frontier justice of their own making, inasmuch as both law and organization, represented by the Wyoming Stock Growers Association, had so far proved ineffective.

By April of 1892, the rustlers also had formed armed bands. Shooting scrapes and lynchings were breaking out, and new dispatches to the East were so full of the ambush battles in the cattle country that Chicago papers and other eastern journals sent "war correspondents" out to cover developments. The stories they wired home occupied front page space for a fortnight or more. By the 12th of the month, things were really popping. A party of some seventy cattlemen was trapped by the rustlers at the TA Ranch, ten miles from Buffalo. When the seriousness of that fight reached the outside, the Johnson County commissioners petitioned for army help from Fort McKinney. President Harrison was also appealed to at the White House. On the 13th orders came and Colonel J. J. Van Horne left Fort McKinney with troops of cavalry and three hours later arrived at the scene.[8] The stockmen, completely hemmed in, agreed to surrender to the military and to be taken to the fort as prisoners. On April 17 they were removed, still as prisoners and under full military escort, to Fort Russell at Cheyenne. Their trial as "an armed band of capitalists with hired war-men" was set for the following January. Three weeks after the trial opened, the Johnson County prosecutor, in a surprise turn, made a motion that all the cases be dismissed. Public opinion in the West had been much aroused, of course, and originally it had been conceded that the cattlemen were well within their rights in defending their property. But sympathy and opinion seemed eventually to turn against them because of the methods they employed, principally that of hiring gunmen from outside the state to augment their numbers.

As soon as I was able, I had my horse taken north to the end of the Burlington tracks, and from there the negro boy rode him home to the ranch. I followed along with a team and buckboard. The weather was cold, as Wyoming springs can be, and it took several days. After a couple of weeks' recuperation, I drove myself over to Buffalo. It was the middle of April, and things were hot there, even though the weather was not.

Buffalo had grown from the little huddle of frame saloons of the Jesse James days and was now a thriving town on the banks of Clear Creek. In view of the good flow of water from the creek I had, two years earlier, built a flour mill there and an electric light plant. I also invested in additional land around the town, and naturally, I felt some concern about my holdings.

As I drove towards the town the mayor, Charley Burritt, met me on the outskirts and told me not to go in, that he could not protect me.[9] I laughed and told him I wasn't looking for protection—I was down to look after my property. Then I drove in across Clear Creek. On the left-hand side of the main street, there was a large livery stable where I usually put up. It was also the rustlers' stronghold, and a number of them were lounging around when I pulled in. I had a shotgun in the buckboard and a six-shooter in my belt. These I promptly took out and handed over to the stable liveryman, Charlie Rounds.[10] He belonged to the rustlers' bunch. I asked him to take care of them and mentioned that I would be in town probably a week. Then, taking my handbag, I crossed the street to the Occidental Hotel.

I was not very warmly welcomed there, either. In fact, I was quickly told about a story circulating to the effect I had brought out a thoroughbred horse from Kentucky with which to lead the cattlemen's raid. Again, I was amused and told my informants that while I might risk my own life, the horse's life was too valuable. He was a racehorse. Besides, I said, being a former sheep man, I hardly thought the cattlemen would let me lead them even though we were all friends.

It was decided, apparently, to let me alone for the time being, but the rustlers put a guard on me. Every place I went, day or night, a man walked behind me with a Winchester. I really had a lot of fun making that fellow a good walker before I was through with him.

Very few men in the whole town dared speak to me. Will Thom, at the bank, Deyo Hasbrouck of the mercantile store, my foreman at the mill, and Frank Grouard from Fort McKinney were my only companions.[11] The cattlemen were not in custody at the fort three miles away, but I thought it best not to go out there. I didn't want my mill burned down—a threat clearly indicated if I so much as stepped out of line.

The day I picked to go home I went to the livery stable in the morning and told the man to have the team ready by noon, that I would start right after dinner. Then I went back to the hotel, but the dining room was full and I had to wait for the second table. While I waited, I played a game of billiards with Frank Grouard, and that made me even later getting my dinner. Just a few people were left at the table when I sat down. One of these, a young man, waited until the others were gone. Then in a very low voice, he told me not to leave at once because "they" were going to "dry-gulch" me at French Creek, six miles out.

Frank Grouard was still in the hotel, so we played some more billiards. The delay, I figured, would make the fellows waiting for me at French Creek a little nervous. At three o'clock I decided to go. At the livery stable, I climbed into the buckboard and was given my shotgun and pistol. When I was out of town, and well out of sight, I threw away all the cartridges in the pistol and reloaded with some from my pocket, reloading the shotgun, too.

My team was a good one so when I neared the French Creek bridge, I tied the reins together and put them over the dashboard, laid the gun across my knee, and let the team drive themselves. That guaranteed a good fast clip. If anyone had looked up from under that old wooden bridge as I thundered across it, they would have been surprised at the reception I had planned.

But nothing happened. Later I found out that three men had been stationed there for over two hours, but being impatient fellows, they gave up, thinking I had been warned, and went away. I missed them by an hour.

When I first contemplated a mill in Buffalo I was going to build it alone. The surveys were completed and the work began when Thomas J. Fisher Jr., the son of a friend of

Father's, came out to live with me at the ranch.[12] He grew enthusiastic about the project and insisted we form a stock company. Thus the Buffalo Mill Company was formed, backed by forty thousand dollars' worth of capital.[13]

The completed mill had a tight floor, forty and a half feet square inside, running along under the main street for 1,500 feet. During the foundation work, we ran into a bed of lignite coal, but we didn't make use of it. Into the penstock running into our basement, I put a Leffel wheel of eighty horsepower. The first year we made a short run grinding wheat, and then a severe winter struck and our penstock completely filled with ice. Just as in a swift-flowing stream, ice crystals formed in the water and ice formed on the rocks at the bottom before it froze the top. This ice closed our floor. Next, we put in an engine and boiler, and when I did this work, I also put in a motor, electric generator, and force pump. The next steps were obvious. We put out water mains and wired the town for electricity.

All this extensive investment seemed fully justified because the Burlington Railroad had not only surveyed into town but had bought the right-of-way and depot site. Then the cattleman's war centering in Buffalo caused the Burlington officials to suddenly reconsider. Practically overnight, they elected to turn north and make Sheridan the terminus for their trains. It was a blow for a number of people, Beck and Fisher among them. Values in Buffalo went to the dogs. All of our work had put us heavily in debt to the First National Bank. The bank demanded payments we couldn't meet and finally, it took over the Buffalo Mill Company. The only part of it I liked came as a sort of aftermath. The bank couldn't hold the property and forced a man to take it over. Within ten years the mill had made *him* so rich he bought the bank and became its president.

When the first Burlington trains reached Sheridan the president of the road, Mr. C. E. Perkins, came out and brought with him Senator John Allison of Iowa. Senator Allison and my father had been associated for many years on the Committee of Appropriations in the United States Senate, and when the party arrived at Sheridan, he insisted they all visit me at the ranch.[14] It was a welcome surprise and resulted in a friendship with Mr. Perkins which lasted as long as he lived. Whenever he came out afterwards to inspect that branch of the road, I joined him. We'd travel around by day and stop wherever night caught us. He was a great and careful railroad man, and those inspection tours were very thorough.

On the morning following Mr. Perkins's first visit, I happened to be driving into Sheridan for ranch supplies when I ran into my friend Wallop. "George," he said, "come with me to the depot. Leiter is arriving from Chicago or Washington, or someplace, to go on a hunt and I know he'll want to see you the first thing he does."

Before long the train puffed in and L. Z. Leiter, his valet, his secretary, and case upon case of liquid refreshment descended from it. It was obvious our two buckboards would be inadequate to convey the company to Wallop's ranch in proper style, so we hired the local stagecoach, loaded it down, hitched our two teams in, and started them off on a dead run.

We made it safely within a mile of Wallop's place when we hit a deep, narrow gulch with such force that the front axle broke with a loud creak and the old coach turned over on its side. Spilled out in the road in this fashion we opened one of the cases to refresh ourselves—only I think we mentioned steadying our nerves—then each one selected a case of his favorite drink to tote and started afoot for the ranch.

That night we had a big dinner with all the proper wine courses and a few extra ones thrown in for good measure. Finally, one of the guests announced he really must go over to his place and fix things up for the night. He seemed to be the only conscientious rancher among us. The next morning Leiter opened the door to have an early look around, and there by the door sill lay our friend sound asleep. After a lively breakfast the rest of us who were ranchers finally got around to see about whether or not the stock had been watered and the cows milked, and all that.

It was fully a year after the railroad had reached Sheridan that I fell to talking one day with C. H. Grinnell who had a place east of Sheridan on Goose Creek. A short distance below his place he had started a coal mine. After looking it over, I decided my next move was to go into the coal mining business, and I thereupon organized a company of ten men and took over the Grinnell property. We each put in our thousand dollars. I was president of the company, Horace Alger was treasurer, and Grinnell remained as foreman and manager. We named it the Sheridan Fuel Company.

We drove a tunnel one thousand feet into the hill above the railroad tracks and ran the coal cars out by gravity. The coal bed was from twelve to fourteen feet thick, light in ash but rather high in water. Although the coal burned well it did not keep well. If exposed to air for any length of time it slacked down. But before the year was out, we were shipping a trainload a day and putting screened coal on the cars at less than seventy cents a ton.

The Patrick brothers had taken three shares in our pool. The general agreement had been that anyone wishing to sell must first offer their share to the company for a period of one month. The Patricks soon made us an offer to either buy or sell. Inasmuch as the company did not take it up before the end of the month, I bought their stock, acquiring a four-tenths interest.

Our best market I felt, after looking the field over, would be the Homestake Mine at Lead, South Dakota, and I spent some time at the offices in Lead and Deadwood getting them to try our product.[15] The Homestake Mine was using enormous quantities of wood. I was convinced we could make them quite a profit if they changed over, as well as making a profit for ourselves. They were practically sold, and everything was about ready for the contract calling for a trainload a day, doubling our business, when I learned that George Holdrege, one of our stockholders and general manager for the Burlington Railroad, had another plan afoot. He brought a couple of men from Omaha to Sheridan to have a business talk with us. It was his idea that we let these two men into the company because they had lumberyards all through Nebraska and Kansas and could handle our coal easily. Because our business depended largely on the friendship of the Burlington route we felt forced to concede to his wishes. We felt secure, anyway, in the thought that we were retaining half the stock. What we didn't know during these negotiations was that one man in our pool had already sold them his share. Not until we issued them stock equal to our own did we find out. Then they reorganized the company and forced us all out. You could make money in the golden West, and you certainly could lose it!

The preceding year I had been working on an idea to make equivalent anthracite out of our lignite slacks, and I had patented a process for that purpose. The Burlington hauled a few carloads of slack for me to their shops at Portsmouth, Nebraska, and loaned me an old shop no longer in use. In it, I built a plant for a continuous process. I ground the slack up fine and with forced feed put it into a line of cylinders which had slowly revolving conveyors. Under these conveyors, I had a fire fed by gas which came off the coal itself. The distillate went to the condensers and the tar that came off I redistilled to get pitch. The pitch I mixed with hot fixed carbon residue, forcing this through the nozzle and cutting it off at convenient lengths. My fuel was thus ninety-eight percent fixed carbon, a fine equivalent to anthracite.

I had heard of a German chemist in St. Paul named Julius Lead.[16] I had him come out, and at every step of the process, he made an analysis. He was accurate and thorough. In the end, I finally concluded that the coal was the least valuable thing I was producing. The by-products of distillation were more important. I also concluded that when the coal was ground to a powder the proper way to burn it was with an air blast, as one would burn fuel oil, rather than condensing it and pressing it into briquettes. The distillation of lignite not only gives several valuable by-products but also many desirable chemicals. Eventually, I am certain, the lignite of

Wyoming will all be distilled before being burned. But it may not be in my day.

Julius Lead was an interesting man. He had a patent burner and a plan for changing crude oils into gas. This interested me, and I bought his patent, but I discovered that I needed a lot more money before these things could be placed properly on the market. To raise the money, I went to Chicago to see my old friend, L. Z. Leiter. However, along about this period his son Joe was involved in the great wheat deal by which he cornered the Chicago wheat market. Eventually, they lost a fortune in it, but when I arrived, beaming with my plans, they were in this thing so deep that Leiter senior couldn't help anyone else. Instead of trying in other quarters I returned to my ranch again and to my other business interests, all of which were loudly demanding attention.

FOURTEEN

Wyoming Politics

In the autumn of 1892, I indulged myself a little more in politics. I was a delegate to the Democratic National Convention in Chicago. The Republicans were convening in Minneapolis ten days earlier, and as a number of my friends were going to the Twin City, I decided to deviate from the straight and narrow path by taking in the Republican convention, too.

It was in Minneapolis one night that I got acquainted with Johann Straus—at least I can thank the Republicans for that. His Blue Danube Waltz was sweeping the country, and they had engaged him, at a handsome fee, to bring his Vienna band out to play at their convention. Straus was the only conductor I ever watched in action who faced the audience instead of his men. And he conducted with a good deal of spirit, besides; it looked, more often than not, as though he were about to take off and fly out of a window. He and I were stopping at the same hotel, and one evening after hearing him I found him alone down in the hotel rathskeller. He was an extraordinarily good beer drinker, and so we had a few pleasant times together.

In Chicago, our Democratic convention was held in a tremendous frame structure, which proved to be anything but waterproof. Just after we had nominated Grover Cleveland for the second term, we had a thunderstorm and the delegate got a complete drenching. A number of us struck for the Turkish baths in the basement of the Palmer House, figuring that would be a splendid place to dry off. No sooner had we got undressed and started through the steam room than a sewer burst and flooded the place. We seized our clothes and ran to the street where, much to the amusement of the passerby, we got dressed. However, we had our revenge in washing up the Republican Party when election time came.

Going back a bit to the time when Cleveland was serving his first term. Wyoming was still a territory, and I had found out that its affairs were being run by a political combine with banking interests in Cheyenne. These banks, in turn, were practically financed by money belonging to the territory inasmuch as that money was being loaned out to our citizens at a high rate of interest. In my desire to clean up this unhealthy situation I went to Washington and stated the conditions to the president.

Senator James Bayard, a friend of Father's and of mine, and Senator L. Q. C. Lamar were both in Cleveland's cabinet, and each of them was an active supporter of mine for the appointment of governor.[1] On our last call at the White House, I was accompanied by Senator Bayard. When we left the Executive Mansion, he told me to go on to Wyoming and that my commission would be there as soon as I was. I got home and found a fair-sized surprise in store for me. A man named Moonlight, from Kansas, had already been appointed governor.[2]

This proved to be the work of a government agent from the Land Office who had gone to the president and stated that I was the biggest land grabber in Wyoming, with huge tracts of government land all fenced. The fencing of the public domain had been given a great deal of publicity at the time and was considered a serious offense. The agent's statement was an entire lie, but he was probably well paid for it by the ring in Cheyenne who, of course, didn't care to see me appointed. I managed to get another agent sent out to examine my place. That man found I not only didn't have any federal land enclosed but that I didn't even have all my own land fenced. But by the time I got myself cleared my opponents had accomplished their end. However, I settled that score in part by doing all I could to help Governor Moonlight, and in a short time, one of the Cheyenne banks closed its doors.

I took my final flyer as a public candidate in 1902 when I ran against DeForest Richards for governor. Again, I was defeated.[3] There was still the United States Senate to run for, but by that time I had reached the conclusion I didn't like the struggle and conflict with men, as represented by politics. On the other hand, the struggle with nature did seem worthwhile. Nature will never cheat or fool you. Perhaps you may fail once or twice, but with nature you always go back and try again, whereas people can never be depended upon the second time if they have failed you the first time. In nature you learn all the answers of life.

It is indeed a happy man who benefits by the experience of others, a wise man who can learn from his own experiences, and a fool who cannot learn from anybody's experience. I knew there was still a great deal for me to do in my own private struggle with nature, as I found it in the West, and so I turned my attention again to the development of some actual part of the country itself.

FIFTEEN

The Shoshone Irrigation Company
and Cody, Wyoming, 1893–1894

On the many prospecting trips to Bald Mountain, I would see the Big Horn Basin stretching out vastly to the west and south. One day an old trapper, Laben Hillberry, pointed out a little mountain peak off in the distance, which I afterwards learned was Cedar Mountain.[1] He told me that a fine river ran through a canyon there and that there was a low divide on the south side of the mountain where water from the river could be diverted and made to irrigate a great tract of land. I asked him how he knew, and he said he had walked over there.

My friend Jerry Ryan had a team and wagon, so I asked him to take Hillberry and go look the situation over.[2] If it were true, I thought it would be an interesting and useful thing to develop. They came back in the fall and said it was all as Hillberry had first reported. Then and there I made up my mind to organize a party for the following summer and survey the country. I had my own instruments, and we had, of course, plenty of men, horses, and wagons about the ranch to make up a sizeable outfit.

In casting around for an instrument man to take, I came across Elwood Mead, who many years later was appointed commissioner of reclamation by President Coolidge.[3] At this time, however, he had just taken on the duties of Wyoming state engineer. I hired him, and then I invited some guests, among them William Hinckle Smith of Philadelphia, John Patrick, two Englishmen visiting me—Captain Stockwell and his brother Andrew Stockwell—Horton Boal of Chicago and one or two others.[4]

When the weather broke late in the spring, we started south through Buffalo and crossed the Big Horn Mountains by way of the one and only wagon road. Then we traveled down the Big Horn River towards the present site of Basin.[5] The river was high, and we couldn't cross there, but we heard of Lovell's Ferry below the mouth of the Stinking Water River, where there would be an iron cable stretched across.[6]

The first night we camped by the river in a grove of trees where a lot of dry logs were lying about. They looked enticing, and we decided to make rafts and have a race down the river. Each man put up twenty dollars and agreed that the one whose raft got under the ferry rope first would win the pot. There was only one condition: we must start at seven o'clock sharp the next morning. Four pairs of us went to work furiously building rafts, but when the starting time arrived Hinckle Smith, my partner, and I were the only two ready to push off. When we were in midstream Captain Stockwell jumped in and swam out to us. The others, seeing we had such a good start, gave up and traveled horseback down some thirty miles along the east bank of the river.

That ride on the raft took us through two canyons, Sheep and Coyote, and it was far from the joy-ride we expected.[7] Several times we hit against the rock walls of the canyons, and our raft would go under while we swam around waiting for it to come up. We had just cleared the second canyon when we hit a logjam and again the raft went under. We succeeded in climbing onto the jam, one of us still clutching the end of the rope, which was attached to the raft now down under us. So, we went to work tearing the logjam apart. In a few hours, the raft slowly rose to the surface.

We started again on our way, happy to find a canteen of whiskey still aboard and one ax stuck fast in a log. That was all the baggage we carried. We were having a little drink and drifting idly down the stream, about a hundred feet from the west bank, when we struck a snag, turned abruptly sideways, and caught on two large limbs of a sunken tree. I slipped into the water and told Stockwell to pass me the ax so that I could chop off one limb. He passed the ax, but not to me. It went into the river. We were now without any means of moving the raft, so we yanked off all the rope and swam for the west shore.

There we landed in a thicket, much to the disapproval of a bull and some cattle, clearly unaccustomed to pedestrians. They were vicious and would paw up the ground, bellow, and charge us. We had to run for it, taking cover behind the larger cottonwood trees, hoping not to come face-to-face with another wild-eyed cow on the other side. After various forays through the brush, we finally parted company with them and started walking north along the riverbank. It was getting late, and as we had had nothing to eat all day, we were delighted to see a cabin on the flat ahead of us. When we got closer, we found it was abandoned and pretty securely boarded up, but we broke in, and inside on a rickety old table we found a rusted tin can with about two inches of sugar and mud in the bottom of it. There was nothing else in the house. We carefully divided this and ate it, and I can tell you it tasted pretty good, at that.

Fortified now we went on, with the intention of swimming the Stinking Water and thus eventually arriving at the ferry. A few miles farther, however, we found another cabin and this time our luck was better. The owner was a hospitable man who invited us to spend the night. He had a saddle of antelope which we finished for him in record time, and then we all turned in.

When morning came, our host advised us that, as the ferry was still several miles away, we would be wise to try the river route again. We borrowed his team, ax, and some barbed wire and in an hour or so built another raft. I had a ten-dollar bill in my watch pocket which I gave our friend as we parted. Then we sailed on down the river and at ten o'clock that day we passed under the ferry rope. Horton Boal was waiting there for us with our horses, and very soon we all caught up with the outfit.

We pressed on westward and that night camped on Sage Creek, five miles below Cedar Mountain that I had first seen. For a couple of days, Mead and I ran preliminary lines while the others amused themselves hunting. Game was fairly good, but the location was not suitable for a permanent camp, so we moved on up through the pass and camped on the Stinking Water River above Cedar Mountain. Back in the pass the next day, I ran a line of levels up to the south fork of the river where we located the headgate of what is now the Cody Canal. Returning to the canyon, we next ran lines eastward, on both sides of the riverbed. All in all, that preliminary survey covered over four hundred thousand acres, stretching as it did to the Greybull River on the south, the Big Horn River on the east, and to the Sand Coulee drainage running into the Clarks Fork River on the north. The latter area was shortly afterwards turned over to the Reclamation Service and eventually, the survey of the south section was more fully developed by a man named Solon Wiley.[8] When the survey of our Cody Canal was finally completed, it covered about twenty-eight thousand acres of irrigable land lying on the south side of the Shoshone River.

My friends and I hunted and made several excursions into the local mountains. Here the game was plentiful and the fishing very fine. When our job was finished, and autumn was again in the air, we started home to Sheridan by the same route. It was then that I added up my expenses for the expedition and found that this pleasant junket had cost me nearly three thousand dollars.

But it had been more than worth it. I returned full of enthusiasm, and with Horace Alger, who was cashier of the bank in Sheridan, I began to figure on building the canal I visualized. In the middle of the figuring, Colonel Cody, Buffalo Bill of the famous Buffalo Bill's Wild West, came to Sheridan. He had an interest in the Sheridan Inn, and his elder daughter Arta was the wife of my friend Horton Boal.[9] Boal, of course, told his father-in-law of our summer's expedition and all about the country over to the west and what I was planning to do. Cody came to me and asked to be let in on it. Naturally, I told him that as Alger and I had been working on the plans together, I would have to consult him first.

Horace was quick to agree that by taking Cody in we

would acquire probably the best-advertised name in the world. That alone, we reasoned, would be advantageous and we thereupon made Cody president of the company we organized. Alger was treasurer, and I was secretary-manager. However, no money was put up then, except the expenses I personally bore.

Cody's partner in Buffalo Bill's Wild West was Nate Salsbury.[10] After a bit, we took him in, and he suggested that inasmuch as the show was paying huge sums annually to Mr. George Bleistein of Buffalo, New York, for lithographing and advertising work, he might come in.[11] Bleistein had two intimate friends, Bronson Rumsey and H. M. Gerrans.[12] Of these three Buffalo men, the first to put any money into the company was Bleistein. He gave a check for five thousand dollars the following spring when we held a meeting of the stockholders and confirmed the officers named and made all seven men directors.

Along in the spring, I went to work on the canal in earnest. I made a contract with a man named Theodore Heckert and placed a camp within a mile of where our headgate was located.[13] The site was chosen on the strength of a fine spring coming out of the hill there. Heckert had between forty and fifty mules and operated his outfit on a force account as the classification of material was rather difficult. In many places, we found the boulders from gravel pits so cemented it was harder to take them out than to take out solid rock. Our hillside work, too, frequently slid and had to be done over and over again. Then I contracted with another crew to riprap the ditch on the riverside and put in the headgate. When that was done, we moved the camp up even closer to the headgate.

Now we had a real crew of men, and saloonkeepers appeared on the scene to try to break in on the camp. I drove them off, in an effort to keep them away from the men as much as possible, for our nearest towns were in Montana—Red Lodge and Billings.[14] It wasn't long before I realized that every payday I was losing a large number of my men, anyway. They'd head for one town or the other to spend their money, and then I'd have to send teams the hundred odd miles to haul out more men or get the same fellows back. So, I had to give up my fight on the saloon-keepers. I let them build near the camp on two promises: first, that their places should be kept quiet and, secondly, that there should be no robbery of the men. In the long run, the men were better off, of course, because they had some protection on the home ground.

Colonel Cody had purchased a bunch of horses from Mike Russell at Deadwood, and as I had quite a bunch still at my ranch, we decided to move them all over to the ditch camp.[15] Cody appointed Frank Grouard, who he, too, had known at Fort McKinney, as his foreman and when Grouard brought the horses over he stayed on to manage Cody's outfit.

That fall of 1894 Cody himself came out to look us over. It was his first trip to the country now named after him, and he was much interested in everything. I remember we made up quite a party to go and meet him at Red Lodge. He had wired that he had been presented with a fine new Concord buggy by the manufacturers and was shipping it west, so in addition to our three rigs, we took an extra team along for him to drive.

When we headed for home, Frank Grouard rode with

Cody, and they took the lead. Mike Russell, who had come down from Deadwood to greet his old friend, rode with me and Johnny Davies, and some of the others brought up the rear in rigs piled high with luggage.[16] Along in the afternoon as we neared Eagle's Nest the road ran across a long sagebrush flat.[17] We were all going like the dickens when I happened to notice that one of the rear wheels on Cody's buggy was skidding. Racing my team abreast with his I yelled to him that there was no snow on the ground and no use of sledding in. It was an odd thing, but that wheel had actually frozen. We had a tough job getting it off. Then we discovered that there was no axle grease in the buggy and none in the other rigs. Nor was there a house for miles. Just then someone saw a herd of antelope in the distance. Grouard borrowed a horse, took his rifle, and rode after one. When he got it back to the roadside, we cracked the main leg bones, took out the marrow, and greased the axle. With that attended to, we drove on.

After staying around camp with us awhile, the colonel got restless and asked me to go with him down in the Grey-bull country. We took his new buggy and with one of his horses and one of mine set out south to visit Colonel Pickett at the Four Bear Ranch.[18]

Crossing the Meeteetse Rim, we saw another fine herd of antelope.[19] Cody had his pet Winchester with him and finally asked me to drive, explaining that he would like to get an antelope to take into Pickett. We hadn't gone far when a bunch of probably two hundred crossed the road a short distance in front of us. We were less than 150 feet from them when Cody jumped out of the buggy and emptied his magazine. He did not get one! I laughed so hard, I nearly fell out of the buggy. After all, this man was celebrated as one of the world's great shots, night after night demonstrating his marksmanship before packed audiences at the Wild West show. Now he climbed back beside me crestfallen. "Damn you, Beck," he said, "if you ever tell this on me I'll shoot you." I told him I didn't think I was in any danger. If he couldn't hit two hundred antelope right in front of him, he couldn't hit me.

However, I kept the story a long time, for Cody was really a wizard with the rifle. The first time he came to my ranch on the Goose Creek he picked up my gun and liked it so well he wanted to try it. I got a hatful of small potatoes and threw them in the air one at a time, watching him hit fourteen straight without a miss.

When we drove into Colonel Pickett's, we found him well provided with meat. He, too, was a fine shot and had named his place from the fact he had killed four bears very close to the spot where his original house stood. That house had been destroyed by a fire in which he lost many valuable books and relics, for Pickett had been private secretary to President Jefferson Davis during the Civil War.

The new house was very comfortable, and he was a hospitable man. We stayed the night, and in the morning, after looking over some of his fine cattle, we went on down the Greybull River to see Dick Ashworth.[20] Ashworth had the adjoining ranch and was also a prominent cattleman. We had noon dinner with him, and he was much put out because he had no bourbon whiskey to offer us. He said the last crowd there had finished it all. But he did have plenty of scotch and burgundy, making it all right with us. Our next stop was at Otto Franc's place.[21] He had the largest number of cattle on the largest place on the Greybull, and being a fine little German he kept everything in beautiful shape.

Towards evening we arrived in Meeteetse. It was the only town west of the Big Horn River and was largely maintained by the patronage of the three ranches we had just visited. It was a rendezvous for all their cowboys and a wild little hamlet. There we spent the night. We didn't even bother with a room because everyone seemed intent on putting on a festival or something, and we concluded we should join in the fun.

The next night we spent in the tiny settlement of Burlington down on the Big Horn River.[22] It was there that we ran across the only sheriff we had seen in a long, long time. His name was Virgil Rice.[23] Rice told us that the Mormon population, in other words, the entire town, was having a dance. Cody insisted that we take in the dance. Virgil and I, by this time, had heard of an old Mormon named Riley who had two daughters.[24] One was the beauty of that whole section; the older one was very much to the contrary. We decided to have some fun with Cody, so we told him at great length about the raving beauty. When we got to the dance, we introduced him to the father, and Cody, falling hook, line, and sinker, said to the old Mormon that he would very much like to dance with his daughter. To the old patriarch that meant, of course, his elder girl. He went and fetched her and then Cody was stuck. She stayed with him all evening like a leech and poor Bill couldn't get away from her. But we agreed that he had probably danced with enough of the world's beauties in his travels to be able to stand up under one dull evening in a little western town.

It wasn't too dull, though. Out in the buggy, we had a good supply of whiskey and cigars, and Cody frequently took some of the Mormons out for refreshment. It was against their religion to indulge in either of these items, but they must have taken the night off because in the morning when we were ready to start, we found there wasn't a thing left except our clothes. Even our friend, the sheriff, failed to recover any of our supply for us, so we started back, across country, to our camp.

En route, at a place called Lone Tree, on Dry Creek, we saw a freighter. We asked him what he was hauling. He replied that it was whiskey for the town of Burlington and Basin. Thereupon we told him to show us some of the Burlington stuff. He objected, but we finally located it and took a case. It turned out to be *the* most awful stuff I ever tried to drink. We had it around for ages, and whenever we found a Mormon in our camp, we'd treat him to some of it in revenge.

After we returned to our camp, Cody found some land he liked around a lake up on the north slope of Carter Mountain, where he had a cabin built and took up a few leases.[25] This place he named Irma Lake, in honor of his younger daughter.[26]

When the ditch work reached the pass south of Cedar Mountain, we found that if we kept the ditch on grade we would run into ground too soft to hold water. It had to be piped over or flumed. Retaining Elwood Mead as our consulting engineer, we learned that the estimate for this work was so high it would be advisable to drop the ditch to a lower level, cross Sulphur Creek, and build a flume about fifteen hundred feet in length around what is known as the Red Hill. From there the ditch ran easterly on grade.

Cedar Mountain and Rattlesnake Mountain, standing as great sentinels, formed our canyon through which rushed the Stinkin' Water River, as it was still officially known on the maps.[27] The Indians discovered it years before and had aptly bestowed the name because of the fumes emanating from remarkable hot sulfur springs down in the riverbed just east of the canyon. Various tribes, including the Sioux and Crow, had long ago made the further discovery of the medicinal properties in this sulfur water. When we came on the scene, the ground around bore evidence of their frequent visits to the healing waters in the many tepee rings and the countless arrowheads still to be picked up.[28]

A few months before I began the ditch work, a Frenchman named Charlie DeMaris had settled at the springs because of his health.[29] Because he attributed his cure from some malignant disease to the waters, he refused to leave the place for any length of time. It soon became a popular spot, also, with our engineers and the crew. Then a fellow named William E. Hymer came down from Red Lodge and started to take out a ditch a mile below the springs to hydraulic for gold.[30] Another outsider named Hap Arnold put up a store building on the river opposite DeMaris's springs, and this mild flurry led Cody to decide to start a town there.[31] With the cooperation of these men, he laid out what he was pleased to call Cody City.[32]

Inasmuch as he had not asked any of our company to come in on this new project, I objected. I decided to lay out another town three miles east of the canyon. After all, if Bill Cody could lay out towns so could George Beck.

I drew a map and taking one of our engineers, Charles E. Hayden, I drove a stake in the ground.[33] Today that spot is in about the exact center of the town of Cody, Wyoming. While Hayden and I were working, we became separated by a few hundred yards. Wishing to consult him I laid the map down, put a rock on it, and walked toward him. Just then a summer whirlwind came along, dislodged the stone, picked the map up, and started it heavenward. Hayden and I followed it as far as we could, but it kept going and we eventually decided our map was recorded in Abraham's Bosom. We drew another.

This one I designated as being of the town of Shoshoni, in Fremont County, Wyoming. Then I sent it down to be recorded in a more suitable place, Lander, Wyoming. But when we applied for a post office, I was notified by the postmaster general that there was a Shoshoni in Fremont County—the post office located at the Shoshoni Indian Reservation. We were told to get another name. I sent in three names—of which Cody was definitely *not* one—but as I was careful to notify each of the company directors each week as to what I was doing, Colonel Cody received a notice along with the rest. He was anxious to correct his error with the crowd, and he was also anxious to have the town named for himself. Mr. Okie Snyder was Cody's secretary, and so Cody sent Snyder to Washington to interview the postmaster general.[34] Snyder bore a letter written on company paper and signed by Cody, as president, requesting that the new town be named Cody and that his previous application on behalf of Cody City, out at the springs, be ignored. It was not long after that before I received formal notification from Washington that we had a post office and that its name was Cody. That's how one town got to be named after one man. As it pleased Buffalo Bill tremendously and did the rest of us no harm, I let it go at that.

SIXTEEN

Developing the Town of Cody and Hunting Trips

We had constructed a real commissary in connection with the ditch camp, but aside from that the first four houses in this brand-new town I built, not that I actually did the work. That was done by George Russell and Jerry Ryan.[1] Russell did the log work and Ryan the stonework, for logs and native stone were our only available materials. Using one or the other we put up a combination hotel-boardinghouse for the workmen, called the Cody Hotel, a schoolhouse, a two-room frame office building now known as the Green Front (it's still my office even if it has degenerated into a pretty fair gentleman's bridge club), and a small stone residence, part of my present home.[2] In the next few months, a mushroom growth of log cabins sprang up and tents of all description. We made further strides when we gallantly laid a few hundred feet of wooden sidewalk to help the ladies keep their skirts out of the dust or mud of our main street.

For the rest, sagebrush flats stretched out in all directions. To make things a little more verdant looking I imported a gardener from the state capital at Cheyenne. The little stone house was a quarter of a mile from the commissary—then the hub of our social life—and I put him and his family out there and plowed up ten acres of ground. Then I told him to try out all the seeds in the catalog and see what he could raise. He was a good gardener, and the results were gratifying, but one day he came to me and said he couldn't live way off out there because he was afraid the coyotes would eat his children, and besides, it was lonesome so far from town. So, I had to build him another house closer to the store, and after a while, I moved out to the stone house.

While I was still living at the boardinghouse-hotel, I had another visit from my Philadelphia friend, William Hinckle Smith. I was occupying a room on the second story right over the dining room. The hotel was a rough place, full of men, muddy boots, and dirty clothes and, I regret to say, my room wasn't much better. Hinckle used to go out to the ditch with me every day, but one day he declined. In the evening when I got home, I went up to my room. It didn't look natural. It was thoroughly cleaned, everything was put in place, a tarpaulin had been put on the floor, a closet made, and the clothes all hung up. Hinckle was there to welcome me. His greeting was "I've cleaned this room up. Now, damn you, you keep it so."

In spite of the town's infinitesimal size, we went right ahead in 1897 and campaigned for the county seat of the newly formed Big Horn County. It was undeniably a premature attack of political aspirations, but nevertheless, when word arrived from Cheyenne that Big Horn County was to be established by the simple expedient of cutting off the northern portion of Fremont County and re-naming it, I again climbed in a buckboard and went out to see the taxpayers. Inasmuch as we would henceforth be residents of the new district and the location of the county seat was still being contested, we saw no reason why Cody should be overlooked in handing out the one plum.

It was quite a jaunt, and a slow one, for the Big Horn Basin alone is a little larger than the whole state of Massachusetts. I didn't skip a ranch or a homestead on my circuit, but even so, we came out second best. The town of Basin, sixty-three miles east of us on the Big Horn River, won the distinction. At the time we were disappointed, but it was just as well for us in the end because another deal came around in 1909 when Big Horn County itself was divided and our section, close to Yellowstone Park, became Park County. Then we did achieve the county seat.

The directors of our Shoshone Irrigation Company had been considerate enough to name two places of business for the transaction of company affairs: one at Cody, the other at the Iroquois Hotel back East in Buffalo. The New York men were all fine sportsmen, and they liked the hunting and fishing we provided in the West, so they came out frequently "on business." Up the South Fork of the Shoshone River—the erstwhile Stinkin' Water, which the state had not elevated with the more formal name—there was some very beautiful country, and an upper meadow, near the headwaters of the river, was a favorite hunting ground for the crowd. As soon as we got together for a board meeting that was where they all wanted to go. Elk, deer, mountain sheep, and bear were all there, with no lengthy excursions to distant points required. We established a sort of clubhouse up in that direction and had George Canfield come over from the Sheridan Inn and run it for us.[3]

Ten miles beyond it up in the mountains was an old mining camp, which we also took over. There we established

Johnny "Reckless" Davies as our representative and to do our assessment work. The minerals there were copper pyrite, molybdenum, lead, antimony, a little showing of gold, and some silver. All told we covered a good piece of ground, but at the time we failed to find enough mineral to pay, although we had enough work down on the claims to patent them. In fact, our mining camp was largely a second hunting center, and we probably got enough fun out of it to balance the ledger.

On one of our hunting parties, we went out from there without encountering our usual good luck. The group included Gerrans, Rumsey, Bleistein, Dr. Carey, Sam Berry, the cook George Grupp, a packer, my dog Leo, and myself.[4] For two days nothing was killed, and we were short of meat. On the afternoon of the second day, I walked out with Leo. Leo was part German uln hound, or mastiff, and part bloodhound. His mother had weighed 185 pounds, and he was no bantamweight at 156 pounds.

A mile out we went over a ridge and saw two elk. I shot one. I had hit rather high and just grazed him but before the elk could get up Leo reached him, and a great fight ensued. An elk weighs between three and four hundred pounds, but Leo caught this animal by the throat, and as it raised up in the air it lifted the dog off the ground. They were moving so rapidly I had difficulty in getting in my second shot, but finally, they came to the ground together. When my bullet went through the elk's head, Leo let go his hold and walked around the stricken animal with the air of a conqueror. I took the tongue and liver into camp and the next day we all went out to see if we could get the other elk.

The cook and packer were sent to haul in elk number one to camp. Leo heard them and made it straight back to drive both men off. I had to go and take possession of the animal before he would allow them to load it. He thought, of course, it was his.

While Hinckle was with me, we took Leo on another hunting trip. A friend of Hinckle's, Frank Bond of Philadelphia, had come out and they wanted to see the Jackson Lake country in the Tetons.[5] A Mr. Mark, A. D. Chamberlain—then the Forest Supervisor—and one of his rangers, a man named Hi Shurtliff, agreed to go with us, saying they knew the trail.[6] We also took Johnny Davies, a couple of packers, and a good outfit of horses.

Then we set off up the South Fork and across the divide to the headwaters of Buffalo Fork. The weather had turned on us, and suddenly there was quite a snow storm. When we broke camp in the morning the forestry men took the lead. The snow was knee deep. After traveling half a day, we looked down into a valley and saw a fine big trail. Down the mountain, we started to get onto it, and there to our surprise, we found the tracks of my dog Leo. We had circled back to our own trail after five hours' hard travel. We thereupon took the guiding out of the hands of the foresters, and following in a general westward direction we finally got down to the Snake River. Going up the river, we found a man who had a cabin at the place where Moran is now located, close to Jackson Lake and on the river. He had a boat, and we tried fishing in the lake without much success.[7]

As the season in the Yellowstone was about to close, we arranged to borrow a wagon, hitch two of our horses to it, and send a man with Hinckle Smith and Bond to the West Thumb of Yellowstone Lake. There they could catch the last steamboat across the lake and stage out from there to Mammoth Hot Springs and then north to the Northern Pacific Railroad.

The night before they left, Hinckle and I walked down by the lake, and he told me he was going to Dakota to sell out the wheat farm he had bought there and go into some other business. I laughed at him and told him the mountain air had gone to his head, that he never would change. But he carried out his resolution. Then making a trip down the Mississippi River, Hinckle saw a run-down railroad, the Choctaw, Oklahoma & Gulf. Traveling over it he observed good coal properties, and he decided that he could make the road pay. With options on it and what property he might need, he went to Philadelphia and laid the proposition before some of his friends. They, too, saw the opportunity and went in with him, making him managing director. He went back to Oklahoma, took up the options, double-tracked the road, and began selling coal to the steamboats on the Mississippi River and to the railroads west. This struck hard at the Atchison, Topeka & Santa Fe Railroad people and they ended by buying the road from Hinckle Smith. He and his friends made a very handsome profit out of his observation and good judgment.

Our party left Moran when the man with the team got back, and we started to find our way back over the mountain.[8] Near the divide, I had taken the lead, and I told the men to stop until I found a pass down on the east side. I put Leo in charge during my absence, instructing him not to let anybody get away. I had been gone probably half an hour when Chamberlain, the Forest Supervisor, declared he, too, would look for a pass. He got about one hundred yards away from the party, whereupon Leo concluded that was far enough. He went after him, took him by the sleeve, and started to lead him back to camp, but Chamberlain shook him off. As soon as Leo saw that the man wasn't going to mind, he grabbed him by the seat of his pants and set him on the ground. Chamberlain got up, brushed himself off, and hurried back to the party, not caring to find out what Leo would do the third time.

Finding a pass, at last, we came down near what is now known as Deer Creek.[9] The second night out we camped at the old mining camp, taking two days to get back when it had taken us over a week going out. Another day and we were back home at the boardinghouse.

SEVENTEEN

Finishing the Cody Canal, Marriage, and Family Life in Cody

Our main ditch was now opposite the town of Cody, and 114 men were at work on it. The board of directors met and voted the needed thirty thousand dollars to complete the job. To raise this money, George Bleistein had taken fifteen thousand dollars' worth of bonds on to Buffalo and Nate Salsbury took the other half to New York. Both men assured me that I would have the money promptly to pay the crews and meet the bills.

But it happened that a financial panic came on in 1893 and continued through 1897. When I sent for funds, none were available. I couldn't stand seeing my bunch of men go unpaid, so I decided to go east myself and get the thing straightened out. In Buffalo, I interviewed the three directors who lived there. Bleistein, who had half our bonds, was a wealthy man, but he explained that conditions were such that he was having difficulty raising sufficient cash to pay the men on his own newspaper and in his lithographing plant. He could not raise an extra cent. And he handed me back the bonds.

In New York, Salsbury gave an even worse report. He, too, handed back his bonds. The outlook was grim, but I decided on one last try. I took the bonds and went to Washington. There I called upon Mrs. Phoebe Hearst, the widow of my old friend Senator Hearst of California. When I told her the trouble I was in, she quickly said, "Why, I'll take the bonds. Go back to my New York office and tell my manager there to give you the money immediately. If he refuses," she added, "have him long distance me. There is a private wire between the office and my house here."

Back in New York I went down to her office and met one of the maddest men I had seen in a long time. He stormed at me, "This is impossible. You can't raise money on government bonds, much less cash on a ditch in Wyoming." I said, "Well, you call Mrs. Hearst in Washington."

She confirmed her order, but he still protested, and finally, she had to demand that he comply with her wishes. When the call was over, he retaliated by announcing he couldn't let me have the money without a ten percent discount. Things were now at such a state I realized I had better not argue over three thousand dollars. He gave me a check on the Wells Fargo Company, and I went over to their banking house and got the twenty-seven thousand dollars.

With the cash stuck in my pocket, I went back to the Hoffman House to pick up my luggage and start west. In the lobby, I ran into Cody. Of course, I couldn't resist telling him of my success. Immediately he and Salsbury begged me to let them have five thousand dollars. They said that if they didn't raise that amount within a couple of days, they would not be able to open their show. I would have it back in sixty days. I knew I wouldn't need all the cash I had within sixty days, so I let them have their five thousand. Times being what they were, it was nine months before I got it back.

Out at the ditch again I paid up my men and contractors, carrying the canal on towards its present terminus near the back of the McCullough Peaks.[1]

Soon our only operating difficulty was in persuading the state to allow us to charge a proper amount for the water rights. We had been started off on a fixed basis of ten dollars an acre. After selling a large amount of land, with water rights, at that figure, it became obvious that the price was not high enough to pay for the construction work. We were then permitted to increase the rate to fifteen dollars. But even that was insufficient. When we were about through, the state allowed us another raise. Most of the land, however, had either been disposed of or contracted for at between ten and fifteen dollars and when we finally closed the books, they showed that the project had cost us nearly twenty-two dollars an acre.

These water-right contracts were made out on a partial payment plan, and drawn up by me, Elwood Mead, and a lawyer from Cheyenne named Burdick.[2] Burdick and Mead wanted to charge the prevailing high rate of interest—which was then twelve percent. But I maintained no farmer could pay that, so we made the interest rate six percent. The important thing was, our contracts were so well drawn that as other canals started throughout the country, they sent to us for our form. Subsequently, it was widely copied throughout the West.

Several years passed before we gathered in enough money to pay Mrs. Hearst her thirty thousand dollars, but we finally succeeded. With this obligation lifted the company turned the land over to the farmers and owners of the water rights. Since then very few changes have been made, and when I recently saw a financial statement attesting to a fine reserve fund back of the Cody Canal, I felt quite a glow of satisfaction over the ditch we dug. Hundreds of thousands of arid acres have been redeemed, and today far more farming and agriculture goes on than even I dared to hope for when I began the work.

Two or three years before I made the call on Mrs. Hearst, I met Miss Daisy Sorrenson. She was living with her sister and brother-in-law, Lilian and Dallas Tinkcom, at their ranch in Marquette near our headgate on the South Fork. She was very pretty and very young, and I maintain I won her with a barrel of gingersnaps. Anyway, I used to take her driving in my buckboard, and she certainly ate an awful lot of gingersnaps.[3]

Besides driving with me, she taught at the local school, consisting of one room and ten pupils of assorted ages. When she discovered that I needed a secretary for the company she volunteered to learn shorthand if I would give her a chance. As good as her word, she went to a business college in Helena, Montana, and returned proficient in typing, bookkeeping, and stenography. Every week after that we turned out fine reports and sent them to all the directors, and when I went east, she ran the business while I was away.

When I came back from the bond-raising mission, we decided to get married. Daisy had been raised in Red Lodge, and some of her family still had a home there, so we had the ceremony there on the 1st of December 1897. She tells me it was a proper church affair with a reception and all the trimmings. I don't doubt her. But I seem to remember more about pacing for hours that day up and down the snowy station platform waiting for the train from

Sheridan. It was bringing Horace Alger up to be our best man, and it was late, as trains were apt to be in the West.

After the wedding, we came back to Cody and moved into the stone house out on the edge of town. The coyotes had frightened away one family, but neither Mrs. Beck nor I were the timid type. We're still in that house, now several times its original size, and we've watched our three children grow up safely, get married, and go away.

With the new century approaching the town began to take on the shape and character of a typical western hamlet. It certainly wasn't a pretty place, but it was practical. We planted a vegetable garden and transplanted a young cottonwood tree from the river by the back door of our home. This was the first tree to grow on this bench and in the town of Cody, and it has grown into a fine old tree today. Cody's first water supply was the river. We'd take a wagon with a big barrel on it down to the river and fill it. Then haul it home and use it rather sparingly. However, we did have nice wide streets, about a dozen of them. I had laid them out one hundred feet wide as a protection against fire and to keep our insurance rates down. Water and the time to turn the ditch water onto the trees and gardens were what it took, and now Cody is a very green western town.

The commissary was still the one store. Among its best customers at this point was Calamity Jane of Deadwood.[4] She was in our midst only a couple of years, and in that time, I know she never came into the commissary to get anything for herself. It was always to relieve the distress of someone else. When I found that out, she got anything she asked for without cost. Perhaps she constituted our first welfare agency, but we never knew her very well, or why she came or when she left. She was a strange, ugly, shy woman.

Some of our other early inhabitants, besides the work crews, were employees of Buffalo Bill's Wild West. A few of them came out when their season with the show ended, worked during the winter months, and then drifted away.

It was still the horse and wagon era, and so Cody promptly built a big frame barn and livery stable on a block of land he bought from the town. Then he figured we needed a newspaper and he persuaded Colonel John H. Peake, of Washington DC, to come out and start one.[5] When Colonel Peake arrived with his family, they were aghast at the size of the town. The other evening Mrs. Peake was telling me about her entry into our midst. She had not been well when they left Washington, and the train trip out to Red Lodge, still our closest depot, had fatigued her greatly. On top of that, she discovered she had a long ride ahead of her by stagecoach. Hour after hour that stage drove over mountain roads and across sagebrush plains. Finally, she thought she could stand it no longer. She looked out and saw nothing—nothing but more sagebrush and rocks. In desperation, she called to the driver to ask when they would reach Cody. "Hell, ma'am," he answered, "you're there now."

The future editor and his family were even more surprised at the newspaper office and living quarters provided. Both were in a lean-to on the west side of Cody's livery stable. However, Peake was a good newspaperman and he started his paper, *The Cody Enterprise.* We all helped him get out the first edition by contributing a variety of articles—the one and only time some of the authors ever saw print. In subsequent editions when news items were scarce, Peake, who was a witty fellow, filled in with breezy comments about the country. He aided materially in advertising and building the town.

Cody also decided to go into the hotel business, but on a larger scale than I had. He was truly a man of vision and foresaw the tourists and hunters who would one day be coming out in numbers. So, he bought another city block and erected on it the large gray stone hotel, which he also named "Irma," for his younger daughter. It was a fine hotel for a little town, with the latest in hotel equipment, brass doorknobs made in the shape of buffalo heads, gas jets, a mahogany bar, fine furniture, and a whole art gallery of paintings depicting the owner in many phases of his career. We worked up a lively and suitable dedication for the opening of that hotel: a parade, a ball, and all the fixings.

We were well supplied with saloons, too, Tom Purcell having the most popular one for a while.[6] Another one was operated by a woman, Poker Nell.[7] Oh, yes, for a long time there were more saloons than there were business houses. That was almost traditional in our land, and the roots of many little western towns went down the deeper for having been planted through the sturdy plank floor of a pioneer bar.

But we didn't neglect our civic duties. We organized a school district and employed a teacher for the stone schoolhouse. She was a highly accomplished Swedish woman, named Miss Vida Weborg.[8] Her education and training had been received in Stockholm, and it was with regret we finally had to part with her because she received offers of much higher salary than we could afford to pay for our first handful of pupils.

It was a town that was a little wild and rough, and so we selected for our first mayor a man who needed no help in keeping the order, Frank Houx.[9] He always looked after the larger disturbances himself, which relieved us of having a police force. He served as long as he wished and when he got tired of the office, I became mayor.

We still didn't have enough people to settle the surrounding farmland. After all, the success of the whole Cody Canal project hung on having the land farmed once it was irrigable. Then two plans were suggested. One was direct and simple. We ran big ads about the Cody country in all the thousands of programs distributed at performances of Buffalo Bill's Wild West.

As for the other plan, we were told that the Polish and Bavarian churches in Chicago had a great number of emigrants on their hands and that the priests could influence these people to the extent that they would gladly settle our land. We got in touch with some of the priests, and they formed a committee to come out and look the situation over. Their delegation seemed well pleased and agreed to take up all of Irma Flat, a fine section of land just out of town. In appreciation of their helpfulness, we returned the compliment by giving the visiting fathers a block of land in town.

The first trainload of settlers to arrive made small down payments, claiming they would need the bulk of their money to improve the places. Salsbury and some of our directors were out when they came, and they thought we should help these people out in an even more practical way, with farm implements and horses and stock. So, we brought a carload of wagons and another carload of machinery and turned them over to the settlers to be paid for out of their crops, retaining title to the property until the machinery was all paid for. We even furnished seed.

When the first year came around, they hadn't made much progress. The next year when we demanded payment, they put on their poorest clothing and came down in a body to see us. They said they couldn't pay. And they all left—all except one man, Joe Vogel.[10] Joe and his wife were both good workers. They did very well, and they remained here for the rest of their lives. They were, therefore, the only people we got out of all our Wild West advertising. It seems that people looking for a new home do not always take seriously the advertising they read in programs. Our next efforts to colonize were along more orthodox lines.

Our land finally filled up with people moving in from Sheridan County and Iowa and Nebraska, with a few Swedish and Norwegian families mixed in. They were the kind to stick, and a few years later we finished the ditch work and turned the farmland over to these sturdy ranchers. When this was being done, and we were closing out the affairs of the Shoshone Irrigation Company, the *Messrs.* Bleistein, Rumsey, and Gerrans elected to take over the commissary and make a permanent store out of it. They sent out Jakie Schwoob from Buffalo, New York, to run it and Harry Weston, too.[11] This they did, and today we still have the Cody Trading Company, founded by the three Buffalo directors, although they no longer operate it.

One evening Tom Purcell, Colonel Cody, and I were

playing poker in Purcell's saloon. Two cattlemen joined us. It so happened that a jackpot was opened, and everybody stayed until the pot finally reached five hundred dollars. We stopped before the call was made and decided, as a good joke, to make the winner contribute the whole jackpot towards the building of a church, for we were still without a place of worship. We all agreed to this. And when it was my good luck to win, I named the Episcopal Church as the beneficiary of the 550 dollars.

We had to organize a guild to receive the money and build the building. When it was completed, we appointed H. R. Weston to read the services in lieu of a rector.[12] But very soon he quit and turned the job over to me. As a lay reader I learned a great deal about the prayer book, but I was even more successful in building up the congregation. This I did by inviting everyone in town who thought he or she could sing to join the choir. A vocal rivalry soon became so keen that we had more church members in the choir stalls than we had in the pews. But the collections were good, and I thought things were going well enough when a little hard luck befell us. Bishop Funston, the Episcopal bishop of Idaho, came by and concluded we should have a proper preacher, so he sent us out one. Within a year the man had the church practically broken up.[13] He had discharged the leader of the choir, and he completely excommunicated me. I was thankful enough for that, but I hated to see the crowd fall away. After another year, we had this rector replaced, and a few years later, we were a well-organized community with a full complement of churches.

EIGHTEEN

The Leiter Ball, the Frederic Remington Visit,
and a Bank Robbery

This chapter should probably be called "Defying the Chaperones When They Were in Power" or: "How Two Westerners Crashed the Leiter Ball."

But name or no name, in the fall of 1900 we directors of the Shoshone Irrigation Company were holding another of our regular meetings, this time back East in Buffalo and with all the members present. When the business was finished, Henry Gerrans, the president of Buffalo's fine Iroquois Hotel, celebrated with an extra-special dinner for us.

In the course of the evening, Colonel Cody mentioned that his daughter Irma was attending a finishing school in New York. Out of deviltry, I asked, "Colonel, why don't you take her to the Leiter ball in Washington? It's being given for their daughters, Nanny and Daisy, who have just returned from India where they have been visiting their other sister, Mary, the wife of Lord Curzon, the viceroy of India. Judging from the newspapers, it's to be the social event of the season."[1]

"I didn't know anything about it," the Colonel replied seriously. And there the subject was dropped.

When we broke up, Cody and Nate Salsbury took the midnight train for New York. Horace Alger and I were to stay over the next day to write up the minutes and balance the company's books. At noon a wire came asking me to come to New York at once. I ignored it. At four o'clock another arrived and was accorded the same treatment. At six o'clock the hotel got one asking for a report on my whereabouts. Alger and I talked it over, and since we had a few days to spare before starting west again we wired Cody we would arrive in Manhattan in the morning.

We reached the old Waldorf-Astoria at seven-thirty and went into breakfast before registering. But Cody was on the lookout for us and joined us before we had a mouthful. "Beck," he said, "you're going to take Irma to the Leiter ball tomorrow night."

"That's a pleasant surprise," I replied, "but I'm not going. I haven't been invited, and I understand it's strictly an invitation affair."

"You must take her," Cody said. "We're in the midst of organizing the show for the next season, and I can't go, and I told her you would take her. She has told the girls at school about it, and I let her have a thousand dollars to buy a dress. If you don't take her, it will break her heart."

I told Cody he had taken on a pretty large risk but that I'd do my best to save Irma's face at school. I had known her since she was a child and I didn't have the heart to refuse since the situation had developed in this way. At the time she was just seventeen, a pretty, wholesome, courageous western girl.

When Alger and I called for her to take her to the train, she was bubbling over with excitement. But Mrs. Cody was not prepared to attend such a party, and as she had heard how strict easterners were about proper etiquette, she was worried about Irma going to the ball without a chaperone. Irma and I assured her that what people might say or do wouldn't bother us and that if we didn't enjoy ourselves, we would leave.

Almost before we knew it, we were in Washington and at the Arlington Hotel. After dinner, I went to see my sister, Mrs. Goodloe. When I told her I was going to ask for an invitation to the Leiter ball she gave me the blowing up of my life, ending with, "George, you're out of your head. I shall call the general and have you put in a lunatic asylum."

"I wish you would," I assured her, "just for the next two or three days, but I'm afraid they might keep me there permanently, and affairs out at the ranch and at Cody can't get along forever without me."

When I left her, I went to call on Mr. Leiter. He was not in. However, I tried again the next afternoon, and the butler escorted me into the library. Old L. Z. Leiter welcomed me like a long-lost friend, and I explained the situation. He said he was delighted I had come and that a formal invitation would be at my hotel by six o'clock. A few minutes past six a messenger arrived with an elaborate, engraved card and Irma's fears vanished.

At nine-thirty we left for the ball. I decided that on the way it might be a good idea to stop by and have my sister inspect my charge so that people would have no room to criticize her on her appearance even if they didn't approve of our flouting the conventions. My sister rose to the occasion graciously and told Irma she looked charming and that she would be as pretty as any girl there. With this encouragement ringing in our ears, we returned to the carriage and soon arrived at the Leiters' handsome DuPont Circle house.

"Now, Irma," I directed, "since you have no chaperone don't waste any time in the dressing room where there will be a lot of curious women; lay off your wrap and come out at once."

I met her outside the dressing room door, and we started up the wide marble stairs. At the top, a large hall led to the double doors of the ballroom. There Mrs. Leiter and her daughters were receiving. The crowd was a brilliant one for the diplomatic corps and had turned out in full force and in full dress. As soon as Mrs. Leiter saw us coming, she did one of the kindest things I have ever known done in Washington society. She left the receiving line and came down the hall to meet us. Welcoming us most graciously she took Irma's arm and thus ostensibly became her chaperone. We walked up to the receiving line feeling a number of pairs of curious eyes upon us.

After chatting there a moment, Irma and I crossed the ballroom. It was large and the guests were now pouring in. We circled around a couple of times looking for some bunch to tie to. Then noticing an elderly lady, Miss Eads, who was something of a social leader and whom I had known when I lived in Washington, we approached her.[2] I introduced Irma. "How do you do," she said coolly, and then she turned to talk to the group about her. After trying several other groups with much the same result, I became a bit discouraged. Irma's pretty cheeks were growing pinker and pinker, but she held her head high and refused to let the rude rebuffs deflate her spirits.

Then, coming to another group, who should I find in the center of it but Mrs. Phoebe Hearst, the senator's widow. She was from the West once, and she knew what this was all about, so she introduced us right and left to her friends. However, they were of the older set. None of them were dancing men, and as Irma longed to dance we started on another tour. We had arrived opposite the entrance when I saw Virginia Lowery, the Duchess D'Arcos, enter the ball-room.[3] I told Irma to sit down and wait for me, and I went to greet Virginia. We had been great friends before she married. After a few pleasant moments reminiscing, I told her about Irma and our troubles. She took prompt action, telling me to fetch Irma while she gathered a number of young men about her.

"Miss Cody," said Virginia, "these young men are all dying for a dance with you so take your choice, but I heart-ily recommend this young Austrian count. He is a fine dancer, although he does not speak English."

Irma's French was of the finishing school variety, but she was good at the sign language. She took on the count, and they danced away a most attractive-looking couple. I drew a sigh of relief and quickly sought the punch bowl.

Soon I ran into some old friends, and I was having a good time, too, in the far corner of the ballroom, when a large door opened and the butler, followed by a line of waiters, announced supper. Everyone waited for Miss Nanny Leiter, the elder of the sisters, to lead the way. She excused herself from the party of gentlemen surrounding her and, walking the length of the ballroom, she took my arm and said, "Will you take me into supper?" I think the whole crowd was as much surprised as I was by this marked attention. "With the greatest of pleasure," I replied, "but I must see that Irma is escorted." "Certainly," said Nanny agreeably. "We will get her."

We found her with the Austrian and told them to follow us. Thus, the wild westerners led the socialites into the magnificent banquet. Seated at the head of the center table we began to enjoy the situation thoroughly because by this time everyone discovered that they knew us, and that, of course, added the spice of amusement to our pleasure.

On the way back to the hotel in the wee small hours, Irma sighed happily, "What stories I'll have to tell the girls at school!" I, also, was pleased with the result although I determined to guard my tongue a little more carefully in the future around that fond father of hers. And I also determined to head for home.

Out in Wyoming, I found Frederic Remington had arrived on his first visit to the Cody country. He was a huge man weighing more than two hundred and fifty pounds, and on this trip, he was accompanied by his wife. She was tiny and very pretty, and he had nicknamed her "Pony Tracks."[4] But this time the man who was already famous for his paintings of Indians and horses did little or no work. He was having a good time in other ways.

On his second visit, he came alone and got down to painting zealously, saying he wanted to capture, especially, the color of the sky and of the sagebrush as he remembered them in Wyoming. In his equipment he had a hundred pounds of art board on which he painted quick little "notes," as he called them—records of the color of the pines—the aspen trees—the lines of a tumble-down cabin—or the early flush of dawn—all to take back to his studio in the East. When it came to drawing, he was the quickest drafter I have ever watched. In ten or fifteen minutes, he would have a whole picture outlined with proper perspective. For a large, heavy person his hands had remarkable agility.

When he started to paint, his rapidity and his accuracy was wonderful to watch. He carried around a small, smooth board with a hole cut in it for his thumb instead of a regulation palette. His pockets would be bulging with tubes of color, and he always had a huge fistful of brushes and pencils. After the scene was sketched he would daub a lot of primary colors on the board and, taking a brush, he'd mix a shade he wanted. Then taking another brush, he'd dab spots of this color all over the canvas. Throwing that brush on the ground, he would take another and start on another color, repeating the process of putting it on in spots wherever the color hit his eye. Finally, he would get so many bright daubs of paint on the canvas that it looked more like a sample of Joseph's coat of many colors than a picture. And then he would begin mixing some dark paint for the shadows. Once he had his shadows in, the picture suddenly stood out—completed. He did several landscapes of the valley of the Shoshone looking north, and even my old buckboard and wagons did their duty as models for future reference.

Nothing so disgusted Fred Remington as to find sawed lumber houses in our country. He felt the West was disgraced by them, that we should have nothing but traditional log cabins. One time we were out driving in the cattle country when he suddenly asked me to stop the horses. Sitting there in the buggy with a sketch pad on his knee he began reproducing the log ranch house we were passing, putting in the mountains in the background, the trees, and the corrals. It was all so familiar to me that when he was done, I said, "What in thunder do you expect to get out of that?" "Thirty-two hundred dollars," he answered. Good Lord, I thought, that would buy the place twice over.

After he had been with me awhile, he wanted to go out on a camping trip. I hired a cook, remembering from his first visit that he was a gargantuan eater as well as a pretty good drinker, and on ahead of us I sent a four-horse team and wagon loaded with everything I thought we could use. The cook and a horse wrangler were sent with the wagon, and they started off early one morning headed for Carter Mountain, up near Irma Lake. Remington and I didn't start in my buckboard until after lunch, but we overtook the wagon about halfway up the mountain. Remington insisted on pausing for a drink. We had with us a nicely spiked five-gallon keg of whiskey. He filled a tin cup and drank it down raw. When we got to camp, he had another before dinner. Then he had several more as we loafed around the big campfire before retiring.

We had two tents, and I had carefully placed mine at a fair distance from him because he could also snore to beat the band. The next morning the rest of us were up and making breakfast preparations before he appeared. When he came out of his tent, he complained of not feeling well and announced he had no appetite—not to bother about him. I told Ben, the cook, to just scramble a couple dozen eggs very lightly, make toast, fry some bacon, and brew the coffee. Then we started to eat.

Remington drifted over, looked at the food, took a piece of bacon and some egg on his plate, and after trying two or three mouthfuls, he said, "Pass me that frying pan." When he got through breakfasting there was hardly a morsel left for the boys. The cook was aghast and wanted to know how much he would have to prepare on days when Remington was feeling fit to begin with.

After a few days spent sketching and painting there, we moved on up to the O. D. Marx ranch at the mouth of Deer Creek on the South Fork of the Shoshone. We had named the day we would be arriving at Marx's ranch and Dr. H. H. Ainsworth, a physician in Cody, was coming up to join us there in a little fishing.[5] Ainsworth was our champion angler, and when we drove into the ranch, we found he had already arrived and had his creel full of trout—perhaps twenty-five pounds in all. And as a boy on the place had caught us fourteen beauties, averaging three-quarters to one pound each, we had a mess of trout, all right.

Ben unpacked his two eighteen-inch frying pans and got busy cooking the whole lot for our dinner. There was plenty of other food besides, but Remington and Ainsworth both announced they were there for all the piscatory pleasure possible and, believe it or not, when they got through only the bones remained. The rest of us had held down to two apiece, all the trout any sane man should eat. Suddenly Ainsworth got up from the table, stepped outside, and parted with the works. Then he went to bed.

Remington finished his dessert and started to smoke a cigar with me. But he never finished the cigar. He, too, bolted in an undignified manner, and then he made straight for the room he was sharing with Ainsworth. Instead of getting into bed he paced the floor for an hour moaning over and over like a phonograph record, "By God, I'm going to die. I'm going to die this time." Then, Ainsworth told me, he stopped in his tracks, reflected a moment, and announced, "But I don't give a damn. They were worth it." The next morning both gentlemen were agreeably alive.

We had planned to go on across the mountains to Bridger Lake via the divide at the head of Deer Creek, but when the time came to go, Remington, decided against crossing at the high elevation. We were already at an altitude of six thousand feet, and he was puffing. When we told him that Bridger Lake would be ten thousand feet, he realized that there were plenty of things for him to paint right there on the river. So, we reorganized, taking the packer with us and leaving the cook to him and promising to be back within a week.

That morning while we were getting ready I put a pack on a horse that I called Chico and turned to pack a second horse. Remington came out and started to sketch Chico as he stood there all loaded. One of the ranch boys, with a real veneration for art, realized that Chico was about to be immortalized by the master. He rushed frantically for a shovel and started digging a post hole, with every intention of setting in a post and then tying Chico to it so that he'd be nice and quiet while he stood for his portrait. But before the hole was half dug Remington had finished the picture. It now hangs over the fireplace in my living room.[6]

Ainsworth and I arrived at Bridger Lake in a change of weather, and on the second day, it began to storm. However, we saw no geese, only ducks. That lake was covered with ducks, and so we put our canvas boat together and soon had our panniers full. There was also a number of moose around the lake, and one young bull became so intrigued with the boat that when it was out of the water, we had to take it up close to the campfire to keep him away from it. After a day or so, as there were still no geese, we decided to return to Remington.

On the way back, we killed an elk to take to Remington as a souvenir, but when we pulled in at the ranch, he had gone. They told us that as soon as the storm came on, he grew restless and wanted to go to town. He loved the sun and was one of the most affable of men when it was pleasant and warm, but when the weather was gloomy, he was miserable. In spite of our plans, he had already headed for the East when we reached Cody.

The Burlington Railroad had already laid plans to bring their roadbed across the mountains by way of the South Fork of the Shoshone and thence down to the Buffalo Fork of the Snake River, thus benefiting by one of the best possible grades across the Rocky Mountains to the Pacific Coast. When they started negotiations for a right-of-way up the river in our direction, Mr. Charles Morrill, president of the Lincoln Land Company, came to see me inasmuch as I was running the town site.[7]

He made a proposition to take over a half interest in the town of Cody. Otherwise, he said, his company would build a town of their own a few miles down the river at a place called Corbett. This would be clearly disastrous for us, and so he and I went east that summer to interview the directors of our company at Buffalo. Then, because Colonel Cody was on tour with his Wild West show, we went on up to Portland, Maine, to confer with him. There we obtained his signature to a contract we had drawn up in Buffalo, selling to the Lincoln Land Company a half interest in the town at ten dollars an acre, our whole township being but one-mile square.

The Lincoln Land Company next acquired another eighty acres across the river from us, on the north side of the Shoshone, and there the Burlington built its station, both companies promising not to build a second town at the depot. I was appointed the land company's local agent in Cody and retained the post until other business affairs of my own claimed my full attention.

But even with these early duties, I was finding it more and more difficult to get back and forth to Sheridan and to my ranch on the Big Goose Creek. Therefore, when William Cameron Forbes, of Boston, Massachusetts, came along and wanted to buy Beckton I capitulated and sold it to him, lock, stock, and barrel.[8] There was a wrench in parting with it because the place was even more beautiful than when I had first seen it, but with the sale completed, I found renewed interests and satisfaction in being a full-time citizen in Big Horn County.

Soon there was enough excitement just living in Cody to make me forget the ranch for a while, at least. On the day after Halloween 1904, I was having a game of chess in the office of Dr. Bradbury.[9] A block up the main street from his office was a new bank I had helped establish along with two Sheridan men, John Winterling and L. H. Brooks, and I. O. Middaugh of Iowa.[10] We called it the First National Bank of Cody, located in a one-story stone building known as the Walls Building, on the corner directly opposite the Irma Hotel.[11] As the doctor and I sat there debating our moves we heard a commotion in the street but dismissed it as a probable continuation of the Halloween celebration. Then a man busted into the doctor's office on the run and told him to bring his instrument case and come at once to the bank, that Middaugh, the cashier, had been shot. We raced to the scene and found him dead in the dust of the main street. He had two bullet holes in him, but before falling, he had managed to make the few hundred feet from the bank in an effort to summon help.

Two holdup men had ridden into town alone, tied their horses to a telegraph pole in front of the office of Judge Walls, around on the side street, and then observing that the teller, C. F. Hensley, was alone in the bank, they walked in.[12] Getting up to the cage they drew their guns and demanded the money. Middaugh was in a back room, where a second door opened out near where the horses were tied. When he heard the noises of the holdup, he made for this door to get help. One of the robbers saw this move, darted to the street, and shot at Middaugh just as he reached the horses. He staggered forward a few paces and was shot again.

The second robber, now alarmed, didn't wait to scoop up the money; he dashed to the street to join his companion in their get-away. Judge Walls had grabbed a pistol and fired at them as they sprang to their saddles. They shot back but missed him. They also took a crack at my friend Jerry Ryan who was working on a new stone building across at the far corner, and as more people appeared, the robbers fired indiscriminately, including a shot that narrowly missed Dr. Frances Lane, a woman physician who had just arrived in town to set up practice.[13] There would have been a good many casualties had they not dropped a couple of automatics in the street as they untied their horses. But once mounted, they lost no time in riding at a gallop for the open country, going south towards the cow town of Meeteetse.

Now a crowd had gathered around the bank, and I offered a large reward for the men, dead or alive. Several posses started in pursuit, but they had not organized well enough among themselves, and when they got separated and began shooting one another they further aided the escape, for of course, the robbers had relays of fresh horses stationed south.

Judge Walls then took up the chase in a professional way. After weeks of work, he located two men answering the description at Vernal, Utah, and had them brought back to the county seat at Basin. There they were identified by several people in addition to Walls. But they never came to trial. An attorney from Sheridan arrived in Basin with quite a sum of money, it is said, and the two men disappeared from the jail. Moreover, they were gone a full week before anyone in Cody was informed of the fact.

NINETEEN

Another Ute Uprising and Famous Guests

Colonel Cody had purchased a few years earlier a fine cattle ranch for himself, the TE Ranch up the South Fork of the Shoshone River. He bought it from an early settler, John L. Burns, for one thousand dollars.[1] Since the colonel's death, the place has changed hands several times for considerations running into the hundreds of thousands of dollars. But that's digressing.

The hunting and fishing around the TE were marvelous, and Cody enjoyed nothing so much as to get out there with a group of congenial fellows after the show season was over. His frequent comings and goings, together with the fact the Burlington was now servicing us with a short line, began to focus more attention on the country and bring us a lot of famous visitors. General Miles made two trips out, General Leonard Wood came, and so did some high-ranking government officials, including Secretary of War Garrison, Secretary of Navy Daniels, Franklin K. Lane of the Department of the Interior, the Hon. James A. Garfield, and others.[2] And one autumn we got all primed for President Theodore Roosevelt.

He had agreed to try our brand of hunting in the company of our congressman, Frank Mondell.[3] Cody was to be their starting point. The up and coming citizens of Louisiana, however, got to agitating and he had to take his hunt that autumn down there. The change eventually worked out to the advantage of the juvenile public, at that, for on this Louisiana hunt Roosevelt killed several bears, starting the famous "Teddy bears" soon afterwards used in his campaigns, and from politics the teddy bear bounded into the toy business.[4]

Buffalo Bill's holidays were not always uninterrupted. Occasionally he was summoned east on business, or the War Department would invite him to confer on a minor outbreak among the few Indian tribes still rebellious enough to flare up once in a while. There had, of course, been no major Indian uprising since the Battle of Wounded Knee in the Badlands and for the most part, all the western tribes were apparently content on their reservations. But along in 1906 some of the Utes became restive, and this led to my accompanying Cody on an amusing expedition "to quell the Utes"—or at least that is what we expected to do when we started.[5]

Their reservation was along the White River in eastern Utah and western Colorado, and for a long time, all had seemed peaceful enough there. Then they made a pact among themselves to migrate in a large body northward through Wyoming towards the Black Hills, probably intending to join up with the Sioux on their reservation in South Dakota. This migration was not suspected until they got into the cattle country of Wyoming and, being short of food, they began killing cattle as well as antelope and other game. Perhaps the scarcity of meat on their own reservation had started the movement, but this method of rectifying matters was in violation of Wyoming's game laws, and suddenly news of their invasion appeared in headlines all over the nation.

Soon a wire came for Cody from General Miles in Washington asking him to go and contact the Utes and if possible induce them to go home thus avoiding, perhaps, the necessity of sending a military expedition after them.

Hank Fulton and I were standing at the Irma Bar with Cody when the telegram was handed to him. He read it and then turned and asked me to go along inasmuch as I was so thoroughly familiar with the part of the state in which they were now reported—I have walked it once or twice in my sheep and cattle days. I said I'd go if Hank would come along for company. When he agreed the three of us took the next train out, the colonel carrying a .30–.40 carbine whereas Hank and I went unarmed.

There had been a lady newspaper reporter hanging around the Irma at the time the wire came. She smelled a fine story in this expedition, and although we told her bluntly we didn't want her along, she nevertheless wired her newspaper for funds and authority to go, and when we got on the train, there she sat.[6]

Along the way, we had more telegrams advising us that the Utes were moving up in the direction of Crawford, and now, more than ever, we wanted to get rid of the lady journalist. So, when the train pulled into Sheridan, we sneaked off and just let her ride on. Then we took the next train on to our destination.

Immediately on arrival, we got in touch with some of the Indians and an army officer only to be told that our services wouldn't be required after all because the Utes had been supplied with food and had agreed to turn around and go back to the reservation. But here the lady scribe caught up with me. It was the end of the week, and not a single train was scheduled to leave in either direction on Sunday. We didn't see how we could stand being cooped up there twenty-four hours, so again we ditched her by hiring a buggy and a team and driving ourselves across the line to Hot Springs, South Dakota. The next day we got an engine and a caboose to come and take us into Deadwood. As long as we were supposed to be away putting down rebellion, we decided we'd better stay away a decent length of time.

We put up at Deadwood's best hotel, and that night in the dining room we noticed a large party at the nearby table. The waiter said it was an opera troupe in town, headed by a woman singer, Miss Marie Hunt.[7] Cody, seeing the possibility of some pleasant professional company, excused himself to us with the remark that he'd just step over "and see some old friends." We watched him introduce himself and as he seemed to be having a fine time we decided to join him and see some friends, too. After dinner, we sat in a box at the local opera house for their performance, and then Cody insisted we take the whole troupe back for an after-the-theater supper. It went on gaily enough, but after a while Hank and I grew sleepy and retired.

We were sharing a huge room in which there were three beds. The next morning when I woke up, I was alone. Hank and the colonel had disappeared and, I noticed, so had the gun. I looked at my watch and found it was late. Downstairs I inquired at the desk for my companions, and the clerk told me they were to be found at Mike Russell's Saloon. Then I asked if I could still get some breakfast and if the opera singer had had hers. The hotel people said no, she hadn't breakfasted, yet. I thereupon dispatched a boy up to ask her to join me. Here, I decided, was an opportunity to have some fun with Cody and the boys.

While we ate, I told the clerk to order me the finest open carriage in town and have it at the door when we finished. It was a landau with a fine pair of horses. We stepped in, and I told the driver to go down the main street and not to stop. As we passed Mike Russell's Saloon some of the crowd from the night before noticed us, but we paid no attention to them, and at the end of the street we turned around and drove back. This time Cody, Hank, Mike, and all the rest were lined up along the curb in front of Mike's, and as we passed they yelled for us to stop. But we professed to be in deep conversation and rode serenely by. The third time we tried pulling Cody's leg, the whole crowd had swarmed out in the street, stretched across in a line to catch the horses and force us to halt. This time they won, and we went into Mike's for an "eye opener."

The colonel and Mike were now so hilarious they sent out and ordered every available carriage in town, piled everyone in, and started a procession up the mountain to Wild Bill Hickok's grave. There we paused long enough to have our pictures taken, Cody apparently thinking to thus honor his old pal Wild Bill by a permanent record of the visit. Mindful of my status as a staid family man I graciously turned the prima donna over to Cody until after the posing was done. With that attended to, we piled in the carriages again and headed back to Mike's.

There I found out why the gun had been missing from our room. Cody made a presentation of it to me, and I observed that he must have taken it bright and early that morning to a jeweler's because the plate on the stock had been changed. It had formerly read: PRESENTED BY THE WINCHESTER COMPANY TO COLONEL W.F. CODY, but now it reads: PRESENTED BY WM. F. CODY TO HIS FRIEND GEORGE T. BECK.[8]

After that ceremony, we took the train out for home—Hank and I did. The colonel felt a sudden urge to go on to New York, and after borrowing all the cash we had, he took off for the East while we rolled over the steel rails to Cody. And that's how the Utes got put down by Buffalo Bill, Hank Fulton, and George Beck. What happened to the stepsister of the press we never did bother to find out.

The next fall we had a brief taste of royalty when Prince Albert of Monaco, a great hunter and sportsman, came west as the guest of A. A. Anderson.[9] Anderson was a New York artist and a Wyoming rancher, with a big place over on the Greybull River. His knowledge of the region was further heightened by his work, some fifteen years before, in establishing the first forest reserve in the state. When the prince's visit to Anderson terminated, he became the guest of Colonel Cody, and Cody outfitted him for a top-notch hunt in our mountains. The prince was a genial fellow and stayed around town a week, during which time he kept me busy taking countless pictures for his personal record.

A few days after he had departed for the mountains Charley Gates arrived, in a private car and with an entourage of his own, to provide a colorful and regrettable episode.[10]

Young Gates's father was John R. "Bet a Million" Gates of Port Arthur, Texas, and the son was wealthy, restless, and generous. He had come hoping to join up with the prince's hunting party, but when he found it had already gone into the hills, he asked me to help get up a party of his own. I had known him before and therefore took considerable pains to get him outfitted and finally I started him off with Ned Frost, whom I considered the best guide and hunter in the country.[11] They were gone a month and returned with all the game listed on their permits. But again, Gates had missed the prince. The Monaco party had come in a few days ahead and had already departed for New York.

Charley Gates was so struck with the country, however, he decided to linger around while Frost went out scouting for a suitable hunting lodge for him to buy. The Gates's private car, meanwhile, remained on a siding over at the depot and Charley took up residence at the Irma.

In Charley's party were a couple of men who appeared exceedingly anxious to get away. They had plans for a European holiday for themselves and Gates, at Gates's expense, and all the week he hung around there was obvious friction among them. Out in the mountains, Gates had not touched a drop but now, sitting around the Irma Hotel day after day waiting for Frost to report on his progress, he began to take an occasional drink.

He was a likable fellow and, as I have said, extremely generous. Among other things, he gave every man in his hunting party a fur coat, and when there were not enough in town to go around he ordered more shipped in. Following that he asked me one day, as a special favor, to get all the preachers in town to come and see him. I sent a boy to round up the handful, and when they were assembled Charley asked each man the total amount of indebtedness against his struggling parish. Then he took out his check-book and cleared up the bills of every church in town.

The last man to leave the room was young Mr. McGin-ley, the rector of the Episcopal church. As he retreated down the hall, I happened to mention that he wanted to get married, poor fellow, but didn't have the money. Gates rushed to the door and called him back. He explained he had just heard he wanted to get married and there was a check for a thousand dollars to go ahead and do it.

By the end of this week of philanthropy, the two men with Gates were behaving more and more oddly. The bar-tender came to me one morning and reported that they had tried to bribe him to put knockout drops in Charley's drinks. He had two glasses of whiskey with him they them-selves had prepared, and which he had refused to serve. I told him certainly not to let Charley have a drop of any-thing, and then I went about my business for the day.

That afternoon Gates took a little snooze in one of the card rooms adjoining the bar, and while he was nodding the two frustrated travelers came in a back entrance and administered a hypodermic of chloral into his arm. In a few minutes, he was unconscious. They watched carefully, and when this occurred, they brought in a couple of hired men to help carry "poor sick Charley" out the back way, put him in a wagon, and take him to the depot to his private car. A deputy sheriff overheard one of the men say that old Charley wouldn't come to until he was out of the state of Wyoming. But the sheriff didn't get to me to report until evening. I started for the depot and encountered the two friends anxiously looking for an oxygen tank and a doc-tor. By noon the next day, Charley was dead.

When the news reached me, I went to the coroner and demanded an investigation. He, the district attorney, and I went to the railroad car, and there the coroner formally ordered an autopsy and placed the car in the custody of the station agent with orders to hold it. Confident that justice would be served I left to go back out to the ditch where serious problems had arisen. When I got back at five o'clock, I learned that the doctor the companions had engaged had connived with them and made a sworn statement that Charley Gates had died of natural causes, whereupon the coroner had released the car. With a special engine attached it had already reached Billings, Montana, and was on its way to Minneapolis, where Gates's mother and his divorced wife lived.

The doctor they had picked up in Cody had gone along with the friends and the body, and we later heard rumors that, in addition to accepting his story, Mrs. Gates had paid him ten thousand dollars for his services.

TWENTY

The Shoshone Reclamation Project
and the Cody Power Plant

Along with the advent of the Burlington Railroad, the Reclamation Service concluded to build a dam on the Shoshone River in the canyon formed by Rattlesnake and
Cedar Mountains and six miles west from Cody. The first
contractors failed. The work was then taken over by the
U.S. Fidelity & Guaranty Company of Baltimore and then,
in turn, gave the contract to the firm of Grant, Smith, and
Locker who completed the project in 1910. It was a remarkable example of engineering, and at the time it was finished it was the highest dam in the world.[1]

I had busied myself, concurrently with the beginning of
the dam construction, by building an electric light plant.
In our earliest surveys of the land, I had noticed a favor-
able bend in the river due north of the future town site.
Now I turned my attention to it and, running some levels across the bend, I found I could get a twenty-foot fall
within one-fourth of a mile, which was sufficient for my
proposed plant. Of course, I tried to organize a company,
but my friends all laughed at the idea, so I mortgaged what
property I had, and with twenty thousand dollars secured
through bonds I put in waterworks to run the light plant,
which has lasted forty years with very little change.

When I started operating the light plant in 1904, I

announced I would give continuous day and night services. The first year I lost heavily, but by the second year, a few progressive people had grown tired enough of trimming the wicks and cleaning the chimneys of their coal oil lamps to try out our newfangled illumination. After that, with the saloons and the hotels in the vanguard changing over to electric lights, the plant became a paying proposition even though I kept our rates down to a minimum.

Of course, just building and operating a light plant left me with plenty of time for other matters, too, among them hunting and prospecting some more. On one of these prospecting trips I was accompanied by Wayne Darlington, an extraordinarily fine mining engineer who had been sent out to me by John Mackay of New York.[2] Many years before, Darlington had worked for Mackay in his mining ventures in the West and then he had gone to China for four years as a consultant to the Chinese government under Li Hung Chang, the great progressive minister of the old emperor.[3]

Now out in Wyoming, Darlington assured me that the main project I had under consideration would take millions of dollars. But when he was through his survey, he said he would like to see a little more of the country and its remarkable resources, so we took two men, a bunch of horses, and started out on a combination business and pleasure exploration. We explored up around Clark's Fork region where a man named Painter had a mine and then back down by the North Fork of the Shoshone River.[4]

Darlington was a great chess player, and as we rode along on horseback we played on a miniature board I had brought from Cuba. One rider would hold the board and make his move, ride up and hand it across to the other player who would then study out his next move. I can recommend chess to thoughtful equestrians, laced at frequent intervals with a little scenery-gazing.

Riding along he also told me of some of his adventures in China, for when he arrived, they had given him a peacock feather to wear in his hat, made him a mandarin, and assigned a lot of men to work under him and study his methods. And, of course, they paid him very handsome fees.

Even with the big fees, he found the cost of tea in Peking a bit stiff. The high government officials had all invited him to their homes to have tea. Naturally, he had to invite them back and give them tea, and that's where his troubles began. He shopped for good tea, and he paid six dollars a pound for it, which seemed a fair price to an American. But in spite of this careful consideration, the Chinese stopped coming. He finally went to one of the foreign residents and asked what in the world was the matter. "Oh," came the forthright reply, "it's that rotten tea you serve." Darlington explained that he paid six dollars a pound for it, and then he was enlightened. The tea he had been entertained with cost three hundred dollars a pound. So, he tried to get some to reinstate himself, but the super-deluxe brand was for restricted patronage, and the best he could buy, a rank outsider, was a tea at ninety dollars per pound. That, he found, he could buy plenty of. And before he left China, to return to America to work again for John Mackay out in Nevada, he felt he had re-won most of his Oriental friends.

Hunting and camping lazily along the North Fork of

the Shoshone, the idea struck me that a good wagon road could be constructed along the river from Cody to the boundary of Yellowstone National Park. Darlington and I thereupon returned to town for a wagon. When he agreed with me that the grade could be made practicable, I went back to Washington in the winter to see about getting a road appropriation.

I had a number of friends on the Appropriations Committee, among them Senator Hale of Maine who had also been a friend of Father's. I went directly to him. He listened attentively and told me to come to the Appropriations Committee the next morning. When I got there, the members poked a lot of fun at me and asked where was this Wyoming? I told them literally in the center of the universe, and then I stated that I wanted forty thousand dollars for the roadwork. Oh, they said, the government always allows more; here, take sixty thousand.

The National Park people, however, were opposed to the construction of an eastern highway and entrance via Cody, and when the appropriation got turned over to them for disbursement most of the sum went to build the Fishing River Bridge within the park itself, and the rest was dissipated on other park improvements.

The next year some of my friends and I got after our Wyoming senators, and they succeeded in securing another large appropriation, and then the work was forced through. My idea had been to build it up Crow Creek, a bit farther to the west, but the park people favored laying the road up Middle Creek, which they did. Today, a quarter of a century later, a quarter of a million people drive over its fifty-three-mile stretch from Cody to the park each summer. This means of course that a quarter of a million tourists come to our town annually, contributing nicely to our growth and prosperity.

On one of the last hunting trips Colonel Cody took in the mountains of Wyoming, way back before the First World War, I joined him as did also Mike Russell from Deadwood, Tom Foley from Omaha, Johnny "Reckless" Davies, and a few local fellows.[5] We also had a very special guest on that trip: Iron Tail, a chief of the Oglala Sioux Indians. Iron Tail toured for years as an attraction with Buffalo Bill's Wild West. He should be even better known to millions of Americans because Earl James Fraser, the sculptor, used him as his model for the Indian profile appearing on the reverse side of our buffalo nickel. He was a fine-looking Indian.[6]

On this trip, I took along my own pack outfit, two or three horse wranglers, and a cook. Cody had a big outfit; we had in all about forty horses. We met up at Pahaska, the colonel's hunting lodge near the Yellowstone Park boundary. The place bore the name the Indians had given Buffalo Bill because of his long hair. From there we went on up the North Fork of the Shoshone River to the mouth of Eagle Creek, crossed the divide, and dropped into the headwaters of Mountain Creek. Before we were across the divide, however, it began to snow violently and seeing ahead any distance was difficult. The colonel and his packers who were leading became badly tangled up in the draws and fallen timber. I had, meanwhile, observed some grassland in the little valley on the north fork of Mountain Creek and I took my outfit, Mike Russell, and Foley and went down there to make camp. Then I sent my packers out to bring Cody in, building a huge camp-fire to light the way.

When morning came, we were practically marooned in a snowfall of three to four feet. But late in the afternoon, the sky cleared sufficiently for Cody and Iron Tail (Ta Ka Nichi Opi) and two other men to go out on horseback to hunt along the south fork on Mountain Creek. Tom Foley and Mike elected to try their luck on foot around where we were camped. Before nightfall, they returned with a deer and after dark Cody and the two men came back, but Iron Tail was not with them. He had shot an elk, Cody reported, and knocked it down, but the elk got up and ran, going across the boundary line into the park. Cody told Iron Tail not to go after it, but the old chief felt that having wounded the animal, it was only right to track him down. Cody was excited because he said if a ranger caught Iron Tail hunting in Yellowstone National Park he would probably arrest our whole party and bring a case against us.

We laid plans to pull out the first thing in the morning, but towards midnight Iron Tail showed up triumphantly bearing the tongue, liver, and teeth of his elk. He wanted a horse to take out to bring back the meat, too, and when Cody refused him one Iron Tail was thoroughly disgusted with Buffalo Bill as well as with a few of the white man's hunting restrictions.

The next morning, we did start off early, Cody and the Indian leading and carefully breaking the trail while the rest of the party and I followed behind with the packhorses. On our way down Mountain Creek, we saw hundreds of ducks frozen in beaver ponds. Their wings had become so covered with ice in the storm they had not been able to get into the air.

Farther on, as we approached the flats near the Yellowstone River, those of us in the rear saw a big moose lying on the hillside less than a hundred yards distant. Cody and Iron Tail had been so intent on watching the trail they had passed him by and were now fully a half mile ahead. But the size of our group stirred the old bull. He got up, shook himself off, and came down before our eyes on the trail Iron Tail and Cody had cleared. Taking advantage of the easy progress he could now make through the snow, he trotted amiably ahead of us until he reached a small side stream flowing into the Yellowstone. This seemed to be his point of transfer, and he turned off just as casually as though hunters frequently came along to oblige him.

When all of us finally reached Thoroughfare Creek, we were further amused to find two boys from Cody out camping and stripped to the waist in a successful effort to be tough in subzero weather.[7] We made camp a mile past them and spent several days hunting. By now Iron Tail, nursing his grudge about the elk, refused to hunt with Cody and he annexed himself to me. We'd ride out together, and soon we developed the habit of taking along the ribs of a deer in a sack tied on behind one of our saddles, and from this wise old Indian I learned the best way to cook them. When we got hungry, we'd find an aspen thicket and make a bed of hot coals from dry aspen wood. Then we would throw the ribs into the coals, kick a few over the top, and wait until the end bones began to burn. They were done then and fit for the gods.

After four or five days, Cody woke up one morning to

find that we had run out of liquor, and he and Johnny Davies struck out for the TE Ranch. I was ready to go in, too, so Iron Tail, Mike Russell, Tom Foley, and the rest of us started in after Cody. Around the head of Ishawooa Creek, the trail was rough, but we made it into the TE on the South Fork of the Shoshone by seven o'clock that night, and the next day the balance of our horses and packers came in.[8]

We were now quite a crowd at the old ranch, and things were merry. Out in their quarter, the cowboys and packs soon got up a poker game of no mean proportions. Someone among them had spotted quite a little money on Iron Tail, so they invited him to join them and after he sat down, they kept urging him to bet. At last when a good big jackpot came up Iron Tail displayed a becoming reluctance to go into it but, egged on, he did, and of course, he won everything on the blanket—the whole works. Then he stood up, stated, "Indian heap sleepy," and went off to bed, leaving behind a completely disillusioned and broke bunch of cowboys.

My friendship with the Indian grew by leaps and bounds, and on his next trip to Cody, he brought me as a present a handsome medicine bag made by his squaw. It is one of the best examples of Indian handicraft I have seen in any collection. To return the compliment I invited him to my house for dinner, and remembering that he liked mutton chops I bought two dozen fine, thick ones, much to the surprise of my two small daughters, Jane and Betty. Their surprise increased to open-eyed amazement when at the table they watched the chief eat eighteen of them and nothing else.

Speaking of food, I recall a memorable stew I once concocted in a rainstorm out on the Meeteetse Rim in the days of early automobiles and the attendant breakdowns, which stranded hungry motorists for hours.

When we found ourselves stalled on this expedition I took a bucket out of the back of the car, climbed over a fence into a corral where I noticed some huge mushrooms growing in an erstwhile sheep pen—remembering how fine sheep manure had been for my strawberries back in the Beckton days—and filled the bucket full. Then I killed three sage hens huddling under some sagebrush, cleaned them and cut them up, dipped up some rainwater, and then set the whole thing to simmer over a brush fire nursed along under an umbrella. It was a truly magnificent stew, well worth waiting for, while we also waited for a passing motorist or a team and a wagon to come to our rescue.

The Indians, of course, cooked wild game better than anyone, although they ate the intestines, and such, raw. It seemed a revolting custom to me when I first watched them do so on Pryor Mountain.[9] But back in those dark days none of us ate that particular part of an animal. Science has since come to the red man's defense in this practice, and now we occasionally pay more for sweetbreads than we do for steaks. But, as I was saying, there has been no improvement to surpass the Indian's simple method of cooking meat—throwing a chunk into the hot coals and allowing them to supply their natural salts while the meat roasts.

Even so, I think I can improve on their venison by adding my own favorite sauce. To make it you sprinkle a haunch of venison with salt and pepper, put it in the oven in a pan with enough hot water around it and two or three slices of pickled pork on top. Baste well for approximately three hours, or until nicely browned. Then make a gravy by dredging some brown flour into the juice in the pan and, stirring well, add a cup of currant jelly. And then it should be served piping hot.

As long as I'm in a culinary mood, I'll give away another of my good recipes because after all, we young bachelors out in the West learned how to cook some specialties of our own. And this tomato omelet never fails to please my guests.

Taking a two and a half pound can of tomatoes—the boon companion of the homesteader—you heat them thoroughly, season with salt, red pepper, butter, and a little sugar. Then you thicken them with enough browned and mashed crackers so that the tomatoes are no longer watery. Next, you take twelve eggs, stir them well, and add them to the boiled tomatoes, stirring the whole business until small bubbles begin to break on top. Pour it onto a hot platter and serve at once to a hungry crowd.

A lot of men I knew and liked out here in Wyoming—Cody and the others—have grown old and died, but the country itself is still young, still beckoning to adventurous men who love its freedom of space and its unlimited resources. In the last three decades cattlemen, ranchers, farmers, hunters, geologists, miners, and oilmen have poured in without causing any congestion in traffic or business—although the oil companies come the closest to taking things over, I suppose.

Today some of the barren flats over which I first rode horseback have become fields of "black gold" sprouting wells and derricks in this profusion, and it's a short enough drive from my front door to my own oil leases. But George Beck and the oil game is another story. . . . Which reminds me, I think I've been talking long enough. I believe I'll get my hat and stick now and go out and look for rocks with some of the young geology students from Princeton who have been hanging around. Remember what I said about prospecting? Once you get the fever, it's a hard thing to shake.

Afterword

Betty Jane Gerber

My brother "Nebe" and I are the grandchildren that George Beck was worried about, but in a strange way, we were the grandchildren most affected by his legacy. We arrived late in his life and were born in Peking, where our father, Nelson T. Johnson, was the first U.S. ambassador to China. My grandfather had sent my mother, Jane Beck, and her brother, George Beck Jr., on an around-the-world trip in 1931. Their second stop was Peking, China. Nelson's family lived next door to Grandfather Beck's sister, Bettie, who was married to General Clay Goodloe (USMC), in the Maryland suburbs of Washington DC. The visit to Peking was extended until within weeks, Nelson and Jane were engaged and then married in October of that year. The round-the-world trip ended on that happy note.

As a family, we visited Cody on two home leaves. The first one occurred in the summer of 1938 through the summer of 1939, when the Japanese occupied Peking. The second leave happened in 1941 when we were on our way to Australia for my father's new posting. These were my only opportunities to personally know my grandfather, George W. T. Beck. I'm afraid it must have been a bit of a shock for him to discover that my brother and I only spoke Chinese and were under the constant care of two Chinese amahs, who seemed determined not to let us fall down. However, the mischievous and humorous twinkle in his eyes and the bear hugs appealed to us immediately. He would take us for daily drives without our minders, and we discovered that the pillows in the backseat were stuffed with gingersnaps (not part of our approved diet). Years later, we learned that he had courted his beloved wife of forty-six years, Daisy May, with a barrel of gingersnaps stashed in his buggy. He was courting us also. We understood the language of gingersnaps. He won our hearts too. During the 1941 stay, Grandfather would take us for a swim at DeMaris Springs before breakfast. Our skin pink and tingling from the bubbles in the water, we would return for a breakfast of eggs, ham, and flapjacks. He felt the waters of the spring were a great palliative and kept a jug of the blue water that smelled like sulfur in the refrigerator on the back porch.

The house where the Beck family lived in Cody, Wyoming, was at 1020 Rumsey Avenue. It was arguably the most historic house in Cody as it had evolved from one of the first edifices in the new town. It was built of large sandstone blocks from the quarry that is now under Beck Lake. The very large living room had a big fireplace, multiple bookshelves, a long table, sofas, and chairs, some of which were Molesworth furniture that was a gift from some of the Cody businesses. There was a player piano with about fifty rolls, which played everything from popular songs to the classics. On social occasions the furniture would be pushed back, and dances were held there. A large mirror with a gilt frame bought by his parents in Paris hung near the dining room. On the shelves were Indian artifacts and other treasured items such as the white ivory or horn statehood gavel with a silver plaque engraved with "G. T. B.-1890" upon it. A picture done by his friend, Frederic Remington, was on the mantel. The wedding portraits of his parents, James Burnie Beck and Jane Augusta Washington Thornton, hung near the mirror.

The dining room and kitchen were the original house. It had a large table that could seat ten to twelve people and was the scene of numerous social gatherings—as was the whole house. Over the table hung a Tiffany-style lamp shade that covered the light. Western pictures were hung on the walls. On the stair landing going upstairs was a full suit of Samurai armor, which his sister Bettie and her husband General Goodloe bought on a trip to Japan. Upstairs were numerous bedrooms and a bathroom with a claw-footed bathtub. A long sleeping porch stretched the length of the house.

On the side yard was a lawn tennis court and beyond was an apple orchard and barn. At the back door of the original part of the house was a large planting of mint, necessary for a Kentucky gentleman to make mint juleps. He was, after all, a Southern gentleman, born and bred with all the attributes that suggests—honorable, honest, generous, dignified, sociable with a respectful regard for the ladies.

George Washington Thornton Beck, a member of the Society of Cincinnati, had a quiet pride in his ancestry and gave each of his children family names. My mother, who was one of the first children born in Cody, was named Jane Augusta Washington Thornton Beck. When she was a small child, she would be given a buffalo nickel if she could say her full name. On the obverse side of that nickel was the face of *Ta Ka Nichi Opi,* Chief Iron Tail, who was often a guest at the family dinner table. While my grandfather imbued each child with this same quiet pride and a reverence for history, he also admonished them "not to live off their relatives, but live up to them." My mother became the family genealogist and developed a love of Scotland. To my aunt Betty, he imparted a knowledge of geology and Indian lore. These two ladies became my mentors.

My grandmother, Daisy May Sorrenson, who brought the saying "ten thousand Swedes were chased through the weeds by one sick Norwegian" into the family lexicon, was an active participant in what resembled "the ladies of the club" in the book of the same name.[1] These were the ladies in a pioneering society who brought education, culture, and a refined sense of propriety to rough circumstances. Daisy and ladies such as "Aunty" Simpson (grandmother of Peter and Alan Simpson, whom you will remember from the foreword to this book), "Mater" Peake (married to Colonel Peake who published the Cody Enterprise), Dr. Frances Lane, and others banded together for strength to raise money for schools, the Cody library, Chautauquas, historical organizations, and churches. Daisy played the piano at home and the organ in church. My grandfather, however, was the winner of $550 in a famous poker game with Buffalo Bill and others and donated it to build the first church in Cody. It is still called "The Poker Church."

George Beck inherited George Washington's "western lands" on the Kanawha River, which are described in an excellent article in *National Geographic* magazine, July 1987, titled "The Potowmack Canal, Waterway that Led to the

Constitution."² The sale of these "western lands" helped finance the founding of Beckton and Cody, Wyoming. Along with the western lands, he inherited George Washington's seal. On the president's birthday, he would take the seal into the schools and make imprints for the children to take home. For years, adults in Cody would show me the imprints they had saved from childhood. "The ladies of the club" would sell imprints at Chautauquas to raise money. That seal is still in my possession, and I consider it a talisman in the quest I began in 1945.

When my family came home that year, it was to Washington DC, where my father oversaw the occupation of Japan after World War II as the secretary-general of the Far Eastern Commission. I now spoke English with an Australian accent, and I knew almost nothing about my country. My grandfather had passed away two years before, but now his life and legacy were at the inspirational core of my search for an American identity and took on a particular aura of importance—my tutors, after all, had learned at his knee. My father's sister, who taught history at the National Cathedral School for Girls, added to this endeavor.

Over the years I was a volunteer docent at the Smithsonian Institution in the halls of Gems & Minerals, Paleontology, and American Indians. I also served on the Council of the American Association of Museums. It was, however, in 1987 when Chief Justice Warren Burger asked my husband, George, and me to help in the bicentennial of the Constitution, that the impact of my grandfather's legacy became fully evident in my destiny.

Some years earlier, we had been shocked to learn that the Beck house in Cody had been destroyed. Preservation of history became a driving force in our efforts. We bought a derelict building in Georgetown whose last name had been "Desperados Discotheque." It actually was a Category 1 National Historic Landmark building where George Washington had met with the landowners to acquire the property to create the constitutionally mandated new federal city, the future nation's capital, Washington DC. We restored it to its former entity, the Forrest-Marbury House.

There were a number of bicentennials that would flow from the Constitution: the presidency, the White House, the U.S. Capitol, and the nation's capital. We created three nonprofits and took leadership positions in each celebration. Senator Patrick Moynihan sponsored the legislation that created the Nation's Capital Bicentennial Commission, of which I was president. George Beck's experience inspired me. He was on the founding board of what is now the Buffalo Bill Center of the West. We proposed a visitor's center for the Washington Monument with an information-technology component called the National Heritage Trail and Travel Center that would serve as a gateway to the nation. September 11, 2001, changed the timing for this, but it is evolving with the new technologies. I testified before Congress for the creation of two new historic trails: the Washington-Rochambeau Revolutionary Route and the Star-Spangled Banner Trail (War of 1812). Other museums still under development are at Langston Golf Course and a proposed Maritime Center. Our heritage trails became First Lady Hillary Clinton's Millennial Trails. We sponsored a musical history of the Shaw neighborhood called "Where Eagles Fly."

George Beck gathered prominent people to plan for

the town of Cody and build the Cody Canal. We sponsored the planning forum called "Historic Georgetown: The Nation's Heritage, The 'Community's Future.'" The Becks sponsored Chautauquas as did other prominent families such as the Simpsons. We, in partnership with the Center of the Book at the Library of Congress and the Smithsonian Institution, sponsored an exhibit of the Chautauqua Book Club Banners with a proposed Book Fair on the Mall the following year. First Lady Laura Bush chose the book fair as her special project, and it is still going strong.

George Beck planted an elm tree on George Washington's bicentennial birthday. We planted newly disease-resistant American chestnut trees in Constitutional Gardens on the Mall. George Beck loved birds, and Beck Lake provided a resting place on the international flyway. We lobbied for the establishment of a park near Mt. Vernon to protect nesting eagles from the land being developed. George Beck surveyed and laid out the town of Cody and the life-supporting irrigation ditch, the Cody Canal. We partnered with the American Association of Land Surveyors, the National Oceanic and Atmospheric Administration (NOAA), and the National Geodetic Survey to identify, mark, and preserve all forty of the Nation's Capital Boundary Stones—our first national monuments.

My grandfather took an interest in helping one of his children's friends, a young woman artist, Olive Fell, get established. In 1980 I was on the founding board of the National Museum of Women in the Arts. We developed walking tours of three historic districts to spread the economic development of tourism in the nation's capital's ten-miles square. We used the concept of an eco-friendly museum that we started in Georgetown, with more than three hundred volunteers doing the historical survey.

In his lifetime, George Beck had started and helped start a number of endeavors, such as bringing electric lights and power to Buffalo and Cody, oil development in the Oregon Basin, promoting mining interests, building and running the first flour mill in Wyoming, raising polo ponies, and overseeing the Cody Canal irrigation project that opened up 28,000 acres to farming. He was a visionary who brought his vision to reality. He also developed the Eastern Gateway to Yellowstone National Park and was a patriot who read the Declaration of Independence every Fourth of July at a Cody town meeting. I am writing this as we are traveling back to Washington DC, after a visit to Cody. We are on U.S. Route 40 in Maryland—The Old National Road. George Washington and his men had cut this road on their way to Fort Duquesne at the start of the French and Indian War. This was the beginning of a struggle for a wilderness empire, and the vision of a country stretching to the western ocean fueled the energy of this endeavor. At its core were the Beckoning frontiers.

1. Photo of a portrait of George Beck's mother, Jane Augusta
Washington Thornton Beck, at the time of her wedding
to James Burnie Beck, 1848.

2. George Beck's father, James Burnie Beck, ca. 1870.

3. George Beck and fellow engineering students at Rensselaer Polytechnic Institute with surveying equipment, ca. 1875.

4. George Beck's house at Beckton, Wyoming, ca. 1885.

5. George Beck with his hunting dogs, ca. 1883.

6. George Beck, ca. 1886. He used this photo later when
he ran for governor of Wyoming in 1891.

7. Cody Canal Headgate located on the South Fork of the Stinking Water River (later renamed Shoshone River), roughly fifteen miles southwest of Cody, 1894.

8. The Shoshone Land and Irrigation Company office on Sheridan Avenue, Cody, 1896.

9. Daisy Sorrenson and George Beck wedding portraits.
They were married in Red Lodge, Montana, in 1897.

10. (*opposite top*) This is the Beck's original
stone house on Rumsey Avenue. *Left to
right*: Grandma Hurd, Jane, and Daisy
holding Betty. Cody, Wyoming, ca. 1900.

11. (*opposite bottom*) George Beck standing
next to his electric light plant, 1905.

12. (*above*) George Beck and William F.
"Buffalo Bill" Cody relaxing at Camp
Foley while on a hunting trip in the hills
near Cody's TE Ranch, 1907.

13. *Left to right:* Jane, Betty, and George "Tee" Beck,
Daisy and George's children, 1910.

14. Daisy Beck with daughters Jane (*left*) and Betty (*right*), 1910.

15. George Beck inspecting an oil well near Cody, Wyoming, ca. 1911.

16. The Beck home on Rumsey Avenue in Cody shortly after the
additions were completed, ca. 1912. Their home became
the social center of the town.

17. George Beck with his daughter Betty Joslin's
children, Betty and Beck, ca. 1940.

18. Oliver H. Wallop, Earl of Portsmouth, and George Beck at
an old-timers' meeting near Sheridan, Wyoming, 1938.

19. George Beck with his daughter Jane Johnson's children, Betty Jane and Nelson, 1938.

20. George Beck, ca. 1940.

21. Cody artist and Beck family friend Olive Fell's
sketch of George Beck, ca. 1935.

APPENDIX 1

Select Letters from William F. "Buffalo Bill" Cody to
George Beck regarding the Cody Canal Project

*The following selection of letters from Buffalo Bill to George
Beck reflect the tension between the two men during the construction of the Cody Canal in northwest Wyoming. Interpreting this correspondence is somewhat challenging due to the
nature of the business partnership and friendship between
Beck and Buffalo Bill. Are some lines in the correspondence
intended to chide Beck for inaction? Or is Buffalo Bill teas-
ing his partner? Events detailed in Beck's memoir reflect the
ambiguities of their relationship, and in an age before emo-
jis, it is difficult to glean Buffalo Bill's feelings towards Beck,
as evident in the following letters.*

*These documents, and many more, are available in digital for-
mat through The Papers of William F. "Buffalo Bill" Cody at
the Buffalo Bill Center of the West, Cody, Wyoming, and can
be viewed at www.CodyArchive.org. The originals are held by
the American Heritage Center at the University of Wyoming in
Laramie, Wyoming. The scanning, transcription, encoding,
and digital display of these letters was supported in part by a
grant from the Wyoming Cultural Trust Fund, a program of
the Department of State Parks and Cultural Resources. Cody's
spelling and punctuation appear as in the original documents.*

Dear George

Your letter gave me great pleasure. And it seemed to
lift a weight off me. That climate out there must be
very productive in regard to liars if I am to beleive one
sentence in your letter or else you have quite a number
of enemies. For I have heard that you were trying to
burry me out of sight and ten thousand other things
from people you little suspect. And coming so seemingly
straight from so many person—and knowing I did not
deserve it I was commenceing to lay pipe to right my
self and fight back for its not my nature to lay down and
quit when I am not in the wrong. No one will apologize
quicker then I will when I am wrong

    I openly confess that I have been dissatisfied with
things you have not done. I have not been dissatisfied
with but one thing you have done. I did not approove
of engageing the Young Lady.[2] Not but that she is a
Lady in every sense of the word. But it was no place for
a Lady. The talk it would create in that wild country
might ruin the Ladys good name. When we get an office
and a proper place for a Lady to work in and for her to
stay Then I would be perfectly willing to give women
the office work to do. But running up and down a ditch
with Hobos makeing all sorts of remarks it was no place
for a woman. And should it ever be my good fortune
to meet the Lady I will tell her so—that it was for her

good I objected George. Its my opinion you could have saved the co a good many dollars if you had been more careful in regard to detail. The Books were not kept as they should have been Everything was run to loose. When a load of goods arrived for us they were not properly checked or looked after. And the way they were disposed of either for our selves sold for cash or credit it was done too carelessly The work of mooveing dirt or stone. I dont think our foremen worked to advantage for instance the two miles that the Graders have been at a whas been to long. George I dont blame you for you have done every thing concientiously But its not your forte You cant look over your work and see and close up leaks you are not careful enough to detail. You start it going and think its being done when its not. probably I am to particular but I cant help it. I want Everything to Moove And every man and horse and tools in their place not left scattered around. And if the men under you know that you know whats going on your self And that they will get rounded it they dont attend to things you would soon see things mooveing differently. And if you would only let them see that you was on to your job You bet your men would soon change for the better. George this is only my opinion given with the best of friendship and I dont want you to take it only as its ment.

George I understand some of those Germans brought out are broke already.[3] I wish you would have a talk with them and find out just how they are situated and if Nagle is treating them squarely. You might say its none of our business But I say it is.[4] I wish you would find out by diging with a spade if you have no well auger by sending three men over on Sage creek I feel sure water can be found let these men dig for water.[5] I think Nagles next colony should be located there. I beleive water can be got withing sixty feet at Irma if some one would tell them to dig.[6] A man must think what can be done for the Advantage of the enterprize & try it where it costs so little. I told Salsbury of this but I fear he has forgotten it.[7]

Foote about the 12th if you can land him he will give you a check for $2000 Stokes owes $1.000 I havent heard a word from any one about how things are or what is to be done or about how much we will have to have this pay day.[8] only that a Doctor wrote me from Red Lodge—& Yegen says we owe him a $1.000 which was news to me.[9] You did not mention it in Chicago. I wish you would try to think up all who we owe. And when these bills come due I am personaly responsable for Omaha people.[10] Graders &c

I am sure if you would give the business thought and action you would be able to keep the credit of our co better. We none of us are to blame if you dont let us know what you do. its your carelessness thats giving our co such a bad name you dont mean to do it but its been your way of doing business all your life. And I should think you had seen the folly of it. Is Alger & Mead there. I havent heard a word from any one.

I hope to God Salsbury wont catch the disease of carelesness & neglect that is so prevelant in that country

Yours—

Col

Lynn. Mass

June-8th 98

My Dear Beck

Bleistein sent $1000 to Alger to day—Says Gerrans will send in few days—Now I will have to hustle Ive $2000 for Hearsts Estate—As Jones wired Flume around up for red bluff would furnish water enough and as he was waiting at Red Lodge. I wired him to close down with work on Dam—I hope and trust we can now get bills all payed. And get rid of the heavy expense out there

I do wish you would let me know how things stand it would take you but a few minutes to do so—

I wish to God I had never seen the Basin—

Yours truly

Cody

Do you know how much cash was paid me for land this spring & who it was paid to? Do you & Alger have a settlement so as to know how things stand?

Apr. 3 [189]6

My Dear George

I recd a letter from Alger this morn. and Answered it.
also wrote You to Marquette. See my letter to Alger of
this date and give me answer to it. George I cannot for
the life of me see where all the money is going to for the
results gained. Our own forces are surely being work to
no advantage. like Burke was working his gang last fall
one plow with six mules and two men standing idle eight
hours out of the ten—but with that I cant see where the
money is going.[11] No wonder Rumsey wanted to shut
down. I am glad my letter about Stokes came in good
time.[12] You see its well to keep one posted punctually.
wish you would learn a lesson from it. Say old Fellow.
if you have come to Sheridan dont for goodness sake
let Rumsey have to wait a week for you to play billiards
before attending to business it will disgust him and this is
a serious time.

I must have a statement of what has been done and
where the money has gone. You did not take time to tell
me in your letter what was being done to the ditch. its
strange you have not mooved from Marquette yet. If the
force had been half managed you would have been away
from those gin Mills long ago—

Yours—
Cody

My Dear B[e]ck

As the time grows near for My going to the Basin—I feel
like letting you know that I hope we may meet as friends.
I admit that at times I have felt hurt at the annoyances of
our troubles there. But I know that you have had a hard
time to do with nothing As our stock holders have fallen
down entirely. And you and I have had to stand the brunt.
And I expect we will still have to do it. As Bleistein writes
me that the Buffalo parties wish to sell out I am perfectly
willing that they should. I donot know how you have fixed
it with the saw mill men and Darrah.[13] And would like to
know if I could before I come out.

    I will be at North Platte

Your truly
W. F. Cody

P.S.

I hope we can have a nice time this winter if we dont
make a cent—we generaly have a good time when we
get together—lets go up South fork to its head & have
a hunt—General Miles will be out with me if he can get
away—

Bill

Speech by George Beck at the Laying of the
Cornerstone for a New City Hall, Cody, Wyoming

*The speech below, part of the George T. Beck Collection at the
University of Wyoming's American Heritage Center, was typed
on notecards.[1] Angle brackets surround Beck's handwritten
corrections and annotations.*

Remarks on Laying of Corner-Stone of New City Hall, Cody, Wyoming—December 6, 1938

Mr. Mayor, City Council, Citizens of Cody and members
of the Masonic Lodge.

You have requested me to make some remarks on the
laying of this corner-stone in the building of your new
City Hall.

Should I look back 45 years I would see a barren expanse
of prarie [*sic*], with little grass, some sage-brush and no
trees,—on a bench high above the river—and four miles
from the mountains. We me, on this preliminary view,
I brought a party of 17. Ten to survey and seven to look
and play.

At the head of my work party I had Elwood Mead as
transit man—later distinguished as an irrigation engineer
and head of the Reclamation Department of our Govern-

ment. As guests, I had Horton Boal, Hinckle Smith, John Palpuck, George and Andrew Stockwell and two others.

Horton Boal was Colonel Cody's son-in-law. He told Col. Cody what he had seen and what I had done by way of preliminary survey. When we went back to Sheridan that fall, the Colonel got so interested that he came to me and asked to be let in. After thinking it over two days, I said "Alright, I will make you President of the company as you are the best advertised man in the world." I made H. C. Alger treasurer and I was Secretary and Manager and built the canal. The other members of our company were—Bronson Rumsey, George Bleistein, H. M. Gerrans and Nate Salsbury.

I camped on the river, near Thompsons <now under the lake>, west of Cedar Mountain and from the low divide south of that mountain ran a line to the South Fork where the headgate is located, then from that divide ran lines eastward on both sides of the main river till we had 400,000 acres within our survey.

As the ditch progressed and we got down opposite our town, where I had located my commissary and the Cody Hotel, I stuck a pole in the center of what is now Sheridan Avenue and 13th St. (where your Xmas tree now stands). Having checked the instruments on the North Star and drawn a map for the town, <all streets 100 ft. wide> I took C. E. Hayden off the ditch work to help me lay it out. I set up the transit where the pole was and I got Hayden to go eastward with the rod. He got so far away that he could not hear me. I laid the map on the ground put a rock on it and started after him. He turned to meet me, we started toward the instrument when a whirlwind came along, picked up our map and took it heavenward. Up and up it went, out of sight, so we conclude that is was recorded in Abraham[']s bosom. We had to make another map— which was recorded in Lander.

The stone Pioneer Building now stands where the commissary building stood, which was the first building in town and is now sometimes called the Green Front. The Cody Hotel was the second building and was not moved. The north half of the block was my horse corral and is the place where you are standing now.

Before the ditch had left the Irma Flat, Mr. William Paxton of Omaha (Paxton and Galleger) an old friend of mine came to see me. I met him at Red Lodge and drove him in my buck-board to our camp. As we came up on this bench from Sage Creek and nearly here, he said "My God, George, What are you going to do with land like this?" I replied, "We are going to make better farms, with more certain crops than you have in Nebraska, and more prosperous and contended [*sic*] people. Then we will build a town. Maybe not as large as Omaha, but MUCH better known for its size."

George W. T. Beck

APPENDIX 3

Summary of a Talk Delivered by Thornton "Tee" Beck about the Beck Family

The following summary was created by an unknown notetaker.
Thornton Beck's talk was delivered on January 29, 1968, most
likely to the Park County Historical Society. The original doc-
ument is also housed in the George T. Beck Collection at the
University of Wyoming's American Heritage Center.[1]

Thornton Beck was born in Cody in 1908, the son of George
T. and Daisy Sorrenson Beck. He had two sisters already,
Betty, born at Red Lodge in 1898, and Jane, born in Cody
in 1900. Mrs. Beck had been orphaned and came from
the east to live with a married sister in Red Lodge. Soon
after she arrived in the west, they moved to the little community of Marquette at the convergence of the North and
South forks of the Stinking Water River. Here she taught
school and later, in 1896, met George Beck who was surveying for a canal to water the new townsite that he and
his friends were laying out on the bench above the river
down below the big canyon. For many years Mrs. Beck
not only kept house but worked as secretary/clerk in the
Cody Canal offices and later, in 1905 when Beck started
the Shoshone Electric Light Company, as his helper in
that endeavor. This Light company served the [town] for
some thirty years, and then, at the instigation of the Rec-

lamation Bureau, Mr. Beck relinquished his first water right on the Shoshone River to them in exchange for a reduced rate for electricity supplied by the big dam [the Shoshone Dam, renamed the Buffalo Bill Dam in 1946].

Mr. Beck reminisced about early day happenings. His father had often told him the story of his being Post Master of the little town/flour mill he started near Sheridan, called Beckton. One day when the Post Office inspector called to see the facilities, he found that Beck had stamps laying out in plain sight on a table and he asked about them. Beck answered that he left them there for the people to use, if they had the money, they left it, if not, the[y] paid him later. The inspector was incensed with this breach of rules and told Beck he couldn't do this, that if he insisted on flouting rules the Post Office would be discontinued. That ended Mr. Beck's Post Master Career.

While George was still at Beckton, he had somewhere [*sic*] of a hundred dogs that he kept for hunting, greyhounds and mixed breeds. He had one man who did nothing but cook up a cornmeal/meat mush for these dogs and see to their care. Among his acquaintances at that place, was an old K[e]ntuckian and George liked to visit the old gentleman. On one of the visits, while they were sitting on the porch of his tiny cabin, several men rode up and were invited in for a meal. After eating, and since darkness had fallen, they decided to spend the night. Beck was also spending the night and as he started to get out his bedroll, he was ordered to put it in a corner. Now Beck was not used to being ordered around and was all set to argue with the man when he caught the Old Man's signal and he took his bedroll to the corner for the night. When they awoke in the morning, the men were gone. The Old Man had informed George that their visitors had been the James boys, and that it was the custom of one of them to always sleep with his feet against the door, his gun in his hand, and that is why he had wanted Beck to go to a corner to sleep.

Many years later, when T. was in Belgium during the Second World War, he was in charge of some thirteen "city boy" soldiers and they had to seek shelter at a farm. The farmer told them they could use a [small] hay filled shack in back, and they bedded down. T. who was new to these men, took the position near the door, placed his feet on it, drew his [L]uger and waited the night. This, he reports, got him in good with his command; it was a lesson he had remembered from his father's story.

When George Beck and Mr. Hayden were laying out the town, they had a plat drawn and put it down on the ground, weighted with a rock. While they paced out and drove stakes at the various intersections, a particularly strong dust devil wind pushed the rock off the plat, and carried it ever upward in a spiral of air. George always said that the plat of Cody was first registered with St. Peter.

While the town was new, Beck lived at the company hotel, the Cody Hotel. He was a messy housekeeper to say the least, and when Oliver Wallop, the Englishman visited town, rooms were at a premium so he bunked in with Beck. He disliked anything disorderly, and he graciously stood the mess of Beck's room for two days and then, while Beck was out one day, he got busy and cleaned it up. When Beck returned he said, "Where *is* everything?" To which Wallop answered, "Now George, I've cleaned this place up, and damn it, see you keep it so!"

Beck and Daisy were married in [1897], just as the new town got started. A German gardner [*sic*] had been imported to do some landscaping, to prove the fertileness of the soil for all prospective home-seekers, and he and his family had a small shack out on the west end of town; the town consisting of mostly tents and a few buildings being constructed at this early date. He tired of the loneliness and moved on and Beck and his bride moved into the primitive accommodations and set up housekeeping They added onto the original one room as the need arose, and finally, in later years when Mrs. Beck was trying to cook in the little lean-to kitchen that was sweltering in the July heat, Dr. Frances Lane, a neighbor and good friend of the family, came over and took an ax and chopped holes in the walls, declaring that George should have fixed it up for health's sake long ago. Then, surveying the damage she had done, she chickened out and took off for home, leaving Daisy to explain what had happened to the "kitchen." Beck took the hint and built a better one. The rock part of the house was built in 1908, just in time for Thornton's arrival.

Once, T. remembered, when Daisy went east, they were left home to cook and care for their father. Beck had a good friend in Chief Iron Tail and he was coming to visit, so the little girls were instructed to get a meal together, all but the meat which George would cook for the old Indian. This the girl's [*sic*] did, but when George arrived home with 24 large chops, they tried to dissuade their father from cooking all of them telling him that he had way too many. However, shooing them into the living room to entertain the old Chief, Beck cooked the meat and when it was done, put it on the table and called everyone to supper. Iron Tail ate nothing but the meat, and kept at it until he had consumed 21 of the chops, the others being taken by the family. The little girls were astounded and when the Chief left demanded to know if this wasn't a breach of Etiquette, but George assured them it was not. It was a compli[m]ent to him that the Chief ate so much.

Albert Felsheim and his father were the stone masons who cut out the sandstone at Beck to build the Beck addition. The story was that Beck had put a twenty dollar gold piece under the fireplace capstone; however, when the old house was raised in the 1960's [*sic*] T. found that it was not a gold peice [*sic*] but a silver dollar.

T. remembered that trotting horses were all the rage until automobiles started showing up. Mrs. Chamberlain and Doc. Lane had Saxons. They were always running their little cars around the dirty streets to the detriment of life and limb and so it was inevitable that some sporting gentleman would think of a race between them. This was held, with T. riding in Doc's car to "balance" it around the corners, and after a race at nose to nose running, Doc pulled out near the finish line to be declared the winner. Other races T. remembers were the ones to the depot whenever a new car showed up in town. This winding road was the local obstacle course to try the mettle of the newcomers. T. learned to drive in Doc's Saxon and the Becks then bought an E. M. F. (Every Mechanical Fault[,] Some said it stood for) from Jakie Schwoob. While driving the EMF one day, T. found a big rock out along Sulphur creek that was shaped like a grinding rock on one side, but had a stick figure on the other. He car[ri]ed it home and George told him he thought it was a burial stone. Dr. McCra[c]ken now has it, and he thinks it is possibly a burial stone of antiquity, some 7–800 years old. It is now at the Museum [Buffalo Bill Center of the West].

One of T.'s pals, Jimmy Kimball, who lived where Margaret and Buster Hamlin do now, was a mechanical genius that T. was always hoping to emulate. He took a piece of wire and hooked it to a nickelodeon in one of the saloons, ran it down the alleys to his house and was able to hear the music when it was playing. T. tried this experiment, but some nice old lady complained about the wire across the street and the sheriff made him tear it down. Later he got even with the sheriff by tossing rotten eggs at him.

To questions from the historical members, T. told about the red brick school house. T. went to school in Texas until the 9th grade at which time he matriculated at the red brick edifice.

George Beck, at the instigation of many towns-people, made a trip to Washington during the Second World War to see about the possibility of converting the Dolomite rock surrounding the town, to magnesium—to be used in airplane manufacturing. But the cost was prohibitive and the project fell by the wayside.

When asked about the wide streets, T. said that his father had often mentioned that they were so made as a fire break and to allow the large freighting teams to turn around.

This concluded T.'s talk, refreshments were served with a general get-together at which time reminiscence[s] were shared.

NOTES

Introduction

1. McLaird, "Ranching in the Big Horns," 157–58. McLaird followed this article with, "Building the Town of Cody." These two articles were based on McLaird's master's thesis, "Western Entrepreneur," submitted to the Department of History and Graduate School at the University of Wyoming.

2. McLaird, "Ranching in the Big Horns," 158.

3. McLaird, "Ranching in the Big Horns," 169.

4. "Good Words for Sheridan," *Sheridan Post*, January 25, 1894, 4. Wyoming Newspapers website, newspapers.wyo.gov.

5. "Local Brevities," *Red Lodge Picket*, January 27, 1894, 3. Chronicling America website, chroniclingamerica.loc.gov.

6. "Local, Personal, and Otherwise," *Sheridan Post*, May 24, 1894, 5; and July 12, 1894, 5. Wyoming Newspapers website.

7. "Local Brevities," *Red Lodge Picket*, September 15, 1894, 3. Chronicling America website.

8. A few histories of Cody, Wyoming, have been published through the years that address the nebulous business and personal relationship between Buffalo Bill and George Beck. See Patrick, *Best Little Town*; Cook, Houze, Edgar, and Fees, *Buffalo Bill's Town*; Houze, *Images of America: Cody*; and Houze, *Cody*. Many Buffalo Bill biographers also addressed Beck and Buffalo Bill's partnership in varying degrees: see Russell, *Lives and Legends*; Snyder Yost, *Buffalo Bill*; Burke, *Buffalo Bill*; Carter, *Buffalo Bill Cody*; and Warren, *Buffalo Bill's America*. For an early history of Cody along with a detailed history of the Buffalo Bill Center of the West (formerly the Buffalo Bill Historical Center), see Bartlett, *From Cody to the World*. For a detailed history of Buffalo Bill and George Beck's efforts that led to the establishment of Cody, Wyoming, see Bonner, *William F. Cody's Wyoming Empire*.

9. Larson, *History of Wyoming*, 305. Larson provides a concise overview of the accomplishments and failures of the Carey Act in Wyoming, see pages 301–6, 348, and 349–53.

10. Larson, *History of Wyoming*, 348.

11. William F. Cody, "The Big Horn Basin," *Big Horn River Pilot*, Thermopolis, Wyoming, October 12, 1898. Wyoming Newspapers website, last accessed October 7, 2018. Buffalo Bill's sister heavily borrowed from this story for her biography of her brother. See Wetmore, *Last of the Great Scouts*.

12. Captain Anson Mills, "Big Horn Expedition August 15 to September 30, 1874" (no publishing information), William Robertson Coe Collection at Yale University, microfilm.

13. Buffalo Bill's Wild West and Congress of Rough Riders of the World (1897), Buffalo Bill Collection MS 6.6.A.1.14, McCracken Research Library, Buffalo Bill Center of the West, Cody, Wyoming.

14. *Rough Rider*, V. 1 # 1 (Buffalo NY: Courier Company, 1899), 12, Buffalo Bill Collection MS 6.3033, McCracken Research Library, Cody, Wyoming. Also available through The Papers of William F. "Buffalo Bill" Cody online archive: http://codyarchive.org/memorabilia/wfc.eph00007.html #bottomBibl. Last accessed October 7, 2018.

15. *Rough Rider*, V. 1 # 1. Many subsequent programs contained various advertisements and articles detailing the progress of the Cody Canal, the town of Cody, Wyoming, and the developing tourist trade to Yellowstone National Park.

16. Buffalo Bill's Wild West, *Historical Sketches and Programme* (1903), 39–41. Wojtowicz collection, McCracken Research Library, Buffalo Bill Center of the West, Cody, Wyoming.

17. "In Windy Wyoming," *Red Lodge Pickett*, March 22, 1901, 7. Chronicling America website.

18. "In Windy Wyoming."

19. "In Windy Wyoming."

20. Rollinson, *Pony Trails in Wyoming*, 292.

21. Towne, "Preacher's Son on the Loose," 44.

22. Rollinson, *Pony Trails in Wyoming*, 292.

23. Hook, "Seven Months in Cody," 5.

24. "Here is something we are printing on the back of envelopes for Cody business men. Don't you want some of them?" *Wyoming Stockgrower and Farmer*, November 10, 1907. Wyoming Newspapers website.

25. Wetmore, *Last of the Great Scouts*, 237.

26. Wetmore, *Last of the Great Scouts*, 237.

27. Lockhart, *Lady Doc.* For biographies of Caroline Lockhart, see Hicks, *Caroline Lockhart*; Furman, *Caroline Lockhart*; Yates, *Western Writers Series: Caroline Lockhart*; and Clayton, *The Cowboy Girl.* For a more in-depth study of Lockhart's connections to Cody, Wyoming, see Fees, "Lockhart, Boomtown, and the Lady Doc," introduction to the reprint of *Lady Doc by Caroline Lockhart.*

28. The biographies on Caroline Lockhart listed above discuss her feud and attacks on Dr. Frances Lane, as well as Lane's purported bisexuality.

29. Lockhart, *Lady Doc*, 47.

30. Lockhart, *Lady Doc*, 45.

31. Lockhart, *Lady Doc*, 47.

32. Andren, *Life Among the Ladies*, 151.

33. The *Wyoming Stockgrower and Farmer* reprinted an article from the *Deadwood Pioneer Times*, dated November 10, on the front page of the November issue of the newspaper under the headline "Buffalo Bill After Indians." The article noted, "Indirectly, he [Buffalo Bill] had some of his friends in various parts of Wyoming give exciting tips to the newspaper correspondents who were eagerly looking for Indian scares." Wyoming Newspapers website.

34. Anderson, *Experiences and Impressions*, 117.

35. McLaird, "Building the Town of Cody," 91.

36. Bonner, *William F. Cody's Wyoming Empire*, 10.

37. Dorothy Johnson, "The Man Who Shot Liberty Valance," *Indian Country* (Boston: Gregg Press, 1979), 89–107; *The Man Who Shot Liberty Valance*, directed by John Ford, Paramount, 1962.

1. Family and Boyhood

1. This refers to Beck's grandson Nelson Beck "Nebe" Johnson (1933–2017). Nebe and his sister Betty Jane Johnson were the children of Nelson Trusler Johnson (ambassador to China from 1935 to 1941 and to Australia from 1941 to 1945) and George Beck's second daughter Jane. Jane and her two children left China for Cody, Wyoming, shortly before the Japanese invasion of Nanking. It was during this trip that Betty Jane and Nelson first met their Beck grandparents.

2. One of the previous editors—possibly George Beck's wife, Daisy, based on the handwriting—noted that James remained with his maternal uncles in Scotland.

3. There seems to be a time discrepancy as to just how long James Beck was with the Chippewa. A previous editor questioned this amount of time, indicating in the margins of the original manuscript that he was with the Chippewa for only a few months.

4. John C. Breckinridge (1821–75) was James Beck's law partner in Lexington, Kentucky. He became a U.S. Congressman in 1851 and subsequently became the youngest vice president up to this time, serving under President James Buchanan (1857–61). During the Civil War, he was a Confederate general and secretary of war for the Confederacy. Beriah Magoffin (1815–85) was governor of Kentucky from 1859 to 1862. Edmund Rice (1819–89) was a local Minnesota politician who became mayor of St. Paul, from 1881 to1883 and again from 1885 to 1887. He served as a congressman to the U.S. House of Representatives from 1887 to 1889. Superior, Wisconsin, was incorporated in 1854, and Duluth, Minnesota, was incorporated in 1857.

5. Lexington, Kentucky, was founded in 1775, and Transylvania University was established in that city in 1780.

6. This was likely Gavin Drummond Hunt (1794–1889).

7. Francis Key Hunt, Esq. (1817–79) was no relation to G. Drummond Hunt, but he was a cousin of Francis Scott Key, who wrote the lyrics of our national anthem. Hunt graduated from Transylvania Law School and was one of the first lawyers in Kentucky. He inherited a million dollars when his father, John Wesley Hunt, passed away in 1849.

8. Jane Augusta Washington Thornton (1824–87) was the daughter of Margaret Buckner and George Washington Spotswood Thornton, who was a nephew of General Washington. She and James Burnie Beck were married on February 3, 1848. Thornton Hill is located near present-day Sperryville along the Thornton River at the foot of the Blue Ridge Mountains and was founded in 1820.

9. Margaret Buckner (1800–36) was the mother of Jane Washington Thornton, who married James Burnie Beck, and therefore the grandmother of George Washington Thornton Beck. She later married Governor James Clark of Kentucky.

10. In handwritten comments, the editor noted the river might be the Hazel River, but Bull Run Creek is located closer to Thornton Hill, Virginia, in the Blue Ridge Mountains.

11. Governor James Clark (1779–1839). In the original manuscript, Beck referred to Governor Clark as George Rogers Clark "the Governor

of Kentucky and a brother of the illustrious Captain William Clark who had earlier made the Lewis and Clark Expedition. Governor Clark, too, had headed another less spectacular expedition which had cleaned the Indians out of Indiana and Illinois," which was incorrect. The family noted in the margins of the original manuscript that this individual was James Clark, a senator and governor from Kentucky, not the famed George Rogers Clark. James Clark became governor of Kentucky in 1836, the same year that Margaret passed away.

12. One of the original editors noted in the manuscript that Jane's grandparents also managed the plantation.

13. Francis Preston Blair (1791–1876) was born in Abingdon, Virginia, but grew up and was educated in Kentucky, where he graduated from Transylvania University with a law degree in 1811. Although he never practiced law, Blair was part of the antislavery movement and active in the newly created Republican party throughout the Civil War. Elizabeth Blair Lee (1818–1906) later became the wife of Rear Admiral Samuel Phillips Lee.

14. Samuel Phillips Lee (1812–97) held the rank of rear admiral in the U.S. Navy. He was a cousin of General Robert E. Lee but refused to join the Confederacy, indicating a division within the Lee family. His marriage into the Blair family made him well known in Washington society. Their house and his father-in-law's house in Washington DC, eventually were joined together, creating the Blair-Lee house, which is now a guesthouse for visiting dignitaries. Montgomery Blair (1813–83) was the son of Francis Preston Blair, the elder brother of Francis Preston Blair Jr., and brother of Elizabeth Blair Lee. He was a lawyer who began his career in St. Louis, Missouri, before moving to Washington DC. He represented the defendant in the Dred Scott case and served as postmaster general of the United States in the cabinet of President Abraham Lincoln. He was a steadfast supporter of the Union. Caroline Buckner Blair (ca. 1810–44) was the first wife of Montgomery Blair. (See Atkins, *We Grew Up Together.*) They had one daughter, Elizabeth, who was born in 1841. Francis Preston Blair Lee (1857–1944) preferred to be called Blair. He was a good childhood friend. He became a Maryland state senator and then governor of Maryland in the early 1900s.

15. Bettie Buckner Beck (1853–1912) was the younger of George W. T. Beck's two older sisters. She married Green Clay Goodloe, brigadier general, USMC. Beck's oldest sister was Margaret Buckner "Maggie" Beck (1849–71) who married James W. Corcoran.

16. The term "carpet slipper" refers to a house slipper whose upper part is made of carpet material or a similar fabric.

17. The language printed reflects Beck's (and others') own language and the use of racial descriptors of the times. We have retained this wording throughout the work, intact for historical reference.

18. Dr. Levi Herr (1828–93) was a veterinarian whose son Levi P. Herr—known as Tick, apparently—was a few years older than Beck.

19. Original editors noted in the margins that Beck's mother helped at a hospital before they left Kentucky.

20. General John Morgan (1825–64). Although born in Huntsville, Alabama, he adopted his mother's home state of Kentucky, having moved there as a young boy. He enlisted in the 1st Kentucky Cavalry during the Mexican War and founded the Lexington Rifles upon his return to Kentucky. He earned the nicknamed "Thunderbolt of the Confederacy" during the Civil War.

21. This seal was passed down through the Thornton family to Beck. Beck visited Cody schools to present a history of George Washington on Washington's birthday and he would allow the students to seal their own letters with sealing wax and the Washington imprint.

2. Post Civil War

1. Regarding his childhood ramblings, one of the original editors, possibly Beck, made this note: "I learned later that my parents let me use the light buggy for they felt sure this was the best way to keep track of me as the neighbors would see me going by."

2. Hamilton Headley (1826–92) was a Kentucky farmer in 1860 whose property was valued at almost $41,000.

3. We were unable to find any information about John Clark.

4. Mud Lick Springs was a spa and resort area that closed in the early 1900s. Its name was changed to Olympian Springs roughly a hundred years earlier but continued to be known locally as Mud Lick Springs.

5. "Thumps" is caused when the diaphragm of the horse spasms due to dehydration. The condition is often mistaken for hiccups.

6. No information could be found regarding Mr. Grimes.

7. William Boyd Allison (1829–1908) was a Republican senator from Iowa who served in the House for four consecutive terms from 1863 to 1871; Beck thought his name was James. Subsequently he was elected to the Senate in 1873 where he served until his death in 1908 prior to the

start of his seventh consecutive term. James G. Blaine, senator (1876–81) of Maine served in the U.S. House from 1863 to 1876 and was later a candidate for the presidency.

8. The original editors indicated in the margins that James B. Beck spoke against impeachment of President Johnson.

9. Baine Dent (1857–1916) was the son of Ulysses S. Grant's brother-in-law Lewis, the brother of Grant's wife, Julia.

10. Dr. Richard Malcolm Johnston (1822–98) was born in Georgia and was an American educator and author. After the Civil War ended, he founded the Penn Lucy School for Boys near Baltimore.

11. James A. Bayard Jr. (1799–1880) served as a Delaware senator from 1851 to 1864 and again from 1867 to 1869 when he was first appointed to fill the seat vacated upon his successor's death and then was elected to fill the unexpired term. His son, Thomas F. Bayard (1828–98), was elected to his father's Democratic Senate seat in 1869. He served three terms, resigning in March 1885 to serve in President Cleveland's cabinet (1885–89) as secretary of state. He later became ambassador to Great Britain for the years 1893–97.

12. Billy Edwards (1844–1907) was born in Birmingham, England, and died in Brooklyn, New York. He was the lightweight champion of the world from 1868 to 1872. In the original manuscript Beck mistakenly thought he was the middle-weight champion.

13. Chamonix and Mer de Glace are in southeastern France near the border with Switzerland. Mer de Glace is a glacier on the north side of Mont Blanc in the French Alps in the Chamonix Valley.

14. Judah P. Benjamin (1811–84) was attorney general from February 1861 until September 1861. In March 1862 Benjamin became secretary of state for the Confederacy. At the end of the war he escaped to England where he practiced law and visited Paris where his wife and daughters were living.

3. A Student at Rensselaer Polytechnic

1. Albert Covington Fowler (1857–1911) entered Rensselaer Polytechnic Institute (RPI) in 1874. He later studied law at Columbia University in New York City, and became a patent attorney. He and his family resided in St. Louis, Missouri, where his wife Mamie also resided.

2. John Morgan Francis (1823–97) was the founder and editor in chief of the *Troy Daily Times*, which was first published on June 25, 1851. He was appointed as minister to Greece in 1871, followed by Portugal, and ended

his diplomatic career as minister to Austria. We believe this reference to Mr. Warren to be Joseph Mabbett Warren (1813–96), a Democratic representative from Troy, New York, to Congress from 1871 to 1873. He entered RPI in 1827 but graduated from Washington—now Trinity—College in Hartford, Connecticut, in 1834.

3. Albyn Prince Dike (1855–1921), in 1879, began his professional career in Skidmore, Nodaway County, Missouri, working for Missouri River Improvements. He later became a merchant in Omaha, Nebraska.

4. Watervliet Gymnasium was the local gym and was named for the town of the same name, which is directly west of Troy on the Hudson River. The name comes from the Dutch word meaning "flowing water" or "water flows."

5. Robert R. Chadwick (1858–1927) graduated from RPI in 1878 with a degree in chemical engineering. He was an assistant in the Geodesy Department for the following four years. Geodesy is a branch of applied mathematics that deals with the measurement of the shapes and areas of large tracts of land in the country. He later became an architect and worked in Pittsburgh, Pennsylvania, and Buffalo, New York. Unfortunately we were unable to find any information about Chenoworth (spelled Chenniworth by Beck). He is not included in the *The History of Rensselaer Polytechnic Institute 1824–1914* by Palmer C. Ricketts, which has a list of all the graduates during those years. In addition, we were unable to find any information about Willets as he is not listed in the *History of Rensselaer Polytechnic Institute 1824–1914*.

6. Donald McLaren (birth and death dates unknown) also graduated from RPI in 1878 with a degree in chemical engineering.

7. Don Carlos Young (1855–1938) graduated from RPI in 1879 with a degree in chemical engineering. He was the architect for the Church of Jesus Christ of Latter-day Saints (1887–93) and designed the temple in Salt Lake City.

8. John Forbes Beale (1850–1923). We believe that this is the man who was the Becks' landlord. He was a lawyer and is buried in Oak Hill Cemetery, Washington DC.

9. Joseph Maull Carey (1845–1924) was probably best known outside of Wyoming for the Carey Act, also known as the Federal Desert Land Act of 1894, which granted millions of acres of federal lands to the states for irrigation purposes. He was an associate justice of the Supreme Court of Wyoming from 1871 to 1876, mayor of Cheyenne (1881–85), and elected

to Congress as a delegate from Wyoming Territory (1885–90) and then as a senator in 1890 when Wyoming became a state. He also served as governor of Wyoming (1911–15). Louisa David (1856–1934) and Joseph Carey were married in 1877.

10. George Hearst (1820–91) was a wealthy businessman who made his fortune in mining throughout the West, including the Comstock Lode in Nevada and the Homestake Mine in South Dakota. He served in the U.S. Senate from 1887 to 1891. He was the father of William Randolph Hearst, the powerful newspaperman from California.

11. Adolph Sutro (1830–98) was a mining engineer who later became mayor of San Francisco. The Sutro Tunnel was a drainage tunnel connected to the Comstock Lode, beginning at Virginia City, Nevada, and running six miles southeast to Dayton, Nevada, where it emptied. Ferdinand Vandeveer Hayden (1829–87) was a geologist known for his surveys of the Rocky Mountains, particularly the Hayden Geological Survey of 1871 of Yellowstone National Park. He also served as a physician for the Union Army during the Civil War. Samuel Pierpoint Langley (1834–1906) was an astronomer, physicist, and an early pioneer in American aviation credited not only with the invention of the unmanned auto-gyro but also for using steam power to fly heavier aircraft. Langley Field in southern Virginia is named after him, among other aviation-related sites.

12. Samuel J. Tilden (1814–86), a Democrat, was governor of New York from 1875 to 1876 before being nominated to run for the presidency in 1876. While he won the popular vote, he was defeated by the Electoral College system.

13. Green Clay Goodloe (1845–1917), known as Clay, was a graduate of the United States Military Academy at West Point. He fought on the Union side during the Civil War. He rose in the ranks of the Marines until he was made a brigadier general in 1883. He was never a captain but was promoted from first lieutenant to major, to colonel, and then to brigadier general.

14. President James A. Garfield was shot by assassin Charles Guiteau on July 2, 1881, and passed away on September 19, 1881.

4. Prospecting in Colorado

1. Horace Greeley (1811–72) was the founder and editor of the *New York Tribune* and a leader of the antislavery movement. The phrase "Go West, young man" was first used by Indiana newspaperman John Soule in 1851 but was popularized by Greeley in his paper as advice to the unem-

ployed. Beck repeated a common misconception that Horace Greeley originated this saying.

2. General Edward Braddock (1695–1755) was the British commander of the army of the thirteen colonies at the start of the French and Indian War. He was seriously wounded during the Battle of the Wilderness (Battle of Monongahela) that took place ten miles east of Pittsburgh on July 13, and he died shortly afterward of his injuries.

3. Joseph Sire Greene (1856–?) was another graduate of RPI in civil engineering, in the class of 1878. He relocated to Leadville, Colorado, to be a mining engineer, then to Pueblo, Colorado, and later to California. He is in the 1930 Census, but not the 1940. Wallace Greene, Joseph Sire Greene's brother, did not graduate from RPI. No other information could be found.

4. Leadville, Colorado, was founded in 1877 during the Colorado silver boom.

5. Evans, Colorado, was founded in 1867 and is located just south of Greeley and northeast of Denver.

6. Sam Woodruff and his partner Joseph Seminole killed R. B. Hayward, a popular Colorado rancher. The two men, attempting to flee from a failed robbery attempt, convinced the unsuspecting Hayward to give them a ride in his wagon. Riding in the back of the wagon, Woodruff choked Hayward to death. Authorities arrested Seminole at his home on the Pine Ridge Reservation and attempted to escort him to Denver only to have him escape by jumping from the train. Eventually he was recaptured and jailed. Woodruff was captured in Iowa and was incarcerated with Seminole. Eventually the two accused men were transferred to a jail in Golden, Colorado. Late in the evening of December 27, 1879, a lynch mob seized the two accused murderers and hanged them from a bridge. Woodruff requested he be allowed to jump from the bridge to hang himself, as opposed to being lifted from the ground. After reciting his last words, members of the lynch mob pushed him off the bridge. Seminole confessed that he and Woodruff were guilty before he was hanged. Information on Woodruff is found in Jessen, *Colorado Gunsmoke*, and Cook, *Hands-Up!*

7. Colonel John Y. Clopper (1837–1908) served in the 2nd Missouri Cavalry, a Union regiment during the Civil War, also known as Merrill's Horse. He was later promoted to lieutenant colonel. Clopper was found

in the 1880 Federal Census living in Denver, Colorado, and is listed as a "stock raiser."

8. John P. Jones (1829–1912) was a Republican senator for Nevada for thirty years from 1873 to 1903. He made a fortune in silver mining and was a cofounder of Santa Monica, California, where he died in 1912.

9. We could not locate any information on either Bird or Haskell.

10. Tin Cup was a lawless mining camp that saw its first gold placer claim in 1859 but then had to wait twenty years before there was a large strike. It was named for the tin cup in which one miner used to carry his gold dust.

11. Italian Peak, Colorado, is in Gunnison National Forest near Crested Butte. It was named Italian Peak because its colors resemble those of the flag of Italy: red, white, and green.

12. Nathan C. Meeker (1817–79) was a newspaperman who worked for Horace Greeley and was the founder of Greeley, Colorado. He asked for and was appointed the Indian agent at the Southern Ute Reservation but never gained the trust of the Indians. Tension between the two factions led to the Meeker Massacre and the Ute War of 1879.

13. Major Thomas Tipton Thornburgh (1843–79), a graduate of West Point Military Academy, was killed by Utes at the Battle of Milk Creek. Fort Fred Steele (1868–86) is located near present-day Rawlins, Wyoming. It was named for Colonel Frederick Steele (1819–68), hero of the Battle of Vicksburg.

14. Colonel Wesley Merritt (1834–1910) was a graduate of West Point who participated in the Indian Wars before being named the superintendent of West Point in 1882 for five years. Eventually he led the VIII Corps in the Battle of Manila Bay in the Spanish-American War in 1898. He retired from the U.S. Army in 1900.

15. Mosquito Pass lies between Fairplay and Leadville in the Mosquito Range of central Colorado, elevation 13,185 feet.

16. Charpiot's Hotel, "Delmonico of the West," was located at 386 Larimer Street and was managed by Jerome S. Riche. It was in existence from 1860 into the 1880s.

17. Cherry Creek River was named for the chokecherries that line its banks. The first Elephant Corral was built in Denver in 1858, although the area had been used for boarding livestock beginning in the 1840s. The first log structure burned down in 1863, so the building that Beck is talking about is the second building, a two-story warehouse with high walls.

5. Working on the Northern Pacific Railroad

1. General Thomas Rosser (1836–1910) was a Confederate major general who was later a railroad construction engineer. In 1898 he became a brigadier general in the Spanish-American War.

2. We could not find any information on Keith.

3. The camp referenced by Beck was the Badlands Cantonment, established in 1879 by the soldiers commanded by Captain Stephen Baker of Company B of the 6th Infantry Regiment. Later renamed the Little Missouri Station, the post remained active until 1883. The buildings were purchased by Henry Gorringe and a group of investors hoping to transform it into a hunting encampment. Gorringe enticed Theodore Roosevelt to the encampment in the fall of 1883 to hunt buffalo.

4. Marquis de Mores (1858–96). The full name of the Frenchman is Antoine Amédée Marie Vincent Manca de Vallambrosa. He was known by his title, the Marquis de Morès, and played a significant role in the development of the North Dakota badlands in the 1880s. He married Medora von Hoffman (1856–1921), the daughter of wealthy banker Louis von Hoffman and Athenias Grymes. Von Hoffman provided much of the funding to the Marquis that enabled him to develop the town of Medora, along with a failed meat-packing plant, a stagecoach line, and a pottery factory.

5. Beck is possibly referring to General Adna Anderson (1827–89), who assumed the role of chief engineer shortly after Rosser resigned. Anderson is given credit for weighing through several surveys to select the final route of the Northern Pacific Railroad. He committed suicide in his hotel room in Philadelphia. By October 1880, trains arrived at the Little Missouri Station.

6. We were unable to find any Gros Ventre by the name Young Man Afraid of Horses. It is possible Beck confused this person's name with the renowned Oglala warrior who fought in Red Cloud's War.

7. Mandan, North Dakota, was founded in 1879.

8. Rosser Creek, North Dakota, was named in honor of General Thomas Rosser.

9. Albert E. Rice (1845–1921) was a Norwegian by birth; he never held the position of governor of Minnesota. However, he was lieutenant governor of Minnesota from 1887 to 1891. Sedgwick Rice (1860–1925) was the son of Edmund Rice, not Albert Rice. He served as a 2nd lieutenant in E Troop, 7th Cavalry beginning in 1883 and served in the military until he was sixty-four, the mandatory age of retirement. He was at the Battle of Wounded Knee, among others, and finished his career as a colonel.

10. We could locate no additional information on Billy Powell.

11. We were unable to locate additional information on Rudy Heinselman.

12. Nelson Appleton Miles (1839–1925) was a graduate of West Point Military Academy who served in the Civil War. Miles commanded troops in various battles on the northern plains and in the southwest during the Indian Wars and in 1895 was named general-in-chief of the army.

13. Cabin Creek was thus named due to the reported presence of a number of trapper cabins.

14. Miles City, Montana, was founded in 1876 and is named for Captain Nelson A. Miles. It is now the county seat of Custer County.

15. Fort Keogh, Miles City, Montana, was named for Captain Miles W. Keogh (1840–76) who was killed at the Battle of Little Big Horn. It was built in 1876 and was occupied until 1924.

16. Mary Hoyt Sherman (1842–1904) married Nelson A. Miles in 1868 and was also the niece of Lieutenant General William Tecumseh Sherman.

17. Beck mistakenly identified Two Moons as a Lakota. Two Moons was a Northern Cheyenne warrior. Two Moons fought with Miles at the Battle of Wolf Mountain and surrendered in 1877, before Beck and his companions entered the region. Miles appointed Two Moons as "head-chief" of the Northern Cheyenne Reservation. Two Moons later negotiated the surrender of the Little Crow band and other "hostile" bands. Yellowstone Kelly, in his memoirs, noted that during the winter of 1880 bison collected in the Yellowstone River Basin due to extreme cold. This attracted several of Sitting Bull's followers from Canada to the Yellowstone valley, escalating violent encounters with enemy tribes, bison hunters, and the United States Army. Yellowstone Kelly described a violent encounter between scouts and Lakota on Mizpah Creek, the drainage west of Cabin Creek in February 1880. It is possible this is the encounter Beck and his companions heard in the distance and witnessed its aftermath. After Kelly's encounter with the Lakota, Miles ordered troops to follow the "hostiles" under the command of Captain Snyder, who later surrounded an encampment of Lakota. Through the Cheyenne chief White Bull, the village surrendered and were escorted to Fort Keogh. See Kelly, *Yellowstone Kelly*.

18. Goose Creek, a tributary of the Tongue River, runs southwest from Sheridan, Wyoming, to the Big Horn Mountains, passing through what was the hamlet of Beckton, the site of Beck's ranch. The name resulted from the presence of numerous geese in this migratory habitat.

19. Fort Custer was located near present-day Hardin, Montana, established in 1877 to police the region after the Battle of Little Big Horn. It overlooks the confluence of the Big Horn and Little Big Horn Rivers. It was in service until 1898. General John Porter Hatch (1822–1901) was a general in the Union Army during the Civil War and the Indian Wars. Beck is likely referring to Charles Francis Roe who served under General Gibbon's Montana Column and arrived on the Battle of Little Big Horn shortly after the battle. His summary of the Battle of Little Big Horn can be found in *Custer Engages the Hostiles* published by Old Army Press. General Alfred Howe Terry (1827–90) was a Union general who served two terms as military commander of the Dakota Territory: 1866–69 and 1872–86.

20. Lieutenant John Jordan Crittenden III (1854–76) was killed in the Battle of Little Big Horn while on temporary assignment with the 7th Cavalry. He was the son of Union general Thomas Leonidas Crittenden and was a native of Kentucky.

21. Beck referred to the Patrick brothers as the Kilpatrick brothers who ran a freight line from Beatrice, Nebraska, to Newcastle, Wyoming. Matt and Al Patrick were early ranchers in the area and ran the stage line between Rock River, Wyoming, and Custer Station, Montana, located on the Yellowstone River.

22. Beck noted the year was 1879; however, the events he describes places him in the area around 1880. O. P. Hanna claimed to be the first settler in the area in 1879. There are two stories of how Soldier Creek got its name. One is that it was named by scout Frank Grouard for leading twenty-five soldiers along the creek to avoid a skirmish with Indians. The other is that it was named for a comment made by a commanding officer when wagons loaded with supplies tried to cross the creek. The officer is reported to have said, "Never mind the wagons, save the soldier." Big Goose Creek and Big Goose Trail were named by early settlers for the wild geese found on the creek. Its origins are in the Big Horn Mountains west of Sheridan. It flows northeast through a valley where it meets up with the Little Goose Creek in the middle of Sheridan. Wolf Creek is located near Sheridan and comes out of the Big Horn Mountains. It was named for the wolves that used to roam the area.

23. The Forbes family bought the ranch in 1898.

24. Albyn Prince Dike; see chapter 3, note 3.

25. Sheridan, Wyoming, was founded in 1882. Its railroad arrived in 1892, as did the Sheridan Inn, in which William F. Cody invested. George

Mandel (1844–1900) was a trapper who was the postmaster of Mandel, Wyoming. In 1882, after just a year, the name was changed to Sheridan in honor of General Philip H. Sheridan.

26. Phillip Mandel (1834–1917) is reported to be the first settler in Laramie, Wyoming. His brother was George Mandel, the trapper and postmaster.

27. Tony Yeltzer (?–1893) was a blacksmith who owned the cabin near Beckton where the first school in Sheridan was held in 1883–84.

6. Homesteading in Wyoming

1. Fort McKinney was located in northeast Wyoming near the Powder River and originally was named Cantonment Reno due to its proximity to the earlier Fort Reno. It was renamed Fort McKinney in 1877 in memory of Lieutenant John A. McKinney (1846–76), killed in November 1876 in a fight at Red Fork of the Powder River. Subsequently the fort was moved fifty miles north on the Clear Creek at the foot of the Big Horn Mountains, deemed to be a safer location for the troops. At this location the fort was in operation from 1878 to 1894.

2. Rock Creek, Wyoming, was a rail station on the Union Pacific Railroad and the terminus of the stage route from Miles City. This route also served as the main shipping point for livestock and supplies to northern Wyoming. Beck mistakenly referred to this as Rock Springs, Wyoming, located in the western section of Wyoming along the Union Pacific line. When the Union Pacific relocated its track, the station name and community changed its name to Rock River.

3. Morten E. Post was a sheep rancher on Pole Creek near Cheyenne who was a Democrat but never held the position of governor of either the territory or the state of Wyoming. The use of "Governor" must have been a nickname. He was active in local Albany County politics.

4. Powder River is in northeast Wyoming and runs southwest through the present-day counties of Gillette, Johnson, and Natrona. The soil along its banks resembles gunpowder; hence its name.

5. Sir Moreton Frewen (1853–1924) was a British financial writer who married Clarita "Clara" Jerome (1851–1935) in 1881. He settled in the Powder River country and founded the Powder River Cattle Company. Mrs. Frewen was the sister of Jennie Jerome Churchill, wife of Lord Randolph Churchill.

6. Captain Charles M. Rockefeller (1844–99) was an officer in the United States Army who served in the Civil War. He was promoted to first lieutenant on March 11, 1878, and to captain on August 15, 1889. At the outbreak of the Spanish-American War in 1898, he was sent to the Philippines where he disappeared two days after his arrival. It is presumed that he was killed, but his body was never found. There is some question as to his relationship with John D. Rockefeller's family. Beck mistakenly referred to Charles as John in the manuscript.

7. Elisha Terrill (1827–97) served as a member of the 1874 Yellowstone Wagon Road and Prospecting Expedition, which left Bozeman to establish a road to the Yellowstone River Basin and to prospect for gold near the Big Horn Mountains. The group fought with several Lakota and Northern Cheyenne bands as they explored the Yellowstone, Rosebud, Big Horn, and Clark's Fork river valleys. The following year, Terrill and a group of men established a trading post named Fort Pease at the mouth of the Big Horn River. He moved to a ranch north of Banner, Wyoming, in 1879, and eventually became its postmaster.

8. Several past residents near Big Horn, Wyoming, claimed the famed outlaws Jesse Woodson James (1847–82) and brother Alexander Franklin "Frank" (1843–1915) "hid out" in the vicinity.

9. Many of the local settlers referred to the African American cook with the derogatory name "N—— Jim." See Garber, *Big Horn Pioneers*.

10. Frank Grouard (1850–1905) was born in French Polynesia. He managed Cody's horses and may have been manager of Cody's TE Ranch during 1896. Grouard was a scout and interpreter for General Crook during the American Indian War of 1876, participating in the Little Big Horn Campaign, the Battle of the Rosebud, the Battle of Slim Buttes, and the Wounded Knee Massacre. He passed away in St. Louis, Missouri.

11. Lake DeSmet is named after Father John Pierre DeSmet.

12. Buffalo, Wyoming, was founded in 1879 and was named after Buffalo, New York. It is the county seat of Johnson County.

13. Massacre Hill was the site of the 1866 Fetterman Massacre near Fort Phil Kearny.

7. Sheepherding and Crow Indians

1. Fort Totten, North Dakota (1867–90), near the border with British Columbia, Canada, was named for Major General Joseph G. Totten (1788–1864) who was chief of the Army Engineer Corps.

2. Red Wing, a Crow Indian scout, was dubbed "One-Eyed Riley" by soldiers due to the loss of one of his eyes. Despite missing an eye, Red Wing was considered by many to be an excellent shot. See LeForge, *Memoirs of a White Crow Indian*, 307.

3. Pryor Creek and Pryor Mountains were named for Sergeant Pryor of the Corps of Discovery.

4. White Horse George moved into the region with his wife Pretty Beads and his daughter Pretty Shell, according to Garber, *Big Horn Pioneers*, 14. This is likely the Crow family to whom Beck refers in this story.

5. Additional information on John Rummel could not be located.

6. James Leffel (1806–66) of Springfield, Ohio, invented the Leffel turbine waterwheel.

7. Matt H. Murphy was one of the early cattle ranchers in the Powder River area.

8. Samuel Hawes Hardin (1846–1921) came to Wyoming in 1880 and was one of the best-known ranchers in Wyoming, raising Hereford bulls. He served in the Wyoming State Legislature representing Sheridan County for a term, elected in 1902. Hardin, Montana, is named for him.

9. Reinhold W. "Billy" Moline (1837–1915) came to the United States from Sweden in 1850.

10. Ben Schneider worked for Beck and liked to prospect.

11. Bald Mountain is located west of Sheridan in the Big Horn Mountains. Dayton Gulch was named for Joseph Dayton Thorn, a Sheridan banker, who founded the town of Dayton, Wyoming, in 1882.

12. The Crow Census of 1885 notes that Yellow Crane was the head of a family of five members and was forty-two years old. Members of his family included his wife No Name, his sister Looks At The Pipe, his granddaughter Takes The Gun, and his stepdaughter Goes To The House. Thanks to Little Big Horn College for providing the database containing this information: http://lib.lbhc.edu/index.php?q=node/96&year=1885&hh1=226.

13. Lodge Grass Creek runs along the Wyoming–Montana border north of Sheridan. Its proper Crow name is Greasy Creek, but there was a mistranslation to English.

14. The Crow Census of 1885 notes that Dancing Woman was age fifty-one and was the head of a family of six members: his wife Plenty Woman, his son Gets Down, his brother-in-law Balls, his son Don't Fall Down, and his mother Hunts the Otter. Yellow Crane died on October 9, 1892. Courtesy of Little Big Horn College: http://lib.lbhc.edu/index.php?q=node/98&year=1885&id=1915.

15. Devil's Canyon is a branch of Big Horn Canyon in northern Wyoming and southern Montana.

8. Return to the East

1. Oliver Henry Wallop (1861–1943) was the 8th Earl of Portsmouth, a British peer who bought a ranch in the Big Horn, Wyoming, area and became a citizen in 1891. He later renounced his American citizenship in order to be seated in the British Parliament in the House of Lords. He is the grandfather of Senator Malcolm Wallop who served three terms in the U.S. Senate.

2. We could not locate any information on John Chamberlain of Washington DC.

3. Palmer House, Chicago, Illinois, was built by Potter Palmer, a wealthy industrialist, as a wedding present to his bride, Bertha Honore. It opened on September 26, 1871, but burned down just thirteen days later in the Great Chicago Fire. Palmer immediately set to work rebuilding, and with a $1.7 million signature loan constructed one of the fanciest hotels worldwide. Beck would have been talking about the second Palmer House.

4. The Rock Creek station was located on the Rock River in Albany County in southeastern Wyoming and was constructed in 1860 as a stage coach station. The Union Pacific reached there in 1868 and used it until 1900 when they relocated the tracks.

5. No additional information pertaining to Major Thomas of Louisville could be located.

6. Colonel Andrew J. Alexander (1833–87) was in the 2nd cavalry and was commander of Fort Custer in the mid-1880s. He died suddenly while traveling by train to his home in New York State.

7. The battlefield site was named Custer Battlefield National Monument in 1946 and subsequently changed in 1991 to Little Bighorn Battlefield National Monument.

8. Rawlins, Wyoming, is county seat of Carbon County. It was named after Rawlins Spring in 1868, which had been named after General John A. Rawlins. The state penitentiary was located there in 1889.

9. William F. "Bear" Davis (1836–1902) started a ranch on Little Goose Creek in 1879, which he sold to Oliver Wallop.

10. John Coates was an old-timer in the Little Goose Creek area.

11. John Howard Conrad (1855–1928) was a banker at Stockgrowers Bank who owned general stores in Buffalo and Sheridan, Wyoming. He

was the post trader at nearby Fort McKinney in the late 1880s. He married Mabel Barnaby in 1884 in Rhode Island.

12. J. M. Lobban (1852?–1910) managed or ran John H. Conrad's store in Sheridan, Wyoming.

13. John D. Loucks (1845–1927) was a cofounder of Sheridan. Loucks was in a cavalry unit during the Civil War and named the town after General Philip Sheridan. Loucks also founded the first newspaper in Sheridan.

14. Kenard Burkitt (1847–1906), whose wife was Lucy, was born in Missouri. He was a founder of Sheridan and is listed in the 1900 Census as a capitalist. Dudley Thurmond (1833–1910) served for four years in the Civil War from West Virginia beginning as a 2nd lieutenant and ending as a captain. He moved with other Thurmond family members to Wyoming, first to Cheyenne and then in 1882 to what would become Sheridan. The land he purchased became a large part of the town, along with John Loucks's land. Thurmond spent the remainder of his life in Sheridan. George Brundage (1832–1912) was born in Ohio and moved to Wyoming in 1881. He married Mary Hall. He was a founder of Sheridan and has a street named after him. His son Howard moved to Cody when it was just beginning and opened a hardware store on Sheridan Ave.

15. Anne Clymer Brooke (1870–1903) from Birdsborough, Pennsylvania, was the wife of Francis Preston Blair Lee. Beck referred to her as Nancy in the manuscript.

16. Margaret Blaine (1865–1949) was the daughter of Representative James G. Blaine. She was in Blair Lee's wedding and later the wife of well-known conductor Walter Damrosch, not Victor Herbert, as Beck says.

17. Mary Ferguson (1860–1940), known as Mamie, married Beck's classmate Albert Fowler in St. Louis, Missouri.

18. William John Thom (1861–1926) was born in Pennsylvania and died in Chicago, Illinois. He was vice president and manager of a bank in Buffalo.

19. No additional information could be found on Mrs. J. Sire.

20. Brown Palace Hotel, Denver, Colorado, was built in 1882 by Henry C. Brown.

9. Trips to the South and to Cuba

1. Beck's mother passed away in March 1887, the infamous Blizzard of 1886–87 likely prevented him from attending her funeral.

2. Senator Thomas Norwood (1830–1913) was a lawyer who represented his state in both the U.S. House and the U.S. Senate as a Democrat for

several terms, eventually retiring in 1889. The name of his home was Harroch Hall located on the Ogeechee River near Savannah. Beck mistakenly referred to him as George in the manuscript.

3. Colonel Andrew Jackson III (1834–1906) was born at the Hermitage, the son of the adopted son of President Andrew Jackson. He graduated from West Point Academy in 1858 and served as a colonel in the 1st Tennessee Heavy Artillery in the Confederate Army.

4. No additional information pertaining to Bishop Spalding of Chicago, Illinois, could be located.

5. The ss *Olivette* was a commercial passenger ship owned by the Plant system. It made three round-trips per week between the Florida cities of Tampa, Key West, and Miami.

6. General Valeriano Weyler was the general governor of Cuba. Beck, or the transcriptionist, printed his last name as Wilder in the original manuscript.

7. Wilhelm (William) Steinitz (1836–1900) was an Austrian master chess player and the first undisputed world chess champion from 1886 to 1894. He was also a highly influential writer and chess theoretician. Tschigorian was a Russian chess champion.

8. d'Hadrez Chess Club, Havana, Cuba, is the name of the host chess club for the international tournament between the Russian champion Tschigorian and the American champion Steinitz in 1889.

9. Sir Horace Curzon Plunkett (1854–1932) was born in Ireland and was known for being an agricultural reformer. He bought a ranch in the Big Horn Basin in the1880s and also invested in other American companies.

10. Nowood Creek is located in Washakie County. It was named by a cavalry unit that camped on its banks and found no wood for their campfires.

11. George Henry MacKenzie (1837–91), a Scot by birth, was a chess champion born in Aberdeen, who came to the United States in 1863 and fought on the Union side in the Civil War.

10. Wyoming Territorial Legislator

1. No further information pertaining to Andrew and Mrs. Gratz could be located.

2. Southern Hotel in St. Louis was built in 1866 and was the premier luxury hotel at the time. It burned in 1877 but was rebuilt in 1881. It closed in 1912 and was demolished in 1933.

3. Johnson County was established in 1875 with Buffalo as the county seat. Subsequently Sheridan County separated from Johnson County in 1888 with the town of Sheridan as its county seat.

4. Henry Asa Coffeen (1848–1912) was born in Gallipolis, Ohio, lived in both Indiana and Illinois, and moved to Sheridan in 1884. Beck was incorrect about Coffeen's first name in the original manuscript.

5. Francis Emroy Warren (1844–1929) was a Republican politician who served several times as territorial governor of Wyoming before being elected as the new state's first governor in 1890. He resigned after only a few months as he'd been elected one of the state's two senators, and he served from 1890 to 1893 in that position. General John J. "Black Jack" Pershing (1860–1948) graduated from West Point Military Academy in 1886 and was the commander of the Allied Expeditionary Force during World War I.

6. Father Francis J. Nugent (birth and death dates unknown) was the pastor of St. Mary's Catholic Church in Cheyenne from 1884 to 1886 when he was sent to Rawlins, Wyoming.

7. No additional information pertaining to Janie Riggs could be located.

8. Cheyenne Club was a social men's club made up of no more than two hundred members and included many of the largest ranch owners in the state. In fact, it was familiar to every notable figure of Wyoming's '80s and '90s "cattle kings," remittance men, and others associated with the territory's livestock business. The club was used as a central meeting place for sociability and conviviality and was built in 1880 at a cost of approximately $25,000. The club folded after the Johnson County War in 1892, which may or may not have been planned in the club itself.

9. Mortimer Jesurun (1860–1933) was born in the Caribbean Netherlands and later lived in Douglas, Converse County. He was an MD who became a trustee of the University of Wyoming in 1907 and was also an ornithologist. In the Civil War, his rank was major, and he served as a surgeon in the 2nd U.S. Cavalry.

10. Charles A. Campbell (?–1896?), Laramie County, served in the Senate from January 15 to March 14, 1890.

11. Clarence Don Clark (1851–1930) was born in New York State and became a teacher and a lawyer, and was a Republican. Clark rose to power in the 1880s in Evanston, Wyoming, and became the new state's first congressman in 1890.

11. Another Trip Back East and to California

1. Joseph Leiter (1858–1932), son of Levi Z. Leiter (1834–1904), was a very wealthy Chicago businessman who invested in real estate. He was one of the founding partners of Marshall Field & Co., an upscale department store. Joseph's daughters were Mary Victoria (1870–1906), Nancy (1872–1930), and his youngest daughter, Margaret Hyde Leiter (1879–1968).

2. James "Gentleman Jim" Corbett (1866–1933), an American heavyweight boxer, was best known for defeating the great John L. Sullivan in twenty-one rounds in a fight held in New Orleans in 1892.

3. Horton Sinclair Boal (1865–1902) was born in Chicago, and in 1888 he moved to North Platte, Nebraska, to open a real estate, loan, and insurance agency. There he met and married Arta Cody, daughter of William F. "Buffalo Bill" Cody, in 1889. They moved to Sheridan, Wyoming, where Boal managed a ranch for Cody. A few years later, he introduced Cody to several future directors of the Shoshone Land and Irrigation Company.

4. Likely Robert "Bob" Fitzsimmons (1863–1917) who defeated Corbett in Reno, Nevada, in 1897 to become the new heavyweight champion of the world.

5. No information could be found regarding Reardon.

6. Chicago Athletic Club opened in 1893 just in time for the World's Exposition held in that city. Its full name was the Chicago Athletic Association. It was a men's-only club until 1972, and while it is still in existence today, the original building will probably be turned into a luxury hotel.

7. Cliff House was a very well-known hotel and restaurant south of San Francisco. The first building, built in 1863, was destroyed by fire in 1894. Rebuilt in 1896, the second building also burned down in 1907. The third version opened in 1909 and still stands today.

8. "Phoebe" Hearst (1842–1919) married George Hearst in 1862. She was the mother of William Randolph Hearst.

9. Frank Locan (1828–1910) was born in Germany and came to the United States in 1848. He eventually settled east of Fresno, California, where he was a large landowner and raised raisin grapes. He and his stepson Charles Bonner formed the Locan Vineyard Company.

10. No further information about Bert Thornton, son of Judge Thornton, could be located.

12. Beckton, Wyoming

1. Frank M. Canton (1849–1927) was elected sheriff of Johnson County, Wyoming, in 1882 and again in 1884. His real name was Josiah—or Joe-Horner. He was a bank robber and killed a Texas Ranger. He officially changed his name to Frank Canton while living in Nebraska and pledged to give up his outlaw ways. He was born near Richmond, Virginia, and lived in Oklahoma, Texas, and Nebraska before moving to Wyoming. Subsequently he moved to Oklahoma, then Alaska, and died upon his return to Oklahoma.

2. Beckton Post Office was established as Milltown Post Office on June 6, 1883, in Johnson County prior to the formation of Sheridan County, and Beck served as postmaster. On June 2, 1884, the name was changed to Beckton with Beck continuing as postmaster. On November 13, 1900, it was discontinued and its mail then handled by the Sheridan Post Office.

3. This is likely Alfred Lambrigger, who settled on Jackson Creek with his three brothers (Gabriel, Alphonso, and Leo) and their families. Garber in *Big Horn Pioneers* notes Alfred's wheat won first place at the Columbian Exposition in Chicago, which fits into Beck's narrative. Beck misspelled Lambrigger's name as Lombrigger and may have confused Alphonso with Alfred.

4. Simon Kearn (1835–?) was a German, not an Austrian, as Beck says.

5. Billings, Montana, was founded in March 1882 and named for Northern Pacific Railway president Frederick Billings.

6. Horace Chapin Alger (1857–1906) was born in Lowell, Massachusetts, the son of a prominent attorney. Alger graduated from Harvard in 1879 and briefly attended medical school before settling on banking and finance as his career, eventually moving to Sheridan, Wyoming, in 1885. He spent the next twenty-one years as an officer of various banks in Sheridan. Alger also had an active political career, serving as Sheridan County treasurer, mayor of Sheridan, and as a member of the Wyoming legislature at various times in the 1890s. He ran unsuccessfully for governor on the Democratic ticket in 1898.

7. James P. Robinson (1844–1916) was the first treasurer of Sheridan County, and mayor of Sheridan in 1890. He was on the board of directors of the First National Bank of Sheridan and held the presidency from 1898 to 1900.

8. George Holdrege (1847–1926) graduated from Harvard in 1869 and became a railroad clerk for the Burlington and Missouri River Railroad Company in Plattsmouth, Nebraska. He worked his way up through the company, eventually becoming general manager of the Omaha office. He oversaw the expansion of the line through Sheridan, Wyoming, where he met George Beck.

Harrison "Harry" Fulmer (1861–1921) was a prominent citizen of Sheridan, Wyoming, who came to Wyoming in 1879 from Nebraska. He was a stage driver for five years before becoming the foreman of a cattle company. In 1902 he left that work to become a druggist and had his own store, Fulmer and Suits, which was highly respected.

C. H. Grinnell (1847–1916) was a businessman, cattle baron, and contractor who helped dig the canal for Little Goose Creek in downtown Sheridan, erected many of the town's substantial homes, and would later become mayor. He was also one of the founders in 1893 of the Sheridan Fuel Co., the first commercial mining company in the Sheridan area.

Charles Nelson Dietz (1853–1933) graduated from Iowa State College and eventually moved to Omaha, Nebraska, where he started the C. N. Dietz Lumber Company. When the Burlington Railroad extended its line to Sheridan, he traveled there to check out the coal reserves and bought six miles of coal land and started the Sheridan Coal Company, which he owned until 1903.

William "Mike" Elmore (1859–1919) was involved with the building of the railroad from Sheridan, Wyoming, across the Crow Reservation and west to Pryor Gap.

9. John William Mackay (1831–1902) was born in Dublin, Ireland, and migrated to the United States as a young man. He went to California in 1851 and became involved in mining. He was one of four partners, all Irishmen, known as the Bonanza Kings, who first made their fortune at the Comstock Lode. Later Mackay invested in cable companies such as the Commercial Cable Company and Postal Telegraph Company.

10. Katherine Duer (1878–1930) was a New York socialite who married Clarence Mackay on May 17, 1898. Later she was president of the Equal Franchise Society and believed equal suffrage would bring improvement in conditions for working women and the welfare of children.

11. Nicola Tesla (1856–1943) was an inventor, an electrical engineer, a mechanical engineer, and a physicist, and he is best known for his work with alternating electrical current.

13. The Johnson County War

1. George Mortimer Pullman (1831–97) was an American industrialist who designed and manufactured the Pullman sleeping car for overnight train travel.

2. William Worcester Lyman (1821–91) was a pewter smith and an American inventor from Connecticut. He invented the first rotating can opener and other kitchen items, but gun aficionados know him for the Lyman gunsight.

3. Similar symptoms confused diagnoses between typhoid fever and malaria; thus, many early physicians referred to one or the other ailment as typho-malaria. Medical progress later allowed for differentiating between the two separate aliments.

4. Meriwether Lewis Clark Jr. (1846–99) was the grandson of William Clark of the Lewis and Clark Expedition. He became interested in horses in 1872, although his family had raised horses for several generations. He was founder of the Louisville Jockey Club and the builder of Churchill Downs in 1875, which he named for his mother's side of the family. The Churchills were one of the "first families" of Kentucky, arriving there in 1787.

5. Newcastle, Wyoming, is the seat of Weston County and was founded in 1889.

6. Johnson County War was a conflict that developed from long-standing disputes between the cattle barons, who owned herds numbering in the thousands, and small ranchers, most running small herds just numbering enough cattle to support their families. Beginning in 1889 it culminated with an invasion by imported gunmen who attacked a cabin near Buffalo, Wyoming, in the Powder River country. The fifty invaders were joined by former sheriff Frank Canton, who at that time was a stock inspector for the Cattleman's Association.

7. Major Frank Walcott (1840–1910) served in the Civil War and in 1870 moved west from Kentucky to Cheyenne, Wyoming. He was a member of the Wyoming Stock Growers Association, made up of the large ranch owners in the state, which blamed small ranchers and homesteaders for the criminal activity in Johnson County, claiming they were stealing cattle from the large ranch herds. In April 1892 he led a group of hired gunman in an invasion of Johnson County, engaging in a shootout at the KC Ranch near Buffalo, Wyoming.

8. Colonel James Judson Van Horne (1834–98) was in the 8th infantry throughout his career. He came west in 1872 after serving in the Civil War and was stationed in the Dakotas, Wyoming, Arizona, and New Mexico.

He died at Fort D. A. Russell near Cheyenne, Wyoming. Fort D. A. Russell opened in 1867 as a cavalry post named for Civil War general David A. Russell (1820–64). Today it is known as F. E. Warren Air Force Base.

9. Charles H. Burritt (1854–1927) was the first mayor of Buffalo, Wyoming, and held office from 1881 to 1897.

10. Charlie Rounds (1855–1906) died in Buffalo, Wyoming, and is buried in the Willow Grove Cemetery.

11. Deyo Hasbrouck (1873–1963), a sheep rancher from Sheridan, Wyoming, married Clara C. Peebler in 1894. In the 1920s, he served on the Sheridan school board.

12. No information other than family friend could be found for Thomas Fisher Jr.

13. Buffalo Mill Company was founded by George Beck in 1886, a year after he built a flour mill on his property in Beckton, Wyoming.

14. Charles Elliot Perkins (1840–1907) worked his way up through the Chicago, Burlington and Quincy Railroad till he became president in 1881 after the Nebraska division of the Union Pacific merged with it. The CB&Q came to Cody in 1901.

15. Homestake Mine, located near Lead, South Dakota, was the largest and deepest underground gold mine in North America.

16. Julius Lead is possibly Julius W. Leede, a German engineer living in Minneapolis.

14. Wyoming Politics

1. Lucious Quintus Cincinnatus Lamar (1825–93) was a congressman from Mississippi until the Civil War, when he served in the Confederate Army as lieutenant colonel until 1862, at which time he entered the diplomatic service of the Confederacy and was sent on a special mission to Russia, France, and England. He was elected a U.S. senator in 1876, resigning in March 1885 to accept a position in President Grover Cleveland's cabinet as secretary of state (1885–88). He was then appointed to the U.S. Supreme Court as an associate justice, a position he held until his death in 1893.

2. Thomas Moonlight (1833–99) was commander at Fort Laramie and governor of the Territory of Wyoming from 1887 to 1889.

3. DeForest Richards (1846–1903) was a banker in Nebraska and then Douglas, Wyoming, before becoming a state senator and then governor of Wyoming from 1889 to 1903. He died in office just four months into his second term. He was also a farmer.

15. The Shoshone Irrigation Company

1. Laben Hillberry (1832–1917) eventually settled in Thermopolis, Wyoming. He later died in Arizona due to complications with asthma.

2. Jerry Ryan (1848–1903) was an engineer by trade who was sent with Laben Hillberry to discover if the Shoshone River could be diverted around the south side of the Cedar Mountain to irrigate a large area of the basin. He became a shareholder in the Shoshone Land and Irrigation Company at its founding in 1895 and was one of the first residents of the town of Cody.

3. Elwood Mead (1858–1936) was a central figure in the history of reclamation projects in the arid West for several decades. Born and raised in Indiana, Mead graduated from Purdue University in 1882 and then received training in civil engineering at Iowa Agricultural College (now Iowa State University). As a faculty member at Colorado State Agricultural College (now Colorado State University), Mead assisted the Colorado State Engineer's Office and quickly became recognized as an expert in irrigation engineering. Mead was appointed Wyoming territorial engineer in 1888, and was Wyoming's first state engineer, serving until 1899. As such Mead was intimately involved in the drafting and administration of Wyoming's water laws. Mead's engineering reports on the Shoshone River provided crucial backing for William F. Cody and his partners in the Cody Canal project.

4. William Hinckle Smith (1861–1943) was a capitalist from Philadelphia who was involved with the Girard Trust and the Penn Mutual Life companies. He was a good friend of Beck's who in later years invested financially in the town of Cody. No additional information could be located on Captain Stockwell and Andrew Stockwell.

5. Basin, Wyoming, was founded in 1896 and became the county seat of Big Horn County the following year, beating out the towns of Cody and Otto in the election.

6. Lovell's Ferry was likely operated by Henry Clay Lovell, a local rancher who settled in the area around 1880. His ranch was the Mason Lovell Ranch, named for himself and his partner, Anthony L. Mason, from Kansas City. The town of Lovell, Wyoming, which was settled by Mormon colonizers in 1900, is named in his honor.

7. It is unlikely that Beck crossed through Coyote Canyon, which is west of Basin and located on the Greybull River. Sheep Canyon is on the Big Horn River and Beck and his party would have floated through the canyon en route to Lovell's Ferry.

8. Solon Lysander Wiley (1840–1926) was born in Vermont and came west at the turn of the twentieth century. He formed the Big Horn Basin Development Company to build an irrigation canal to bring water from the Shoshone River and deliver it to what eventually became the Oregon Basin Oil Field. Work began on it in mid-1903. He invested much of his personal fortune in this venture, but it was not enough, and the canal and the town he named for himself never succeeded.

9. Arta Lucille Cody (1866–1904) is the eldest of William F. Cody's four children, of which only two lived to adulthood. She married Charles Thorp after Horton Boal's death.

10. Nate Salsbury (1846–1902) was an actor. After Cody and Doc Carver split up, Salsbury joined Buffalo Bill's Wild West, becoming a partner as well as vice president and manager of the show until his death on December 24, 1902.

11. George Bleistein (1861–1918) was born in Buffalo, New York, the son of German immigrants. While still in his teens, Bleistein began work for the Courier Printing Company in Buffalo and rose through the ranks to become the firm's president in 1884. Bleistein's company provided printed materials for Buffalo Bill's Wild West in the 1890s and early 1900s. Bleistein was one of the town founders of Cody, invested in the Shoshone Land and Irrigation Company, served on its board of directors, and had other business interests in the Big Horn Basin.

12. Bronson Rumsey II (1854–1946) grew up in Buffalo, New York, the son of Bronson Case Rumsey (1823–1902), who owned a successful tannery business. As an investor and board member in the Shoshone Land and Irrigation Company, Bronson Rumsey II was one of Cody's town founders. Among other business interests in the Big Horn Basin, Rumsey was one of the original partners in the Cody Trading Company.

Henry M. Gerrans (1853–1939) lived much of his life in Buffalo, New York, where he was co-owner of the Iroquois Hotel Company from the late 1880s to the early 1920s. Gerrans appears to have been prominent in Buffalo's civic affairs, as he was on the board of directors for the Pan-American Exposition of 1901, which was held in that city. He invested in the Shoshone Land and Irrigation Company in the 1890s. Gerrans also invested in oil fields and other business interests in the basin in addition to the irrigation venture.

13. Beck identified this individual as Charley Eckert, but this was likely Theo or Theodore Heckert, a railroad contractor who owned grading

equipment used in land development. In 1895 George Beck, chief surveyor Charles Hayden, and Heckert set up a grading camp and started construction of the headgate and flume of the Cody Canal.

14. Red Lodge, Montana, was founded in 1882 and a post office established in 1884. The railroad line was completed in 1889 and Red Lodge became the closest railroad shipping point to Cody and the rest of the Big Horn Basin.

15. Michael "Mike" R. Russell (1847–1930), born in Tipperary, Ireland, met Cody in Kansas in the late 1860s. Russell moved to Deadwood, South Dakota, in 1877 where he was a rancher, had mining operations, and was owner of the Buffalo Saloon. About 1895 Russell sold Cody cattle, horses, and his "TE" brand, which Cody used to establish his TE Ranch on the South Fork of the Shoshone River, southwest of Cody, Wyoming. Russell was probably Cody's oldest and closest friend and remained friends with the entire Cody family long after Cody's passing, frequently traveling to the town of Cody to visit them.

16. John "Reckless" Davies or Davis (1864–1914), a native of South Wales, came to the South Fork area in 1891 after mining coal in Red Lodge and established what is now the Majo Ranch. He became a guide for many of Buffalo Bill's hunting parties. He passed away at the age of fifty from ptomaine poisoning after eating tainted green beans while at Pahaska Tepee, Buffalo Bill's hunting lodge near the east entrance to Yellowstone.

17. Eagle's Nest was a stage stop on the stagecoach trail from Red Lodge, Montana, to Meeteetse, Wyoming. Thomas Lanchbury built the stop with overnight capabilities for passengers, drivers, and animals. Mrs. Emma Lanchbury was well known by her guests and local residents for her cooking skills.

18. Colonel William D. Pickett (1827–1917) was born in Alabama, grew up in Kentucky, and fought for the Confederacy during the Civil War. In 1883 he bought land along the Greybull River in Meeteetse, Wyoming. The Four Bear Ranch name stemmed from an incident when Pickett killed four bears in one evening.

19. *Meeteetse* is supposedly a Shoshone Indian word that means meeting place or resting place. The town was settled around 1887.

20. Richard "Dick" Ashworth (1856–1901) was an Englishman who started a cattle ranch on the Greybull River in 1881. Subsequently he and his partner, James C. Johnston, started the Hoodoo Ranch on Sage Creek.

21. Count Otto Franc von Lichtenstein (1846–1903), known as Otto Franc, was a cattle baron who in 1881 founded the Pitchfork Ranch, named

for his cattle brand. He was found on his ranch dead from a bullet wound from his own shotgun, which was stuck in a fence.

22. Burlington, Wyoming, was founded in 1893 by Mormons and named for the Burlington Railroad in hopes to entice the railroad to connect to their town.

23. No additional information on Virgil Rice could be located.

24. Thomas K. Riley (1844–1923) may be the Thomas K. Riley listed in the 1900 Census for Burlington who was a butcher. He had two daughters named Eileen and Christeen.

25. Carter Mountain is a part of the Absaroka Mountains located southeast of the town of Cody along the east side of the South Fork branch of the Stinking Water (Shoshone) River, named in honor of Judge William Carter of Fort Bridger, one of the first to bring cattle into Big Horn Basin. Carter was also the first to refer to the area as Shoshone.

26. Irma Louise Cody (1884–1918) was Louisa and William F. Cody's youngest daughter for whom he named the Irma Hotel. She passed away during the Spanish influenza epidemic in October 1918, just three days after her husband Fred Garlow.

27. Rattlesnake Mountain is located on the north side of the Shoshone River west of Cody and along the canyon. It was so named because of the numerous rattlesnakes living there. Cedar Mountain forms the south wall of the Shoshone Canyon. Although named for the presence of numerous cedar trees, this mountain is also known as Spirit Mountain. Many argue that Buffalo Bill's last wish was to be buried on Cedar Mountain, so his remains would overlook Cody, Wyoming.

28. Despite Beck's enthusiasm for picking up arrowheads, this is a practice now forbidden on public lands.

29. Charles DeMaris (1827–1914) settled two miles west of the present town of Cody near the geothermal springs named in his honor. DeMaris filed for and received water rights at the site and built a hotel.

30. William Ebert Hymer (1853–1933) was born near Rushville, Illinois, and settled in Nebraska in 1878, where he became one of the first merchants in the new town of Holdrege in the early 1880s. When the bank opened he was the first cashier and later its president and went into receivership. In March 1895 he moved to what would become Cody, Wyoming, and became a partner in the Shoshone Land and Irrigation Company. He contributed little capital and was eventually forced out of the venture by the other partners. He went on to other business ventures in and around Red Lodge, Montana, where he died in 1933.

31. Harrison Preston Arnold (1840–1923), known as "Hap," came from Billings in 1895 to open a general mercantile store in Cody City overlooking DeMaris Springs. In 1902 Arnold relocated his business to the main street of Cody, Wyoming, and advertised it as the "Good Stuff" store.

32. Cody City was William F. Cody's initial attempt in 1895 at starting a town along the Stinking Water River. It was located a short distance west of present-day Cody, Wyoming.

33. Charles E. Hayden (1866–1938) was a surveyor, assistant manager for the Shoshone Irrigation Company, and the resident engineer of the project. In May of 1896 George Beck and surveyor Charles Hayden staked out the town site of Cody, Wyoming. He is not related to the famed western explorer Ferdinand Vandeveer Hayden.

34. Okie Snyder (1856–1909) was hired by William F. Cody to observe Beck and the progress of the Cody Canal. He resided on Irma Flat on the South Fork but died in Emden, Illinois.

16. Developing Cody and Hunting Trips

1. George S. Russell (1850–1922) was the carpenter, along with Jerry Ryan, who built most of the initial buildings of the new town.

2. Cody Hotel was the first hotel in Cody, Wyoming. It began as a tent hotel on the south side of Sheridan Avenue, between Thirteenth and Fourteenth Streets as they are now known. It subsequently moved across the street where a wooden building was erected. The Green Front was the nickname given to George Beck's office in the Shoshone Land and Irrigation Company's building.

3. George Canfield (1836–99) and his wife Lucy were the first managers of the Sheridan Inn when it opened in 1893.

4. Sam Berry (1847–1929) was a hunter and a guide, a murderer—for hire—and an outlaw who spent five years in Wyoming's Territorial Prison for murder. He spent many years wandering around Wyoming before turning up in the Meeteetse/Cody area in 1897. George P. Grupp (1860–1942) was born in Germany and arrived in the United States in about 1880. His wife Louella was also German. Together they managed a restaurant in Cody. No information could be found on Dr. Carey.

5. Frank S. Bond (birth and death dates unknown) became president of the Philadelphia and Reading Railroad Company in 1881, a position he held for one year.

6. No information on Mr. Mark could be located. A. D. Chamberlain was the supervisor of the Yellowstone Park Timber Land Reserve, Shoshone Division, from 1898–1902. In 1908 the name of this reserve was changed to the Shoshone National Forest. Hi Shurtliff (1846–1903) was a forest ranger in the Shoshone National Forest west of Cody, originally from Massachusetts.

7. Moran was a small town named after Mount Moran of the Teton Range, which was named for the famed artist Thomas Moran. The town was relocated in 1959.

8. This would be Moran Junction.

9. Deer Creek is a small creek that runs out of Carter Mountain south of Cody toward the west.

17. The Cody Canal, Marriage, and Family Life

1. Named for Pete McCulloch, a Scottish immigrant who drove Judge Carter's cattle herd into the Big Horn Basin.

2. Charles W. Burdick (1860–1927) was a prominent Cheyenne lawyer, and served as the first Wyoming state auditor (1890–94) and later as Wyoming secretary of state (1895–99).

3. Daisy Sorrenson Beck (1875–1956) was born in Fort Dodge, Iowa, and when orphaned at age ten was raised by her sister Lillian and brother-in-law Dallas Tinckom in Red Lodge, Montana. She married George W. T. Beck in 1897.

4. Calamity Jane (1852–1903), whose real name was Martha Jane Canary.

5. Colonel John H. Peake (1848–1905) came to Cody at the behest of William F. "Buffalo Bill" Cody from Washington DC to be publisher of the town's newspaper, *The Cody Enterprise*. He had previously worked for the *North Platte Enterprise* in the early 1870s. Anna Peake (1856–1953), Colonel Peake's wife, also known as "Granny" Peake by the townspeople of Cody, took over the newspaper after her husband's death.

6. Tom Purcell (1854–1901) was the owner of Purcell's Saloon where the "Poker Church" poker game was held, which Beck won and decided the money should be used to build an Episcopal church. Purcell subsequently moved to Roy, Washington, where he passed away.

7. "Poker Nell" owned a saloon in Cody until her insanity caused her to be committed to an asylum in Basin, Wyoming. Dr. Will Frackelton, a dentist, noted he mounted two diamonds in her two front teeth to distract

her opponents during poker games. She was married to Harry Bruce, who was later convicted of killing a man in Thermopolis, Wyoming.

8. In the original manuscript Beck mistakenly identified the teacher's first name as Paula. Vida Weborg was the first teacher in Cody before she returned to her native Sweden.

9. Frank Houx (1854–1941) was the first mayor of Cody, Wyoming. He was a prominent Democrat and served as Wyoming secretary of state as well as governor of Wyoming when John B. Kendrick resigned to assume a seat in the U.S. Senate.

10. This would be John "Joe" Vogel (1872–1963).

11. Jacob M. "Jakie" Schwoob (1874–1932) managed the Cody Trading Company and also served as a state senator. He was also a tremendous promoter of Cody, Wyoming, the Buffalo Bill Museum, and the Cody–Yellowstone Road.

12. No information could be located on H. R. Weston.

13. Bishop James Bowen Funston (ca. 1856–1918) was the first Presbyterian-Episcopal bishop of Idaho.

18. The Ball, the Visit, and a Bank Robbery

1. The Leiter family resided in a three-story mansion with fifty-five rooms on DuPont Circle in Washington DC. Levi Leiter (1834–1904) worked as a bookkeeper for Cooley, Wadsworth & Company and later amassed a fortune by investing in Chicago real estate. He married Mary Theresa Carver (1844–1913). The marriage produced one son, Joseph Leiter (1868–1932), and three daughters: Mary Victoria (1870–1906), Nancy "Nannie" Lathrop Carver (1873–1930), and Margaret "Daisy" Hyde (1880–1968). The family was well connected to British nobility, for Mary Victoria married British statesman George Curzon who served as viceroy of India, and "Daisy" married Henry Mollineux Howard, the 19th Earl of Suffolk and 12th Earl of Berkshire. An article in the Washington DC *Evening Star* dated December 26, 1901, reported the Leiters invited five hundred guests to the ball and noted their new purchases and gifts from India.

2. It is possible that "Miss Eads" was either Eliza Ann Eads How (1846–1915) or Martha Eads Switzer (1851–1901). Their father, James Buchanan Eads (1820–87), was from Missouri and he served as a Lincoln advisor in fortifying the Mississippi River. Later he designed the jetty system that narrowed the Mississippi River, clearing the silt out of the main channel to ensure year-round travel for larger ships. He also designed the Eads

Bridge in St. Louis. Beck would have been familiar with Eads's engineering career and legacy.

3. Virginia Woodbury Lowery (ca. 1840–1934) married José Brunetti y Gayos (1839–1928), the 15th Duke of Arcos of Spain. He served as plenipeteniary of Spain in the United States from 1889 to 1902. Virginia Lowery's family from New Hampshire was both wealthy and politically well connected. The Duke's competitor for Virginia's hand in marriage was Admiral George Dewey.

4. Eva Caten (1859–1918) married Remington in 1883.

5. O. D. Marx was part owner of the Cody Hotel, and Dr. Ainsworth was a local physician. No additional information could be located.

6. This painting is currently in the collections of the Whitney Western Art Museum at the Buffalo Bill Center of the West in Cody, Wyoming.

7. Charles Morrill, was the president of the Lincoln Land Company. This company, headquartered in Lincoln, Nebraska, built up the towns along the Burlington Railroad lines.

8. The Forbes family purchased Beck's ranch in 1898 and continues to ranch the region.

9. Dr. James T. Bradbury (1865–1952) practiced medicine in Cody with Dr. Frances Lane. They held a contract with the U.S. government to treat the men working on the Shoshone Dam beginning in 1904.

10. John Winterling (1848–1917) was a banker from Sheridan, Wyoming. Lyman H. Brooks (1860–1931) was born in Canada. He was one of the founders of Sheridan, Wyoming. I. O. Middaugh (1868–1904) was a banker from Wheatland, Wyoming.

11. The Irma Hotel was built by William F. "Buffalo Bill" Cody and named for his youngest daughter, Irma. It opened on November 18, 1901.

12. Charles Furse Hensley (1867–1950) was a bank teller at the First National Bank in Cody during the robbery in 1904, as noted by Beck.

13. Dr. Frances Lane was a local female physician who was known as the Lady Doc. Caroline Lockhart published a scathing novel based on Francis Lane with the title *The Lady Doc.*

19. Another Ute Uprising and Famous Guests

1. John L. Burns (1842–1929) of Red Lodge, Montana, was a former stagecoach driver who purchased the Belknap Ranch and sold it to Buffalo Bill.

2. Garfield was the secretary of agriculture, and this visit was to see the reclamation project.

3. Frank Wheeler Mondell (1860–1939) served in the House of Representatives from 1899 until 1923. He came to Wyoming in 1887 and helped develop the town of Newcastle, Wyoming, along with oil and coal interests in the area. Mondell was chairman of the Committee on Irrigation of Arid Lands for the 58th and 59th Congresses.

4. It is likely Roosevelt also dodged the hunting trip to avoid General Miles due to tension between the two men.

5. The Ute Uprising occurred in 1906. Soldiers from Fort Meade suppressed the "uprising," which consisted of a handful of Ute who left their reservation to hunt near the Black Hills.

6. This female reporter was possibly Caroline Lockhart (1871–1962), a reporter for the *Boston Post* and the *Philadelphia Bulletin*. She arrived in Cody, Wyoming, in 1904, and made it her home. Eventually she purchased *The Cody Enterprise* and wrote a number of fictional novels that included many characters modeled after her Wyoming neighbors, including the Becks, in *The Lady Doc*.

7. Marie Hunt owned a stock company that performed various plays in Deadwood.

8. This firearm is now on display at the Buffalo Bill Museum at the Buffalo Bill Center of the West in Cody, Wyoming.

9. Prince Albert of Monaco was invited by Meeteetse artist and rancher A. A. Anderson to hunt west of Cody, Wyoming. They established a hunting camp, carved away some bark from a tree, and painted "Camp Monaco" on the exposed wood. The Camp Monaco Tree stood on its original location until 1994 when it was relocated to the Buffalo Bill Center of the West in Cody, Wyoming.

10. Charles Gilbert Gates (abt. 1876–1913) lived in Port Arthur, Texas, and his occupation was listed as "broker" in the 1910 Census. His nickname was "Spend-a-Million Gates" and he was the son of John Warne Gates—"Bet-a-Million Gates"—whose occupation in the same census is listed as "farmer."

11. Nedward Frost (1881–1957) came to the Big Horn Basin with his family in 1886. He grew up hunting and fishing, which led to him and his cousin Fred Richard forming the Frost and Richard Company.

20. The Shoshone Project and the Power Plant

1. This dam was completed in 1910 under the supervision of the Reclamation Service, later renamed the Bureau of Reclamation. In 1946 the

Shoshone Dam was renamed Buffalo Bill Dam in recognition of the centennial of Buffalo Bill's birthday.

2. Wayne Darlington (1862–1942) was raised in the heart of Philadelphia during the Civil War and went on to become a mining engineer, politician, and businessman after graduating from the Schofield School at Yale University in 1883 followed by postgraduate work at the Royal Mining Academy in Frieburg, Germany. He worked in China, Mexico, the far West, Alaska, and eventually Idaho where a rural community was named after him. In 1889 he became a mining engineer to the emperor of China and Viceroy Li Hung Chang.

3. Li Hung Chang (*Li Hongzhang*) (1823–1901) was a leading viceroy of China in the nineteenth century who made strenuous efforts to modernize his country. He hired mining engineer Wayne Darlington in 1889.

4. John R. Painter (1861–1936) operated a mine, a ranch, and a post office on the upper Clarks Fork of the Yellowstone River.

5. Tom Foley was a friend of Buffalo Bill's who ran a saloon in Omaha, Nebraska. This 1907 hunt was depicted in a painting titled *Camp Foley* by artist R. Farrington Elwell. The painting, which currently resides in the collections of the Buffalo Bill Center of the West in Cody, Wyoming, illustrates Buffalo Bill, George Beck, and Tom Foley resting outside a canvas tent.

6. Chief Iron Tail (1857–1915) was an Oglala Sioux who fought at the Little Big Horn and later at Wounded Knee. He performed with Buffalo Bill's Wild West and became very close friends with Cody, and the two went on many hunts together. He was one of the models used for the Indian head nickel designed by James E. Fraser.

7. Thorofare Plateau marks the headwaters of many creeks, providing a "thoroughfare" for wildlife and early travelers between drainages of the Snake River, Big Horn River, and Yellowstone River.

8. *Ishawooa* is a Shoshone word meaning "the wolf's penis." This name identified a feature now known as Castle Rock, located along the South Fork of the Shoshone River. Mae Urbanek noted in her book *Wyoming Place Names* that the name means "lying warm" in Shoshone, the less-offensive definition adopted by local settlers. Ishawooa Pass divides the headwaters of the Yellowstone from the South Fork of the Shoshone. The mountain has a patch of snow that when melted to the low-water point resembles a horse head with reins.

9. Pryor Mountain and Pryor Gap were named for Sergeant Nathaniel Pryor from the Lewis and Clark Corps of Discovery.

21. Afterword

1. See Santmyer, ". . . *And Ladies of the Club.*"

2. "The Potowmack Canal, Waterway that Led to the Constitution," *National Geographic* (July 1987).

Appendix 1

1. William F. Cody often did not write the year on his letters; however, he did record the month, day, and his location. This information was matched with the touring schedule of Buffalo Bill's Wild West to determine the year. The Wild West performed in Dayton, Ohio, on July 5, 1896.

2. The "Young Lady" to whom Cody refers is Daisy May Sorrenson, a young woman who was a teacher in Marquette, Wyoming, and whom Beck hired to work for Shoshone Irrigation Company. Beck later married Sorrenson in Red Lodge, Montana on December 1, 1897; they had three children: Betty (born 1898, later Mrs. Doyle and Mrs. J. M. Roberson), Jane (born 1900, later Mrs. Nelson T. Johnson), and George Thornton Beck Jr. (born 1908).

3. "Germans" refers to the fifty or so German migrant families who arrived to settle in the Big Horn Basin; they were represented by S. V. Nagle.

4. S. V. Nagle, an associate of the firm of F. A. Nagle Commission Merchants of Chicago, attempted to recruit settlers to the lands in the Big Horn Basin that were to be irrigated by the Cody Canal.

5. Sage Creek lies east of Cody, Wyoming, trending north–south and flowing into the Shoshone River northeast of Cody.

6. "Irma" likely refers to Irma Flat, an area in the South Fork Valley outside Cody, Wyoming, that was named after Cody's daughter, Irma.

7. Nathan "Nate" Salsbury (1846–1902) was a veteran of the Civil War who later became an actor and a successful theatrical producer and manager. He joined Cody in 1884 as co-owner of Buffalo Bill's Wild West. His show business skills contributed greatly to the venture's success until his death in 1902.

8. "Foote" is Robert Foote (1834–1916), a Wyoming Senate Democrat representing Johnson County, Wyoming, from 1895 to 1897. Foote led the effort against the Carey Act in Wyoming. "Stokes" is possibly Edward S. Stokes (1841–1901), at one time a railroad and oil magnate and businessman. Stokes was an owner of Hoffman House, an elegant hotel in Manhattan where Cody was often a guest. Cody may have wanted Stokes to invest in the Cody Canal.

9. Red Lodge, Montana, lies sixty-five miles north of Cody and was the closest rail line to Cody, Wyoming. The "Doctor" is not identified. "Yegen" refers to P. Yegen and Co., a Red Lodge mercantile from which supplies were purchased for the irrigation project.

10. "Omaha people" are unidentified.

11. "Burke" refers to Carlton Burke, a foreman working on the irrigation project.

12. Likely Edward Stokes, see note 8.

13. Hudson W. Darrah (1864–1929), a sawmill owner with other business interests in and around the town of Cody, Wyoming, had a history of legal disputes with the Shoshone Irrigation Company.

Appendix 2

1. Remarks on Laying of Corner-Stone of New City Hall, Cody, Wyoming—December 6, 1938, box 30, folder 9, George T. Beck Collection, Number 00059, American Heritage Center, University of Wyoming.

Appendix 3

1. Thornton Beck Talk, January 29, 1968, box 7, folder 7, George T. Beck Collection, Number 00059, American Heritage Center, University of Wyoming.

BIBLIOGRAPHY

Anderson, A. A. *Experiences and Impressions: The Autobiography of A. A. Anderson*. New York: MacMillan, 1933.

Andren, Gladys. *Life Among the Ladies by the Lake*. Cody WY: Rustler Printing and Publishing, 1984.

Atkins, Annette. *We Grew Up Together: Brothers and Sisters in Nineteenth-Century America*. Champaign: University of Illinois Press, 2000.

Bartlett, Richard A. *From Cody to the World: The Fist Seventy-Five Years of the Buffalo Bill Memorial Association*. Cody WY: Buffalo Bill Historical Center, 1992.

Blackstone, Sarah J. *The Business of Being Buffalo Bill: Selected Letters of William F. Cody*. New York: Praeger, 1988.

Blair, Pat, Dana Prater, and the Sheridan County Museum. *Images of America: Sheridan*. Charleston SC: Arcadia, 2008.

Blevins, Bruce H. *Big Horn County, Wyoming: Facts and Maps Through Time*. Powell WY: WIM Marketing, 2000.

———. *Park County, Wyoming: Facts and Maps Through Time*. Powell WY: WIM Marketing, 1999.

Bonner, Robert, and Beryl Churchill. *Home in the Valley: Powell's First Century*. Cody WY: WordsWorth, 2008.

Bonner, Robert E. *William F. Cody's Wyoming Empire: The Buffalo Bill Nobody Knows*. Norman: University of Oklahoma Press, 2007.

Brown, Mark H. *The Plainsmen of the Yellowstone: A History of the Yellowstone Basin*. Lincoln: University of Nebraska Press, 1969.

Burke, John. *Buffalo Bill: The Noblest Whiteskin*. New York: G. P. Putnam's Sons, 1973.

Burt, Struthers. *Powder River, Let 'er Buck*. New Nork: Farrar & Rinehart, 1938.

Carter, Robert A. *Buffalo Bill Cody: The Man Behind the Legend*. New York: John Wiley & Sons, 2000.

Chamberlin, Agnes B. *The Story of the Cody Club, 1900–1940.* New York: J. J. Little & Ives, 1940.

Cheney, Roberta Carkeek. *Names on the Face of Montana.* Missoula MT: Mountain Press, 1983.

Christiansen, Cleo. *Sagebrush Settlements.* Lovell: Cleo Christiansen, 1967.

Churchill, Beryl Gail. *Challenging the Canyon: A Family Man Builds Dam.* Cody WY: WordsWorth, 2001.

———. *The Dam Book: The Construction History of Corbett, Buffalo Bill and Wilwood Dams.* Cody WY: Rustler Printing and Publishing, 1986.

———. *Dams, Ditches and Water: A History of the Shoshone Reclamation Project.* Cody WY: Rustler Printing and Publishing, 1979.

Clayton, John. *The Cowboy Girl: The Life of Caroline Lockhart.* Lincoln: University of Nebraska Press, 2007.

Cody, William F. *Buffalo Bill's Life Story.* New York: Farrar & Rinehart, 1920.

———. *The Life of Hon. William F. Cody, Known as Buffalo Bill.* Edited by Frank Christianson. Lincoln: University of Nebraska Press, 2011.

Cook, David J. *Hands-Up! Or Twenty Years of Detective Life in the Mountains and on the Plains.* Denver: W. F. Robinson, 1882. Reprint, Norman: University of Oklahoma Press, 1958.

Cook, Jeannie, Lynn Johnson Houze, Bob Edgar, and Paul Fees. *Buffalo Bill's Town in the Rockies: A Pictorial History of Cody, Wyoming.* Virginia Beach VA: Donning, 1996.

Davis, John W. *Wyoming Range War: The Infamous Invasion of Johnson County.* Norman: University of Oklahoma Press, 2010.

De Barthe, Joe. *The Life and Adventures of Frank Grouard.* St. Joseph MO: Combe, 1894.

Fees, Paul. "Lockhart, Boomtown, and the Lady Doc." Introduction to *The Lady Doc by Caroline Lockhart.* Reprint, Cody WY: WordsWorth, 2003.

Fillerup, Melvin M. *Sidon: The Canal that Faith Built.* Cody WY: Ptarmigan, 1988.

Foote, Stella. *Letters from "Buffalo Bill."* El Segundo CA: Upton & Sons, 1990.

Furman, Necah Stewart. *Caroline Lockhart: Her Life and Legacy.* Cody WY: Buffalo Bill Historical Center, 1994.

Garber, Vie Willits, ed. *Big Horn Pioneers.* Big Horn WY: Big Horn Public Schools, 1961.

Gillette, Edward. *The Iron Trail.* Boston: Christopher, 1925.

Hanna, Oliver Perry. *An Old Timer's Story of the Old Wild West.* Casper WY: Endeavor, 1926 (1984).

Hedren, Paul L. *After Custer: Loss and Transformation in Sioux Country.* Norman: University of Oklahoma Press, 2011.

Hicks, Lucille Patrick. *Caroline Lockhart: Liberated Lady, 1870–1962.* Cheyenne WY: Pioneer, 1984.

Hook, James W. "Seven Months in Cody, Wyoming, 1905–1906." *Annals of Wyoming* 26, no. 1 (January 1954): 3–24.

Houze, Lynn Johnson, *Cody: Then & Now.* Charleston SC: Arcadia Publishing, 2011.

———. *Images of America: Cody.* Charleston SC: Arcadia, 2008.

Jessen, Ken. *Colorado Gunsmoke: True Stories of Outlaws and Lawmen on the Colorado Frontier.* Loveland CO: J. V. Publications, 1986.

Johnston, Jeremy M. *Images of America: Powell.* Charleston SC: Arcadia, 2008.

Jordan, Roy A., and S. Brett DeBoer. *Wyoming: A Source Book.* Niwot: University Press of Colorado, 1996.

Kahin, Sharon, and Laurie Rufe. *In the Shadow of the Rockies: A Photographic History of the Pioneer Experience in Wyoming's Big Horn Basin.* Powell WY: Northwest Community College, 1983.

Kelly, Luther S. *Yellowstone Kelly: The Memoirs of Luther S. Kelly.* Edited by M. M. Quaife. Lincoln: University of Nebraska Press, 1973.

Kensel, W. Hudson. *Dude Ranching in Yellowstone Country: Larry Larom and Valley Ranch, 1915–1969.* Norman OK: Arthur H. Clark, 2010.

———. *Pahaska Tepee–Buffalo Bill's Old Hunting Lodge and Hotel, a History, 1901–1946.* Cody WY: Buffalo Bill Historical Center, 1987.

Kluger, James R. *Turning on Water with a Shovel: The Career of Elwood Mead.* Albuquerque: University of New Mexico Press, 1992.

Larson, T. A. *History of Wyoming.* 2nd rev. edition. Lincoln: University of Nebraska Press, 1978.

Leforge, Thomas, as told by Thomas B. Marquis. *Memoirs of a White Crow Indian.* Lincoln: University of Nebraska Press, 1974.

Lindsay, Charles. *The Big Horn Basin.* Lincoln: University of Nebraska, 1932.

Lockhart, Caroline. *The Lady Doc.* Philadelphia: J. B. Lippincott, 1912.

MacLean, Col. French L. *Sitting Bull, Crazy Horse, Gold, and Guns: The 1874 Yellowstone Wagon Road and Prospecting Expedition and the Battle of Lodge Grass Creek.* Atglen PA: Schiffer, 2016.

McLaird, James D. "Building the Town of Cody: George T. Beck, 1894–1943." *Annals of Wyoming* 40, no. 1 (1968): 73–105.

———. "Ranching in the Big Horns: George T. Beck, 1856–1894." *Annals of Wyoming* 39, no. 2 (1967): 157–85.

Mills, Captain Anson. "Big Horn Expedition August 15 to September 30, 1874." (No publishing information), William Robertson Coe Collection at Yale University, microfilm.

Murray, Ester Johansson. *A History of the Northfork of the Shoshone River*. Cody WY: Lone Eagle Multimedia, 1996.

Overton, Richard C. *Burlington Route: A History of the Burlington Lines*. New York: Alfred A. Knopf, 1965.

――――. *Burlington West: A Colonization History of the Burlington Railroad*. Reprint, New York: Russell & Russell, 1967.

Park County Story Committee. *The Park County Story*. Lubbock TX: Craftsman, 1980.

Patrick, Lucille Nichols. *The Best Little Town by a Dam Site*. Cheyenne WY: Flintlock, 1968.

――――. *The Candy Kid: James Calvin "Kid" Nichols*. Cheyenne WY: Flintlock, 1969.

Pisani, Donald J. *To Reclaim a Divided West: Water, Law, and Public Policy 1848–1902*. Albuquerque: University of New Mexico Press, 1992.

Ricketts, Palmer C. *History of the Rensselaer Polytechnic Institute, 1824–1894*. New York: John Wiley and Sons, 1895.

Roberts, Phil. *Cody's Cave: National Monuments and the Politics of Public Lands in the 20th Century West*. Laramie WY: Skyline West, 2012.

Roe, Charles Francis. "Custer's Last Battle." *Custer Engages the Hostiles*. Fort Collins CO: Old Army Press, N.d.

Rollinson, John K. *Pony Trails in Wyoming*. Caldwell ID: Caxton, 1941.

――――. *Wyoming Cattle Trails*. Caldwell ID: Caxton, 1948.

Russell, Don. *The Lives and Legends of Buffalo Bill*. Norman: University of Oklahoma Press, 1960.

Santmyer, Helen Hooven. *". . . And Ladies of the Club."* New York: Putnam's, 1982.

Sheridan County Extension Homemakers Council. *Sheridan County Heritage*. Pierre SD: State, 1983.

Slack, Judy, Bozeman Trail Museum, and Big Horn City Historical Society. *Images of America: Big Horn City*. Charleston SC: Arcadia, 2011.

Smith, Helena Huntington. *The War on Powder River: The History of an Insurrection*. Lincoln: University of Nebraska Press, 1966.

Stands In Timber, John, and Margo Liberty. *Cheyenne Memories*. New Haven CT: Yale University Press, 1998.

———. *The Complete John Stands In Timber Interviews.* Norman: University of Oklahoma Press, 2013.

Towne, Charles Wayland. "Preacher's Son on the Loose with Buffalo Bill Cody." *Montana: The Magazine of Western History* 18, no. 4 (October 1968): 40–55.

Urbanek, Mae. *Wyoming Place Names.* Missoula MT: Mountain Press, 1988.

Walker, Tacetta B. *Stories of Early Days in Wyoming.* Casper WY: Tacetta B. Walker, 1936.

Wallop, Gerald, Earl of Portsmouth. *A Knot of Roots: The Autobiography of a Man Whose Life Spans Three Continents and Two Worlds.* New York: New American Library, 1965.

Warren, Louis. *Buffalo Bill's America: William Cody & The Wild West Show.* New York: Random House, 2007.

Wasden, David J. *From Beaver to Oil: A Century in the Development of Wyoming's Big Horn Basin.* Cheyenne: Pioneer, 1973.

Weibert, Don L. *The 1874 Invasion of Montana: A Prelude to the Custer Disaster.* Billings MT: Benchmark, 1993.

Welch, Charles A. *History of the Big Horn Basin.* N.p.: Deseret News, 1940, reprinted in 1998.

Wetmore, Helen Cody. *Last of the Great Scouts: The Life Story of Col. William F. Cody "Buffalo Bill."* Chicago: Duluth, 1899.

Woods, Lawrence M. *Wyoming's Big Horn Basin to 1901: A Late Frontier.* Spokane: Arthur H. Clark, 1997.

Wooster, Robert. *Nelson A. Miles & the Twilight of the Frontier Army.* Lincoln: University of Nebraska Press, 1993.

Yates, Norris. *Western Writers Series: Caroline Lockhart.* Boise ID: Boise State University, 1994.

Yost, Nellie Snyder. *Buffalo Bill: His Family, Friends, Fame, Failures, and Fortunes.* Chicago: Swallow, 1979.

INDEX

Battle of Wolf Mountain, 301n17
Battle of Wounded Knee, 240, 300n9,
304n10, 324n6
Bavarian immigrants. *See* Germans
Bayard, James A., Jr., 33, 190, 295n11
Bayard, Thomas F., 295n11
Beale, Forbes, 47
Beale, John Forbes, 296n8
Beatrice NE, 178, 302n21
Beck, Bettie Buckner. *See* Goodloe,
Bettie Buckner Beck
Beck, Daisy May Sorrenson: back-
ground of, 283, 320n3; Buffalo Bill's
referral to, 272, 325appendix1n2;
courtship and marriage of, xxvii, 218,
262, 286, 320n3, 325appendix1n2;
editing of husband's memoir, xxvi,
liv; granddaughter's memories of,
264; occupations of, 218, 283; Simpsons' memories of, ix, x, xiii
Beck, Ebenezer P., 6
Beck, George Thornton, Jr.,
"Tee," ix, xiv, 149, 261, 283–88,
325appendix1n2
Beck, George W. T.: ancestry and progeny of, 263–64; athletic pursuits of,
34–35, 41–46; autobiography manuscripts of, xxv–xxvi, xxviii, xliii, xlvii,
l–li, liii–lv; birth and early life of, 5;
boats and boating of, 30, 31, 47–48,
51; boxing of, 34–35, 41, 159–62; on
Buffalo Bill's first trip to Big Horn
Basin, xxxvi; cattle of, 118; as church
reader, 224; clothing of, 127–28; collection of arrowheads, 204, 318n28;
construction projects of, 83–84, 110–
12, 133; cooking by, 107, 255–58, 286–
87; dancing of, 35, 48–49; death of,
xii, xiv; demeanor of, xii, xiii, xxv,
xxvii, l, liv, 263; dogs of, 54–55, 60,
78, 101–3, 110, 117, 118, 128–31, 139–
42, 151–52, 210–13, 284; and dolomite conversion, 288; education of,
xxx, 20, 32–33, 40, 47; engineering
career of, 65, 67–69; establishment
of Cody, xxxviii–xxxix, 204–5, 285;
exotic pets of, 113, 132; farming and

gardening by, 108, 167–70; as father's
secretary, 47, 139, 154, 157; fictional
portrayal of, xliv–xlvi; fondness for
scallops, 39; as "Governor," xxxi;
grandmother of, 292n9; hair of, 13–
14; horses of, 24–26, 71, 79–83, 91,
110, 118–19, 124, 135, 168–69, 177–78,
180, 181, 234, 268; illness of, 26, 177–
78, 313n3; inheritance of, 53; at irrigation project site, 194–96; legacy of,
265–68; marriage and family of, 218,
283, 286, 293n15, 320n3, 325appen-
dix1n2; as mayor of Cody, 222; medical remedies of, 12; messiness of,
285; painting of, 324n5; partnership
with Buffalo Bill, xxxii–xxxiv, xxxvii,
xl, xlii, xlviii–l, liii–liv, 271; physical
appearance of, x, xi, xiii; poker playing of, 155, 223–24, 264, 320ch17n6;
political career of, xxxi, 153–54, 156–
57, 159, 189–91; as postmaster, 167–
68, 284, 311n2; prospecting by, 62,
65, 91, 119–23, 126, 136, 163, 167, 172,
250–51, 259; on ship to England, 36–
37; shooting by, 23–24, 103–4, 114;
Simpsons' memories of, ix; speech at
city hall cornerstone laying, 279–81;
visitors to ranch of, 91–93; wanderlust of, 20, 23, 53, 294n1; as western
entrepreneur, xxviii, l–liv; wildlife
encounters of, 61, 85–86, 91, 102–3,
109, 125–26, 168
Beck, Helen, 6
Beck, James Burnie: advice on son's
future, 65; background of, 6–7,
291n2; at boat launching, 47; courtship and marriage of, 10–11, 292n8;
in Cuba, 143–45, 149; death of, 51,
157; estate of, 159; friends of, 182–83,
190, 292n4; gift of gun from, 23; and
impeachment of President Johnson,
295n8; impression of son's clothing, 127; law education of, 8; letter
of introduction for son, 39; meeting
with Abraham Lincoln, 19, 20; political career of, xxix, 8–9, 26, 27, 51,
154; protection of property during

Blaine, Margaret, 135, 307n16

Blair, Caroline Buckner, 27, 293n14

Blair, Elizabeth. *See* Lee, Elizabeth Blair

Blair, Francis, Jr., 293n14

Blair, Francis Preston, 10, 28, 293n13, 293n14

Blair, Montgomery, 19, 27, 293n14

Blair-Lee house, 293n14

Bleistein, George, xi, 198, 215, 223, 275, 277, 280, 316n11

Bligh's coal mine, 70. *See also* coal, lignite

Blizzard of 1886–87, 139, 307n1

Blue Ridge Mountains, 292n8, 292n10

Boal, Horton Sinclair: background of, 310n3; George Beck's visit within Chicago, 159, 161; and irrigation project, xxxii, xxxiii, xxxiv, 194, 196, 280; wife of, 316n9

Bonanza Kings, 312n9

Bond, Frank, 211, 212, 319n5

Bonner, Charles, 165–66, 310n9

Bonner, Robert E., xlix–l

Book Fair on the Mall, 267

Boone, Daniel, 47

Boston MA, xli, 107, 236

Boston Post, 323n6

Bozeman MT, 304n7

Bradbury, James T., 236–37, 322n9

Braddock, Edward, 53, 298n2

Breckinridge, John C., xxix–xxx, 7, 8, 11, 14, 32, 157, 292n4

Bridger Lake, 234

Brooke, Anne Clymer, 135, 307n15

Brookland MD, 149

Brooklyn NY, 40, 71, 85, 89, 295n12

Brooks, Lyman H., 236, 322n10

Brown, Henry C., 307n19

Brown Palace Hotel, 137, 307n19

Bruce, Harry, 320ch17n7

Brundage, George, 135, 307n14

Brundage, Howard, 307n14

Brunetti y Gayos, José, Duke of Arcos of Spain, 322n3

Brunswick GA, 139, 141

Buchanan, James, 8, 292n4

Buck (servant), 11, 12

Buckner, Caroline. *See* Blair, Caroline Buckner

Buckner, Margaret, 9, 292n8, 292n9, 292n11

buffalo, 74–76, 79, 301n17

Buffalo Bill Center of the West, xviii, lv, 266, 271, 288, 322n6, 323nn8–9, 324n5

Buffalo Bill Dam. *See* Shoshone Dam

Buffalo Bill Museum: gun in, 323n8; promotion of, 321n11. *See also* Buffalo Bill Center of the West

Buffalo Bill's Town in the Rockies (Cook, Houze, Edgar, and Fees), xlix

Buffalo Bill's Wild West: Buffalo Bill's shooting in, 201; fame of, xvii; financing of, 216; as marketing tool, xxxiv, xxxvii, xxxviii, 222, 223; partners and employees of, 198, 220, 253, 316n10, 324n6, 325n7; in Portland ME, 235; printed materials for, 316n11; tour schedule of, 325appendix1n1. *See also* Cody, William F. "Buffalo Bill"

Buffalo Fork, 211

Buffalo Fork, Snake River, 235

Buffalo Mill Company, 183–84, 314n13

Buffalo NY: boxing in, 160; irrigation project partners in, 198, 209, 223, 225, 235, 277, 316n11, 316n12; Robert Chadwick in, 296n5; storekeeper from, 223; Wyoming town named for, 304n12

Buffalo Saloon, 317n15

Buffalo WY: bank in, 136, 307n18; Charlie Rounds in, 314n10; chess playing in, 146; development of, xxxii; fight at ranch near, 179, 313n6, 313n7; founding of, 304n12; fundraising for canal in, 215; George Beck's property in, 153, 180–83; hotel in, 129; inspection party in, 194; James Gang at, 96; lights and power in, 268; mayor of, 314n9; store in, 134, 306n11

Bull Run Creek, 9, 292n10

Burden Iron Works, 43, 44, 45
Burdick, Charles W., 217, 320n2
Burger, Warren, 265
Burke, Carlton, 276, 326n11
Burkitt, Kenard, 135, 307n14
Burkitt, Lucy, 307n14
Burlington and Missouri Railroad Company: George Holdrege with, 312n8
Burlington Railroad: and coal business, 186–87; in Cody, xl, xlix, 235–36, 239; horse on, 180; interests in Buffalo wy, 183; in Sheridan, 183, 184, 312n8; town named for, 318n22; towns along, 322n7. *See also* railroads
Burlington wy, 202–3, 318n22, 318n24
Burns, John L., 239, 322n1
Burns, Walter Noble, li–lii
Burritt, Charles H., 180, 314n9
Bush, Laura, 267

Cabin Creek, 73, 301n13, 301n17
Cairo il, 8
Calamity Jane, li, 219–20, 320n4
California, 119, 159, 163–66, 297n10, 298n3, 310n9, 312n9
Campbell, Charles A., 155, 309n10
Camp Foley (Elwell), 324n5
Camp Monaco Tree, 323n9
camshaft, 69
Canada, 73, 301n17, 322n10
Canadian Pacific Railroad, 68. *See also* railroads
Canary, Martha Jane. *See* Calamity Jane
Canberra, Australia, 149
Canfield, George, xxxiii, 209, 319n3
Canfield, Lucy, 319n3
Canfield, Sherman, xxxiii
Canton, Frank, 167, 178, 311n1, 313n6
Cantonment Reno, 303n1. *See also* Fort McKinney
Carbon County, 133, 306n8
Carey, Dr., 210
Carey, Joseph Maull, xxxii, 49, 296n9
Carey Act, xxxii, xxxiv, xxxv, 325n8
Carlyle, John G., 9
Carter, William, 318n25, 320n1

Carter Mountain, 203, 232, 318n25
Carver, Doc, 316n10
Carver, Theresa Mary. *See* Leiter, Theresa Mary Carver
Castle Rock, 324n8
Caten, Eva, 230, 322n4
Catholics, 153–54, 309n6
Cedar Mountain, 193, 196, 203, 204, 249, 280, 315n2, 318n27
Center of the Book, 267
Chadwick, Robert R., 42, 296n5
Chamberlain, A. D., 211, 213, 320ch16n6
Chamberlain, John, 128
Chamberlain, Mrs., 287
Chamonix, France, 37, 295n13
charcoal, 57. *See also* coal, lignite
Charpiot's Hotel, 64, 299n16
Chautauquas, 264, 265, 267
Chenoworth (rpi student), 42, 296n5
Cherry Creek River, 64, 299n17
Chesapeake Bay, 48
chess, 93, 145–47, 236, 250–51, 308n7, 308n11
Cheyenne Club, 154–55, 309n8
Cheyenne wy: attorney from, 217, 320n2; banks in, 190, 191; Dudley Thurmond in, 307n14; Frank Walcott in, 313n7; gardener from, 207–8; George Beck's trip from, 64; politics and politicians in, xxxi, 153, 296n9; priest in, 309n6; prisoners in, 179; sheep purchase in, 86
Chicago: Democratic National Convention in, 189; dogs sent to, 128; fundraising in, 188; George Beck in, 159–60, 274; Horton Boal in, 310n3; Leiters in, 310n1, 321n1; meatpacking industry in, 68; news of Johnson County War in, 179; Palmer House hotel in, 306n3; settlers from, 222, 325appendix1n4; William Thom in, 307n18; World's Fair in, 169, 310n6, 311n3
Chicago, Burlington and Quincy Railroad (cb&q), 314n14
Chicago Athletic Club, 160, 310n6

shooting by, 200–201; as town namesake, xlvii–xlviii, 205–6. *See also* Buffalo Bill's Wild West

CodyArchive.org, xviii, 271

Cody Canal: construction of, xxxviii, 198–99, 215–17, 319n34; correspondence regarding, 271–77; Daisy Beck's work on, 283; George Beck's role in building, liv, 267, 268; location of headgate of, 196, 198; partners in building, 198, 279–80, 315n3, 316n13, 325n8; promotion of development near, xxxvii–xxxviii, xlix, 325appendix1n4; success of, xxxv, 217–18, 222; supplies for, 326n9; survey of site for, xxxvi, 196–97

Cody City, 204–6, 319n31, 319n32

Cody Club, xxxviii, xl

The Cody Enterprise, xlix, 220–21, 264, 320n5, 323n6

Cody Hotel, 207, 280, 281, 285, 319n2, 322n5

CodyStudies.org, xviii

Cody Trading Company, 223, 316n12, 321n11

Cody WY: bank robbery in, 236–38, 322n12; Beck family and friends in, ix, 261, 283, 291n11; Beck home in, x, xiii–xv, 219, 262–63, 265, 286, 287; Buffalo Bill's remains near, 318n27; campers from, 255; Camp Monaco Tree in, 323n9; Caroline Lockhart in, 323n6; Charley Gates's doctor in, 247; churches in, xxxviii–xxxix, 224, 245–46, 264; city hall cornerstone laid in, 279–81; construction in, 207, 319n1, 319n2; as county seat, 208–9, 315n5; doctors in, 322n9; establishment and promotion of, xxxvi–xxxviii, 265, 315n4, 319n33, 321n11; farming in, 222–23; fictional portrayals of life in, xliv–xlvi, liii; founders of, xi, xxxiii, xxxix, xliii, xliv, xlvii–xlviii, 267, 279–80, 316n11, 316n12; Fourth of July in, 268; gun in museum in, 323n8; hotel in, 221; Howard Brundage in, 307n14; Iron

Tail in, 256; maps of, 205, 280–81, 285; Mike Russell in, 317n15; mining company near, 209–10; mountains near, 318n25, 318n27; newspaper in, xlix, 320n5; paintings in, 322n6, 324n5; post office in, 205–6; research materials in and about, xviii, xlix, lv; residents and visitors in, xli–xlii, 219–23, 253, 268, 281, 315n2, 320n5, 323n6; sale of land in, 235–36; saloon in, 320ch17n7; Sam Berry in, 319n4; schools in, 221–22, 321n8; store in, 319n31; streets in, 288; transportation to and from, xxxix, xl, 252, 314n14, 317n14; water projects in and near, 209, 215, 249; William Ebert in, 318n30; women's role in building, 264

Cody-Yellowstone Road: promotion of, 321n11. *See also* Yellowstone highway

Coffeen, Henry Asa, 153, 309n4

Colorado: Ames ladies in, 137; crime in, 298n6; Elwood Mead in, 315n3; George Beck's first dollar earned in, 60; gold strikes in, 58; horses in, 54; Joseph Sire Greene's career in, 298n3; Mosquito Range in, 299n15; prospecting in, 136; sheep shopping in, 86

Colter's Hell, xxxiv

Columbia University, 47, 295n1

Columbus OH, 27

Commercial Cable Company, 312n9

Comstock Lode, 297n10, 297n11, 312n9

Confederacy, xxix, xxx, 14, 37, 293n14, 295n14

Confederate Army: members of, 14, 292n4, 300n1, 308n3, 314n1, 317n18; raiding of homes, 17; return to homes after war, 27, 157; in Silver Spring MD, 28

Congress Hotel, 160

Congressional Record, 10

Conrad, John Howard, 134, 135, 136, 306n11, 307n12

Constitutional Gardens, 267

Cook, Jeanne, xlix

Frankfort KY, 9, 10
Fraser, James E., 253, 324n6
Fremont County WY, 205, 208
French and Indian War, 268, 298n2
French Creek, 182
Fresno CA, 164–65, 310n9
Frewen, Clarita "Clara" Jerome, 303n5
Frewen, Sir Moreton, 87, 88, 303n5
Frontier Thesis, xxviii
Frost, Nedward, 245, 323n11
Frost and Richard Company, 323n11
Fulmer, Harrison "Harry," 173, 312n8
Fulton, Hank, 241–44
Funston, Bishop James Bowen, 224, 321n13

Garber, Vie Willits, 305n4, 311n3
Garfield, James A., 51, 239, 297n14, 322n2
Garlow, Fred, 318n26
Garrison, Secretary of War, 239
Gates, Charles Gilbert, 244–47, 323n10
Gates, John Warne "Bet-a-Million Gates," 244, 323n10
Genesee River valley, 7
Geneva, Switzerland, 37
Georgetown, 266, 268
Georgetown mining camp, 56
George Washington University. See Columbia University
Georgia, 33
Geraldine W. and Robert J. Dellenback Foundation, xviii
Gerber, Betty Jane Johnson, x, xi, xiv, xxv, xxvii, lv, 149, 261–68, 291n1
Gerber, George, 265
Germans, 222, 273, 286, 325appendix1n3
Germany, 310n9, 311n4, 316n11, 319n4, 324n2
Gerrans, Henry M., xi, 198, 210, 223, 225, 275, 280, 316n12
Gibbon, General, 302n19
gingersnaps, xxv, xxvii, 218, 262
Girard Trust, 315n4
The Globe, 10
gold, 204, 210, 299n10, 304n7

Golden CO, 298n6
Golden Gate Park, 163
Goodloe, Bettie Buckner Beck: background of, 293n15; birth of, 11; and brother's dancing, 34; education of, 20; inheritance of, 159; marriage of, 51; memorial volume sent by, 157; neighbors of, 261; suit of armor from, 263; threatened by intruder, 13; travel to Cincinnati, 19; visits to, 149, 227
Goodloe, Green Clay, 51, 149, 261, 263, 293n15, 297n13
Goose Creek, 74, 81, 82, 185, 201, 301n18
Goose Creek Canyon, 110, 111
Gorringe, Henry, 300n3
Grand River, 59
Grant, Jesse, 29
Grant, Julia, 295n9
Grant, Smith, and Locker, 249
Grant, Ulysses S., 29–30, 295n9
graphite, 62
Gratz, Andrew, 151–52
Gratz, Mrs. Andrew, 151–52
Greasy Creek, 305n13. See also Lodge Grass Creek
Great Britain: ambassador to, 295n11; Horace Plunkett's title in, 146; immigrants from, 134; Judah Benjamin in, 295n14; Leiter relations to nobility in, 321n1; L. Q. C. Lamar in, 314n1; Oliver H. Wallop in, 128, 133, 306n1; promotion of western hunting in, xxxviii; Thornton land holdings in, 36, 37, 38; wool business in, 107
Great Lakes, 7
Great Plains, xxxi
Greece, 295n2
Greeley, Horace, 53, 297n1, 299n12
Greeley CO, 299n12
Greene, Joseph Sire, 54, 59, 60, 298n3
Greene, Wallace, 54, 59, 86–88, 90–91, 136–37, 298n3
Green Front, x, 207, 281, 319n2

Key, Francis Scott, 292n7
Key West FL, 149, 308n5
Kilpatrick brothers. *See* Patrick, Matt and Al
Kimball, Jimmy, 288

LaCrosse WI, 32
Lady Doc (Lockhart), xlv–xlvi, liii, 322n13, 323n6
"lady newspaper reporter," xlvii, 241–42, 244, 323n6. *See also* Lockhart, Caroline
Lake, Stuart N., lii
Lake DeSmet, 96, 304n11
Lake Superior, 7, 64
Lakota Indians, 301n17, 304n7
Lamar, L. Q. C., 190, 314n1
Lambrigger, Alfred "Alph," 169–70, 311n3
Lamour, Louis, lii
Lanchbury, Emma, 317n17
Lanchbury, Thomas, 317n17
Lander WY, 205, 281
Land Office, 190–91
Lane, Frances, xlv, xlvii, 237, 264, 286, 287, 291n28, 322n9, 322n13
Lane, Franklin K., 239
Langley, Samuel Pierpoint, 50, 297n11
Langston Golf Course, 266
Laramie Peak, 87
Laramie WY, 271, 303n26
Larson, T. A., xxxv
The Last of the Great Scouts (Wetmore), xliii–xliv
lead, 62, 210
Lead, Julius, 187, 188, 314n16
Lead SD, 186, 314n15
Leadville CO: atmosphere in, 56; founding of, 298n4; George Beck and friends in, xxx, xxxi, 54, 58–60, 63; mining in, 54, 298n3; Mosquito Pass near, 299n15; value of lead ore in, 62
Lee, Blair: at dance, 49; family of, 10, 293n14; George Beck's friendship with, 27–29, 31, 41; marriage of, 135, 307n15, 307n16; trips West, 131

Lee, Elizabeth Blair, 10, 27, 293n13, 293n14
Lee, Francis Preston Blair. *See* Lee, Blair
Lee, Robert E., 31, 293n14
Lee, Samuel Phillips, 10, 27, 31, 151, 293n13, 293n14
Leede, Julius W., 314n16
Leffel, James, 305n6
Leffel wheels, 111, 183, 305n6
Leiter, Daisy, 174, 225, 226, 228
Leiter, Joseph, 159, 310n1, 321n1
Leiter, Levi Z., 159, 184–85, 188, 227, 310n1, 321n1
Leiter, Margaret "Daisy" Hyde. *See* Howard, Margaret "Daisy" Hyde Leiter
Leiter, Mary Victoria. *See* Curzon, Mary Victoria Leiter
Leiter, Nancy "Nannie" Lathrop Carver, 174, 225, 226, 228, 229, 310n1, 321n1
Leiter, Theresa Mary Carver, 228, 321n1
Lewis and Clark Expedition, 292n11, 305n3, 324n9. *See also* Clark, William
Lexington Gun Club, 23
Lexington KY: Civil War in, 19; dog kennel near, 128; founding of, 292n5; George Beck's early life in, 5, 11, 13, 23, 26; George Beck's friends from, 151; James Burnie Beck's travel to, 8, 20; law practice in, 292n4; mountain climbers from, 37; preparation for military school in, 35; transport of James Burnie Beck's body to, 157
Lexington Rifles, 294n20
Library of Congress, 267
Lichtenstein, Otto Franc von. *See* Franc, Otto
The Life and Legend of Wyatt Earp, lii
The Life and Times of Judge Roy Bean, lii
Li Hung Chang, 250, 324n2, 324n3
Lincoln, Abraham, xxix, 19–21, 29, 293n14, 321n2
Lincoln Land Company, 235–36, 322n7

Paxton and Galleger, 281
Peake, Anna "Granny," 264, 320n5
Peake, John H., 220–21, 264, 320n5
Peebler, Clara C., 314n11
Peking, 251, 261
Pen Lucy, 33
Penn Mutual Life, 315n4
Pennsylvania Railroad, 174. *See also* railroads
Perkins, Charles Elliot, 184, 314n14
Pershing, John J. "Black Jack," 153, 309n5
Persia, shah of, 38
Philadelphia and Reading Railroad Company, 319n5. *See also* railroads
Philadelphia Bulletin, 323n6
Philadelphia PA: Adna Anderson in, 300n5; Beck family in, 14, 19–21; coal investors in, 212; George Beck's friends in, 194, 208, 211, 315n4; sportsmen's club investor in, 174; Wayne Darlington in, 324n2
Philippines, 93, 151, 304n6
Pickett, William D., 200, 201, 317n18
Pikes Peak, 137
Pine Ridge Reservation, 298n6
Pioneer Building, 281
Pitchfork Ranch, 317n21
Pittsburgh PA, 296n5, 298n2
Plattsmouth NE, 312n8
Plunkett, Horace Curzon, 146, 308n9
Poker Church, 264. *See also* Episcopal churches
Poker Nell, 221, 320ch17n7
Pole Creek, 303n3
Polish immigrants, 222
Ponce de Leon Hotel, 143
Pony Express Bob, 160
"Pony Tracks." *See* Caten, Eva
Port Arthur TX, 244, 323n10
Portland ME, 235
Portsmouth NE, 187
Portugal, 295n2
Post, Morten E., 86, 90, 303n3
Postal Telegraph Company, 312n9
Potomac River, 48, 51
Poughkeepsie NY, 43

Powder River, xxxi, 87–88, 117, 301n16, 303n1, 303n4, 313n6
Powder River Cattle Company, 87, 303n5
Powell, Billy, 71, 79
Pretty Beads, 305n4
Pretty Shell, 305n4
Prim (servant), 11, 12, 14, 18
Princeton University, 41, 259
Pryor, Nathan, 305n3, 324n9
Pryor Creek, 103, 305n3
Pryor Gap, 312n8, 324n9
Pryor Mountain, 122–23, 257, 305n3, 324n9
Pueblo CO, 298n3
Pullman, George Mortimer, 177, 313n1
Pumpkin Buttes, 87
Purcell, Tom, 221, 223–24, 320ch17n6
Purcell's Saloon, 320ch17n6
P. Yegen and Co., 274, 326n9
pyrite, 210

Quaker School, 20

Rabbit Creek Canyon, 136
railroads: accommodations on, 97–99; Buffalo Bill's negotiations with, xxxiii; camps of, 67, 71; coal consumption of, 212; construction of, 68, 69; in Cuba, 148; effect on western development, xxxii; in Sheridan, 302n25; Thomas Rosser with, 300n1. *See also* Burlington Railroad; Northern Pacific Railroad; Pennsylvania Railroad; Philadelphia and Reading Railroad Company; Union Pacific Railroad
Rappahannock County VA, 9
Rappahannock River, 60
Rattlesnake Mountain, 204, 249, 318n27
Rawlins, John A., 306n8
Rawlins Spring, 306n8
Rawlins WY, 62, 133, 299n13, 306n8, 309n6
Reardon (boxer), 160
Reconstruction period, 27, 29, 157

Salsbury, Nate: assistance to Cody settlers, 222–23; background of, 316n10, 325n7; influence in Cody, xi; and irrigation project, 198, 215, 225, 274, 280; loan request of, 216

Salt Lake City UT, 296n7

Sand Coulee drainage, 197

San Francisco CA, 163, 166, 297n11

Santa Monica CA, 299n8

Savannah GA, 139, 307n2

Saxon (automobile), 287

Scarlett, Margaret Webster, xviii

Scarlett, W. Richard, III, xviii

Schneider, Ben, 119, 120, 124, 126, 305n10

Schwoob, Jacob M. "Jakie," l, 223, 287, 321n11

Scotland, 6, 8, 37, 151, 264, 291n2, 308n11

Seminole, Joseph, 298n6

servants, 18–19

Shaw neighborhood, 266

sheep: cattlemen's attitude toward raisers of, 181; disease of, 88–90, 117–18; and dogs, 101, 102, 106; driving of, 86–88; end of George Beck's business with, 107–8; manure of, 257; purchase in Iowa, 97; raising of, 85, 93, 168; Wallace Greene's involvement in business of, 136; of William Thom, 136

Sheep Canyon, 194, 315n7

Sheridan, Clare, 87

Sheridan, Philip H., 302n26, 307n13

Sheridan Coal Company, 312n8

Sheridan County WY, 110, 153, 223, 305n8, 311n6, 311n7

Sheridan Fuel Company, 185, 312n8

Sheridan Inn, xxxiii, 209, 302n25, 319n3

Sheridan Post, xxxiii

Sheridan WY: attorney in, 238; banks and bankers in, 236, 305n11, 311n7, 322n10; Boals in, 310n3; burial of Oliver Wallop in, 128; coal mining business in, 186; community of, xxxi; creeks in, 301n18, 302n22; devel-opment of, xxxii–xxxiv, 153, 312n8; Deyo Hasbrouck in, 314n11; Dudley Thurmond in, 307n14; establishment of, 134–35; first school in, 303n27; founders of, 307nn13–14, 322n10; George Beck's travel to and from, 236; Harry Fulmer in, 312n8; Henry Asa Coffeen in, 309n4; history of, 302n25; Horace Alger in, 219, 311n6; irrigation project planning in, 197, 280; lady reporter in, 241; location of, 81; newspaper in, 307n13; post office in, 311n2; railroad in, 183, 184, 312n8; store in, 134, 306n11, 307n12

Sherman, Mary Hoyt. *See* Miles, Mary Hoyt Sherman

Sherman, William Tecumseh, 301n16

Shoshone area, name of, 318n25

Shoshone Canyon, 318n27

Shoshone Dam, 283–84, 322n9, 323n11

Shoshone Indians, 317n19, 324n8

Shoshone Land and Irrigation Company: advertisement of property, xxxvii; Buffalo Bill's introduction to directors of, 310n3; business locations of, 209, 225, 319n2; closing of, 223; Daisy Sorrenson's work with, 325appendix1n2; engineer on, 319n33; legal disputes with, 326n13; shareholders in, 315n2, 316nn11–12, 318n30; support for project of, xxxv

Shoshone National Forest, 320ch16n6

Shoshone River: Buffalo Bill's ranch on, 239, 256, 317n15; hunting and camping on, 211, 233, 253; irrigable land near, 197; at Ishawooa Pass, 324n8; mountains near, 318n25, 318n27; naming of, xxxv, 209; painting of valley of, 231; prospecting near, 250; railroad along, 235, 236; Sage Creek at, 325appendix1n5; water projects on, 249, 283–84, 315nn2–3, 316n8, 323n11. *See also* North Fork, Shoshone River; South Fork, Shoshone River; Stinking Water River

Shoshoni Indian Reservation, 205

Watervliet Gymnasium, 41, 296n4
Wayne, John, li
Weborg, Vida, 221–22, 321n8
Wells Fargo Company, 216
West, American: Albyn Prince Dike's
business in, 89; clothing in, 57; cooking
by bachelors in, 258; development of,
xxviii, xxx, xxxii, l–liii; Frederic Remington's impressions of, 231; George
Beck's experiences in, 35, 53, 70–72;
George Hearst's mining enterprises in,
297n10; history of, xvii, xviii; image of,
xvii, xxvii, li–liii; railroad rates for moving to, 97–98; reclamation projects in,
315n3; saloons in, 221; social customs
in, 133; train schedules in, 219; treatment of southerners in, 5; water rights
contracts in, 217; Wayne Darlington in,
324n2; William Thom's interest in, 135–
36; winter weather in, 139
Weston, Harry, 223
Weston, H. R., 224
Weston County, Wyoming, 313n5
West Point Military Academy: Andrew
Jackson III at, 308n3; appointments
to, 33–36; Clay Goodloe at, 297n13;
George Beck's desire to attend, xxx, 33,
34; John J. Pershing at, 309n5; Nelson
Miles at, 301n12; Thomas Thornburgh
at, 299n13; Wesley Merritt at, 299n14
Wetmore, Helen Cody, xliii–xliv
Weyler, Valeriano, 145, 308n6
W. F. Cody Hotel Company, xxxiii
W. F. Cody Transportation Company,
xxxiii
wheat, 110, 112–13, 115–16, 127, 169–70,
183, 188, 311n3
Wheatland wy, 322n10
"Where Eagles Fly," 266
White Bull, 301n17
White Horse (Crow), 122
White Horse George, 108–9, 305n4
White House, 19–20, 28, 190, 266
White River, 240
Whitney Western Art Museum, 322n6.
  See also Buffalo Bill Center of the West
Wild Bill Hickok, li

Wild West shows. See Buffalo Bill's
  Wild West
Wiley, Solon Lysander, xxxv, 197, 316n8
Wilkerson, Anna May "Fannie," 167,
  178
Willets (RPI student), 42, 45, 46,
  296n5
William F. Cody's Wyoming Empire (Bon-
  ner), xlix
Willow Grove Cemetery, 314n10
Winston Brothers, 68
Winterling, John, 236, 322n10
Wolf Creek, 77, 302n22
Wolf Mountains, 74
Wood, Leonard, 239
Woodreve, 149
Woodruff, Sam, 54–55, 298n6
wool. See sheep
World War I, 309n5
World War II, 265, 285, 288
Wyatt Earp (Lake), lii
Wyoming: Carey Act projects in, xxxv,
  296n9; cattle in, 118, 178–79, 305n8,
  309n8, 313n6; Charles Burdick's gov-
  ernment positions in, 320n2; contribution to Cody papers project, xviii;
  first forest reserve in, 244; first mill
  built in, 111; Frank Canton in, 311n1;
  Frederic Remington's visit to, 39,
  230; George Beck's legacy in, 268;
  Irish cattle rancher in, 146; J. J. Van
  Horne in, 313n8; lignite in, 187–88;
  naming of Shoshone River, xxxv; Oliver H. Wallop's death and burial in,
  128; politics and politicians in, xxxi,
  49, 152–53, 156–57, 189–91, 303n3,
  305n8, 309n5, 309n11, 311n6, 314n3,
  325n8; road building in, 252; shipping routes in, 303n2; sportsmen's
  clubs in, 173–74; state engineer in,
  193–94; statehood of, xxxi, 154, 156,
  296n9; Thurmond family in, 307n14;
  treatment of George Beck in, 5; Ute
  migration through, 240–41; Wallace
  Greene in, 136; water rights and laws
  in, 110, 217, 315n3, 318n29; weather
  in, 180; women's right to vote in, 156